everyday

everyday FOOD LIGHT

The Quickest and Easiest Recipes, All Under **500** Calories

FROM THE KITCHENS OF MARTHA STEWART LIVING

Clarkson Potter/Publishers
New York

Published in the United States by Clarkson Potter/Publishers,
an imprint of the Crown Publishing Group,
a division of Random House, Inc., New York.
www.crownpublishing.com
www.clarksonpotter.com
www.marthastewart.com

CLARKSON POTTER is a trademark and POTTER with colophon
is a registered trademark of Random House, Inc.

The recipes and photographs in this book originally appeared
in issues of EVERYDAY FOOD magazine.

Library of Congress Cataloging-in-Publication Data is available upon request.

ISBN 978-0-307-71809-9
eISBN 978-0-307-95319-3

Printed in the United States of America

Book and cover design by Jeffrey Kurtz
Photography credits appear on page 373.

10 9 8 7 6 5 4 3 2 1

First Edition

To all of you who want to eat delicious food
but want to watch your calories, maintain a healthy lifestyle,
and live a good long life!

CONTENTS

WINTER 31

SPRING

SUMMER ₁₉₇

INTRODUCTION

When it came time to start working on the third volume in the *Everyday Food* cookbook library, the editors and I quickly agreed on what it should offer: a collection of low-calorie, low-fat dishes for all of us who want to eat healthy yet flavorful meals, every day. The "light" issue of the magazine, published each January, is always a top seller on newsstands and a favorite among our subscribers (as we learn from their many appreciative letters and e-mails). You'll find a year's worth of recipes, organized by season, each with fewer than 500 calories (and a minimal amount of fat). We hope you try them all!

And since we know how helpful it is to have the nutritional break-down beside each recipe, that's where you'll find it in this book, just like in the magazine. We've also shared our favorite low-fat cooking methods (like steaming and roasting), kitchen tools, and flavor boosters—plus tips for making smart substitutions and other ways to lighten up your favorite dishes (look for "Why It's Light" in the headnote). Our goal with this book, and with the magazine, is to help you create quick, delicious, and healthy dinners on your own, all through the week.

Martha Stewart

GOLDEN RULES FOR EATING LIGHT

1 **RETHINK YOUR ROUTINE:** Instead of frying or sautéing, try lower-fat techniques such as poaching, steaming, grilling, or roasting.

2 **MAKE SIMPLE SUBSTITUTIONS:** Use yogurt instead of sour cream; instead of the full-fat versions, use reduced-fat cream cheese and mayonnaise, and part-skim mozzarella and ricotta cheese.

3 **PAY ATTENTION TO PORTIONS:** A serving of protein should be the size of a deck of cards, and a serving of starchy foods (like pasta and rice) should be the size of a tennis ball.

4 **GO EASY ON THE OIL:** Rather than pouring oil straight into a pan when cooking, parcel it out with a measuring spoon. Or use a pastry brush to lightly coat the pan (and food) with oil before roasting.

5 **UP YOUR VEGETABLES:** Increasing the number of vegetables on your plate and reducing the amount of meat is an easy way to cut out fat and add nutrients.

6 **OPT FOR LEAN PROTEIN:** Opt for lower-fat meats, such as skinless chicken and turkey breast, or beef and pork tenderloin (instead of rib eye and Porterhouse), and eat more fish and meatless proteins like beans and tofu.

7 **SLIM DOWN YOUR SALADS:** To keep your salad more healthful, make your own vinaigrette using less oil than store-bought versions, or use low-fat buttermilk in creamy dressings. Toss the salad with just enough dressing to coat, and cut down on fatty additions such as cheese and croutons.

8 **ADD FAT-FREE FLAVOR:** Instead of relying on fats like butter and oil, enhance your dishes with vinegar, citrus, spices, and fresh or dried herbs.

9 **FILL UP ON FIBER:** Beans, whole grains, and legumes are relatively low in calories yet packed with fiber, which helps keep you feeling fuller longer.

10 **CHOOSE SWEETS WISELY:** Make a low-fat treat for dessert, such as angel food cake or granita, or enjoy just a few squares of bittersweet chocolate.

POACHING

This gentle form of low-fat cooking deserves more popularity in the home kitchen: It is simple to do, requires basic pots and pans, and yields food with a wonderful silken texture. Cooking in gently simmering liquid keeps the food moist without adding any fat, and also preserves its flavor. Poached chicken or fish can be shredded, sliced, or flaked, and is ideal for adding to salads, sandwiches, soups, tacos, and more.

To poach, place ingredients (including any aromatics; see list below) in a pot and cover with water or broth. Bring just to a boil, then reduce heat to the barest simmer. Chicken is done when it's no longer pink inside and an instant-read thermometer inserted in the thickest part of the meat registers 160°F; fish should begin to turn opaque and register 140°F (overcooking will result in rubbery chicken or fish).

RECIPES

SUGGESTED AROMATICS

Fresh or dried herbs

Whole spices, such as peppercorns

Fresh ginger

Garlic cloves

Onions, shallots, leeks, or scallions

Citrus slices, zest, or juice

Carrots

Celery

Fennel

Soy sauce

Wine

Broth

POACHING TIPS

CHOOSE A POACHING LIQUID You can poach meat in water, broth, wine, or any other liquid, but choose one that won't overpower the flavor of the meat. For example, use a light broth for delicate fish, and wine for chicken or richer-tasting fish such as salmon.

ADD AROMATICS To enhance flavor, you can embellish the poaching liquid with whatever aromatics you have on hand, such as herbs, spices, fruits and vegetables, or wine. Try fresh ginger with soy sauce, or orange and rosemary.

USE THE RIGHT POT Make sure the food, poaching liquid, and aromatics fit comfortably in the pot, with room to spare at the top (to avoid bubbling over).

BRING LIQUID TO A SIMMER Poaching liquid is at the right temperature when small air bubbles start to form at the bottom of the pot and just a few bubbles break the surface of the liquid; it should not come to a boil. Partially cover the pot to keep the liquid at a simmer. In place of a lid, you can use a round of parchment paper cut to fit the pot.

SAVE THE BROTH Once the meat is cooked, reserve the resulting broth; it can be used to make soup or sauces, or be incorporated into another dish such as a braise or stew.

TRY POACHING FRUIT Though meats are most commonly poached, the technique works wonderfully for fruit, too, to make a simple, not-too-sweet dessert. Pears take well to poaching, as do apples, stone fruits, and figs. Fruit and aromatics can be poached in wine or a simple syrup made by boiling equal parts water and sugar until the sugar melts.

STEAMING

Long a favorite technique for low-calorie cooking, steaming—another "wet-cooking" method similar to poaching—is also an excellent way to prepare meals that are clean-tasting and exceptionally moist and tender throughout. Since steam is hotter than boiling water, vegetables cook more quickly and retain more nutrients when steamed rather than boiled; they also maintain their brightness and texture.

To prepare for steaming, place a metal or bamboo basket in a saucepan filled with 1 inch of salted water (the bottom of the basket should not touch the water). Bring to a boil, add vegetables, lower the heat, and cover with a tight-fitting lid. The cooking time will vary depending on what you're steaming; generally, vegetables are done when they are tender yet still crisp, and can be pierced easily with a knife. Although this technique is used primarily for vegetables and fish, chicken can also be steamed with excellent results. Another way to steam food is to cook it in parchment, as described on page 18.

RECIPES

STEAMING TIPS

CHOOSE A STEAMER BASKET A multilevel bamboo basket, common in Asian cooking, is an excellent alternative to a metal steamer basket. If you don't have a metal or bamboo steamer basket, you can use a heatproof sieve or colander that fits inside a lidded saucepan. Just be sure the bottom isn't dipping into the boiling water.

LAYER BAMBOO STEAMERS Since an Asian-style steamer has several layers, you can cook multiple foods simultaneously. Place foods that need more time to cook, such as starchy vegetables, in the bottom basket, closest to the heat source, and more delicate foods, like fish, in the top tiers. Line each basket with lettuce or cabbage leaves to keep foods from sticking to the bamboo.

GET CREATIVE There are other ways to steam food besides in a basket—any method that creates and traps steam will cook food quickly and evenly. For example, fish or chicken can be steamed atop a bed of vegetables or rice in a lidded pot (see page 350), or on a plate set in a covered skillet with simmering water.

GIVE FOOD SOME SPACE Whatever vessel you use, make sure it's big enough so that the vapor can circulate around the food. If the steamer is too small, the food will not cook as quickly or evenly.

KEEP THINGS SMALL Steaming works best for vegetables and for small, uniformly even fillets of fish, boneless chicken breasts, and shellfish. Larger pieces will overcook on the outside before the interior is cooked through.

ENHANCE THE FLAVOR As when poaching, you can add aromatics such as alliums, herbs, whole spices, ginger, and fruits and vegetables to the liquid to subtly flavor steamed foods. Try mint and lemon slices for fish, or fresh dill and citrus peel for chicken.

COOKING IN PARCHMENT

Despite its French name, cooking *en papillote,* or in parchment, is among the easiest and healthiest ways to prepare meats and vegetables. The method is simple: place the food on parchment paper, pleat or twist the edges to seal, then place in the oven, where the food cooks in its own juices (or with some liquid added for extra flavor).

You'll find parchment paper at the supermarket near the foil; do not substitute waxed paper, which will not seal the food properly. When assembling, group ingredients—meats and vegetables—with similar cooking times, and add a few flavorings (see below) before folding up the packets following one of the methods shown (opposite). Always set the packets on a rimmed baking sheet in case of leaks; the food is ready when the packets have puffed up. Open the packets carefully, preferably at the table, to allow the hot steam (and heady aromas) to escape.

RECIPES

SALMON IN PARCHMENT WITH GREEN BEANS AND LEMON ZEST **169**

BROCCOLI, SNAP PEAS, AND ASPARAGUS IN PARCHMENT **185**

POTATOES, LEEKS, AND CARROTS IN PARCHMENT **185**

EGGS WITH MUSHROOMS AND SPINACH **297**

SUGGESTED AROMATICS

Fresh or dried herbs

Whole spices, such as peppercorns

Red-pepper flakes

Fresh ginger

Garlic cloves

Onions, shallots, leeks, or scallions

Citrus slices, zest, or juice

Fennel slices

Soy sauce

Wine or vinegar

CLASSIC

This method is ideal for delicate ingredients, such as raw eggs and lean fish.

1 Fold a sheet of parchment in half and cut into a half-heart shape. Unfold and place ingredients in middle of one half, alongside fold.

2 Fold other half over and pleat tightly around edge to seal.

TWIST

This basic method is the easiest for everyday cooking: just fold and twist ends.

1 Place ingredients in center of a sheet of paper. Fold long ends of paper over ingredients, like a letter.

2 Tightly twist short ends to seal, then turn them up.

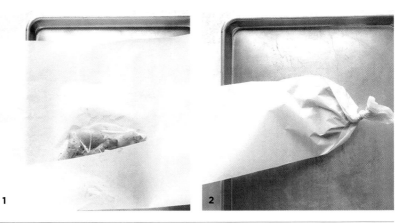

ENVELOPE

Attractive and neatly folded, this compact style is great for entertaining.

1 Place ingredients in center of a sheet of paper. Bring long ends of paper together and fold down three times to make a seam.

2 Tuck short ends underneath to secure (tie packet with twine if desired).

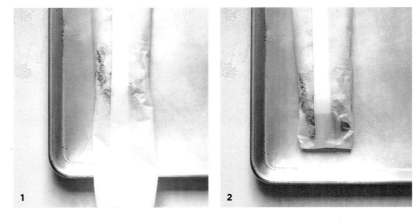

STIR-FRYING

This traditional Asian cooking method lets you prepare meats, vegetables, and other foods quickly at high temperatures, with only a small amount of oil, so they are crisp yet tender. Besides chicken, beef, pork, and tofu, you can stir-fry a wide range of vegetables, including mushrooms, broccoli, peppers, and bok choy and other greens, as well as rice. Follow the steps on the opposite page for great results every time. The same principles apply whether you're cooking meat, vegetables, tofu, or rice.

STIR-FRYING TIPS

KEEP INGREDIENTS UNIFORM Cut ingredients into similar-size pieces so that they cook at the same rate; or, when necessary, work in batches to accommodate different-size ingredients (this will also help you avoid overcrowding the wok).

USE THE RIGHT OIL Opt for an oil that can withstand cooking at high heat, such as safflower or peanut oil.

TIME IT RIGHT Add meats and vegetables that will take the longest time to cook first, followed by those that cook more quickly, so that everything will be done at the same time.

FINISH WITH A PAN SAUCE Use the pan drippings to make a quick sauce for drizzling over the dish.

CHOOSE THE RIGHT PAN (A)

You can use a wok, a heavy-bottomed pan (not nonstick), or a cast-iron skillet. It should be at least 12 inches wide to prevent overcrowding the food.

HAVE EVERYTHING READY BEFORE YOU BEGIN (B)

Because stir-frying is a quick cooking method, always chop, slice, or otherwise prepare the ingredients before you turn on the heat. Group them near the stove, within easy reach.

GET THE PAN HOT (C)

Before you start cooking, it's important to heat the pan until very hot. When the pan is hot, carefully add the oil and swirl it around, then immediately begin adding the other ingredients.

KEEP IT MOVING (D) To

cook foods quickly and evenly without scorching, you'll need to continually stir them as they cook. Once the stir-fry is done, transfer it right away to a serving dish so the food doesn't overcook.

ROASTING

Roasting works magic on vegetables, intensifying their sweetness and caramelizing edges. It's also a great method for cooking all kinds of meat; the exterior turns crisp and golden brown, while the interior remains succulent and juicy. Because the flavors are concentrated, you need few other ingredients—just a splash of oil and a sprinkle of salt and pepper. Fresh or dried herbs—or ground spices—are other nice additions. Once your food is in the oven, it requires little monitoring—just a toss halfway through roasting time.

RECIPES

ROASTING TIPS

USE A STURDY PAN The sides should be 1 to 3 inches—high enough to catch juices but low enough for steam to escape. A rimmed baking sheet is fine for vegetables; a higher-sided roasting pan is better for larger cuts of meat.

ROAST EVEN-SIZED PIECES Cut vegetables into same-size pieces for even cooking. Leave space between vegetables; overcrowding the pan will cause the vegetables to steam rather than brown.

TOSS YOUR INGREDIENTS Tossing occasionally during roasting helps foods cook evenly.

ROAST THINGS TOGETHER Cook vegetables and meat at the same time, enhancing the flavor of both, to make a complete meal. Spread sturdy vegetables such as potatoes, onions, or garlic in a roasting pan and place the meat—such as a whole chicken or pork loin—on top. The vegetables will infuse the meat with flavor as it cooks; they also form a makeshift rack, keeping the meat from sticking to the pan.

START AT ROOM TEMPERATURE Allow a roast to come to room temperature before you start cooking by letting it sit out for one to two hours; otherwise, you'll end up with meat that is unevenly cooked.

CONTROL THE HEAT For small cuts of meat, maintain a high temperature to the end; for larger cuts, lower heat partway through (about 350°F) to keep them from burning on the outside before they're completely cooked through.

USE AN INSTANT-READ THERMOMETER Check the internal temperature of meat at about three-quarters of the total suggested cooking time, then every five to ten minutes afterward to keep from overcooking. Insert the thermometer into the thickest part of the meat, avoiding any bone. Cook beef to a minimum temperature of 145°F (for medium-rare); pork, 160°F, and poultry, 165°F.

TAKE ADVANTAGE OF PAN DRIPPINGS After roasting meat, use the drippings in the pan to make a simple sauce. Pour liquid such as wine, water, or broth into the pan, and simmer, scraping up the flavorful browned bits with a wooden spoon, until reduced and thickened.

GRILLING

Summertime eating is all about ease, and there's no better way to prepare delicious fuss-free meals than on the grill. The dry heat from the grill sears meat and imparts a smoky flavor. While the meat cooks, the fat drips off and falls through the grates. Beyond the smoky taste that results from the hot grill, it's easy to season foods before cooking with marinades, brines, or spice rubs—all of which are high in flavor but not in fat. In addition to meat and poultry, vegetables, seafood, tofu, and even fruits take well to grilling, so you can prepare a complete meal all in one stop.

RECIPES

TEMPERATURE GUIDE FOR CHARCOAL GRILLS

Gas grills make it easy to heat the grill to a specific temperature, since they have settings and a built-in thermometer. To gauge the heat of a charcoal grill, hold the palm of your hand carefully over the charcoal, as far from the briquettes as the food would be (about 5 inches). You should be able to hold your hand there for only 4 to 5 seconds for medium heat, 3 to 4 seconds for medium-high heat, and 2 to 3 seconds for high heat. To maintain the temperature of a charcoal grill, add a couple handfuls of coals every half hour.

LIGHTING THE GRILL

For a gas grill, simply ignite and adjust the heat as described at right. For a charcoal grill, fill a chimney starter with coals, then light them. Allow a coating of white ash to form on the coals, then empty into the grill. To increase the heat, add more coals. Once the coals are hot, spread them in the center or on one side.

DIRECT HEAT VERSUS INDIRECT HEAT

Whether you grill over direct or indirect heat depends on what you are cooking. Direct heat, the zone immediately above the heat source, sears and quickly cooks smaller pieces of meat as well as vegetables. Indirect heat, the zone near but not right over the heat source, cooks more slowly, and is better for larger cuts of meat. Sometimes you may want to use both types of heat— direct heat to sear the meat first, then indirect heat to finish cooking it all the way through.

For direct heat (A), set up the heat source (gas or charcoal) evenly across the center of the grilling area. Use direct heat to cook steak, chicken pieces, kebabs, sausages, burgers, and vegetables.

For indirect heat (B), set up the heat source on one side of the grill and place the food on the other. Cook whole chickens and turkey breasts, pork shoulders, and brisket over indirect heat.

GRILLING TIPS

START WITH A CLEAN GRILL Heat grill before cleaning the grates—they're easier to clean when hot. Use a wire brush to clean grates before cooking and immediately after.

OIL THE GRATES Lightly oil the hot grates just before you grill (so the oil doesn't burn off), using a grilling brush or a clean rag dipped in oil, holding it with long tongs.

BRING TO ROOM TEMPERATURE Steaks, chops, and chicken at room temperature will grill more evenly.

USE SKEWERS Use two-pronged skewers for foods that are likely to spin when being turned on the grill, such as shrimp and scallops. You can achieve the same result by threading the food through two skewers at once. Wooden skewers need to be soaked in water for 30 minutes before grilling, to prevent them from scorching.

GET A NICE SEAR When searing foods, keep the lid of the grill open. Don't flip often or move food around too much; instead, let meat form a crust before moving it. When you do move a piece of meat, use tongs or a spatula; piercing it with a fork will cause the juices to run out, as will pressing down on meat.

TEST FOR DONENESS Use an instant-read thermometer to test the doneness of meat without cutting into it. Insert thermometer into the thickest part, to bring up base line, avoiding the bone.

LET MEAT REST Allow steaks, chops, and chicken to rest for 10 minutes before serving.

PRACTICE FIRE SAFETY Position grill at least 10 feet away from anything that could catch fire. If flare-ups occur, close lid and vents to extinguish flames. Wait 24 hours to dispose of ash to be sure there are no hot embers.

TOOLS FOR LOWER-CALORIE COOKING

1 **STEAMER BASKET** You can cook vegetables or fish quickly in a steamer basket. Choose either a lightweight metal insert with folding perforated sides, which fits into most lidded saucepans, or a lidded bamboo version, which sits inside a skillet. In either type, the basket is suspended over (not in) boiling water, and steam rises through the holes and is trapped by the lid, cooking the food inside.

2 **GRILL PAN** Similar to cooking on an outdoor grill, searing on a grill pan requires little, if any, fat. Stove-top pans have ridges that give food grill marks, plus they allow fat to drain off. Choose a cast-iron pan and season it, if necessary, according to the manufacturer's instructions.

3 **ROASTING PAN** Sturdy and practical, roasting pans are designed for cooking large pieces of meat; they are also very useful for roasting vegetables. The sides of the pan are low enough to allow meat to brown while retaining the flavorful cooking juices; a rack fitted inside helps the meat brown on all sides, and prevents it from stewing in the juices. Choose a heavy-bottomed pan without a nonstick surface for the best browning.

4 **SALAD SPINNER** It's easy to wash and dry all types of lettuce with one of these inexpensive and effective tools. A salad spinner dries leaves in seconds. You can store washed and dried lettuce in the sealed container for several days in the refrigerator. Salad spinners can also be used to dry just-washed leafy greens and other vegetables before stir-frying or sautéing.

5 **CAST-IRON SKILLET** An old-fashioned cast-iron skillet is as close as it gets to a perfect pan. The pan's heavy base distributes heat evenly, beautifully browning meats, fish, and vegetables, whether you use it on top of the stove or in the oven. Once seasoned, the surface is naturally nonstick, eliminating the need for excess oil or butter. To season a skillet, rub the entire surface of the pan with oil, and heat it in a 300-degree oven for an hour. To clean it, sprinkle the inside with coarse salt, rub with paper towels, and wipe clean (do not use soap). You can rinse it in water if needed; just be sure to dry it thoroughly before storing to prevent rust. Do not cook acidic foods such as tomato sauce in a cast-iron pan, as they will erode the seasoned surface.

6 **IMMERSION BLENDER** Puréeing is a good way to give vegetable soups a creamy consistency without adding cream (or other high-fat ingredients). An immersion blender purées right in the pot, so there's no need to transfer hot foods to a blender or food processor. Its detachable components make it easy to clean. Choose a model with a cord; cordless versions often lack the power of plug-in models.

7 **CITRUS REAMER OR JUICER** A hand-press juicer or a reamer extracts the most juice from each fruit. To use a hand-press juicer, place half a lemon or lime in the cup, with the cut side facing the holes. Clamp down over a bowl. To use a reamer, simply insert the ridged cone in the center of a citrus fruit half, and twist to release the juice. Before halving the fruit, roll it on a work surface under your palm a few times (or microwave it for 10 seconds) to loosen the juices.

8 **CITRUS ZESTER** Citrus zest brightens all kinds of savory dishes, minimizing the need for higher-calorie flavor enhancers like oil or butter. Although this tool was originally intended for woodworking, its tiny, razor-sharp teeth make it perfect for grating citrus fruit (as well as hard cheeses, fresh ginger, and whole spices such as nutmeg). For citrus, zest only the outer layer of the skin; the white pith underneath has an unpleasant bitter taste. Remember to remove zest before extracting juice.

9 **INSTANT-READ THERMOMETER** The lower fat content of lean meats makes them more susceptible to drying out when they are cooked. An instant-read thermometer takes away the guesswork. To use, insert the thermometer into the thickest part of the meat near the end of the cooking time, avoiding any bone. An analog thermometer is inexpensive and easy to read; for just a bit more money, a digital version offers faster and more precise temperature readings.

10 **PARCHMENT PAPER** Parchment is used to create envelopes that efficiently steam food in the oven, a technique called cooking en papillote (see page 18). The paper is treated with silicone, so it is nonstick; it is also heatproof and grease-resistant. That's why parchment is often used to line cookie sheets and cake pans, instead of coating them with oil or butter. It's available bleached (white) or unbleached (brown).

LOW-FAT FLAVOR BOOSTERS

1 **MARINADES** Marinating meat, poultry, and fish not only adds flavor but also improves the texture, tenderizing meat and helping chicken, turkey, and fish stay moist during cooking. Follow this formula for making marinades: In a small bowl, whisk together an acid, such as lemon juice or vinegar; some oil or liquid, such as buttermilk; and seasonings of your choice, such as garlic, salt, pepper, spices, or herbs. Marinate meat and poultry for at least 30 minutes at room temperature in a nonreactive baking dish or resealable plastic bag; if marinating longer (up to 24 hours), refrigerate, turning food occasionally. Seafood should be marinated for only 15 to 30 minutes. Because it's not safe to consume marinades used on raw fish or meat, set some aside before marinating if you plan to baste food during cooking. Use a clean brush to apply.

2 **DRY RUBS** Spice rubs are mixtures of salt, sugar, spices, and dried herbs used to season meat, poultry, or seafood before cooking, especially when grilling. Rubs are quick and easy to assemble; they can also be more flavorful and economical than commercial blends. Unlike marinades, rubs can be applied just before cooking or up to several hours ahead. Use your fingers to rub the mixture on the meat, coating lightly—aim for about 1 teaspoon for every ¾ pound.

3 **VINAIGRETTES** Store-bought salad dressings are often loaded with fat, salt, sugar, and preservatives; making your own enables you to control the fat and calories as well as the flavor. When you use good-quality ingredients, you don't need as much dressing to satisfy your taste buds. The standard ratio of oil to vinegar in classic vinaigrettes is three or four parts oil to one part vinegar; including Dijon, honey, and other thickeners means you can cut back on the oil. For low-fat creamy dressings, swap in low-fat yogurt or buttermilk for mayonnaise and sour cream.

4 **HERBS** Fresh or dried, herbs add a welcome (calorie-free!) layer of flavor to just about any dish, whether as a main ingredient or a garnish. Add fresh herbs at the end of cooking—or, if using as a garnish, just before serving. Dried herbs are more potent than fresh, so you'll need to use less.

5 **SPICES** Ranging from fragrant and mild (cinnamon, cardamom) to aggressively hot (cayenne), spices do wonders in enhancing dishes, especially when scaling back on the fat content. If you can, buy whole spices and grind them as needed—their taste will be more pronounced, and they'll last longer in the pantry. Keep ground spices in their jars in a cool, dark place for up to one year.

6 **CITRUS JUICE AND ZEST** Grapefruits, oranges, lemons, and limes are among the kitchen's most versatile ingredients and can be used to flavor meat, fish, poultry, and vegetable dishes as well as dressings and desserts. Citrus juice adds acidity while zest contributes brightness. The sour undertones in citrus enhance almost all other flavors. Lemon juice is an excellent substitute for salt—a squeeze will perk up dips, sauces, and stews. Before zesting fruit, remove any waxy coating by washing the skin lightly, and buy organic citrus whenever possible.

7 DIJON MUSTARD With zero fat and only about five calories per teaspoon, Dijon is a boon to anyone wanting to cut back on calories but not flavor. Besides being a tasty sandwich spread, Dijon is an essential ingredient in vinaigrettes, where it acts as a thickener so less oil is needed, and adds sharpness to marinades. It can also be used in sauces for meats and some vegetable dishes, and as a flavorful alternative to mayonnaise when making chicken, tuna, egg, and potato salads. Another tip: try spreading some mustard on a pork chop or chicken cutlet, then top with bread crumbs and bake to a crisp crust.

8 YOGURT AND BUTTERMILK Low-fat yogurt and buttermilk are great stand-ins for other, more fattening types of dairy; they're also handy when making dips, dressings, and marinades (in fact, they are ideal for marinades, as their lactic acid tenderizes the meat). Both can be stirred into soup to mimic cream's silkiness. Yogurt has less fat than sour cream and tastes great drizzled over baked potatoes. Low-fat yogurt has half the cholesterol and saturated fat of the whole-milk kind, but is still rich and creamy; Greek-style yogurt has the best texture, and is higher in protein than regular yogurt. Buttermilk has less cholesterol than whole milk but just as many nutrients; despite its name, it doesn't actually contain any butter. Most buttermilk sold in the supermarket is labeled low-fat.

9 ASIAN FISH SAUCE AND SOY SAUCE Fish sauce (nuoc nam and nam pla) and soy sauce are staples of Asian cuisines. Though it's made from fish—usually anchovies— fish sauce doesn't taste strictly "fishy"; instead, it's salty and tangy. Soy sauce (made from soybeans) has a similar flavor profile. The two can be used, separately or in combination, in stir-fries, soups, noodle dishes, marinades, and dipping sauces. They pair well with other Asian ingredients such as cilantro, ginger, rice vinegar, and chiles.

10 SALSA America's favorite condiment is also a low-fat ally in the kitchen. Use it, naturally, in tacos, enchiladas, and quesadillas, but also to top off eggs, fish, poultry, and beef. There's a salsa for every palate; choose among red or green, chunky or smooth, mild, medium, or hot. Some salsas contain vinegar or lime juice for tanginess; those made with fruit, such as mango or pineapple, are slightly sweet. Green salsas get their color and zestiness from tomatillos (cousins to tomatoes) and green chiles. It's easy to make your own, but fresh salsas are a good shortcut; look for them in the refrigerator section, next to other sauces and spreads.

1

WINTER

Start the year off right by dialing back on rich foods and opting instead for light, invigorating dishes. Winter greens, cauliflower and other cruciferous vegetables, potatoes, and citrus fruits will see you through the season. Pair them with simple preparations of meat and fish—steaming in parchment is an especially easy and effective cooking method—for a meal that will leave you satisfied without feeling stuffed.

You can enjoy comfort food too without overindulging: bulk up meat-centric dishes with lots of added vegetables or beans, or incorporate small portions of high-calorie ingredients like cheese or bacon. A few tricks and savvy substitutions can lighten up all-time favorites like fried chicken, lasagna, and even pineapple upside-down cake.

WHY IT'S LIGHT Using light mayonnaise (and a bit of water) in the dressing considerably reduces the calories and fat. Lime juice and chili powder contribute unexpected flavor notes while still keeping the whole thing light.

CAESAR SALAD WITH SPICY SHRIMP

SERVES 4 ■ PREP TIME: 30 MINUTES ■ **TOTAL TIME: 30 MINUTES**

4 corn tortillas (5-inch)

2 teaspoons vegetable oil, such as safflower

1½ teaspoons chili powder

Coarse salt and ground pepper

¾ pound medium shrimp, peeled and deveined

⅓ cup light mayonnaise

2 tablespoons fresh lime juice

2 tablespoons grated Parmesan cheese, plus more for serving

4 anchovy fillets, rinsed and minced

1 to 2 tablespoons water

1 large head romaine lettuce (1½ pounds), torn into pieces

1 Preheat oven to 375°F. Place tortillas on a baking sheet. Dividing evenly, brush both sides with 1 teaspoon oil; sprinkle with ½ teaspoon chili powder, and season with salt and pepper. Bake until golden brown and crisp, turning once, 8 to 10 minutes. Let cool, then break into pieces.

2 Heat broiler. In a large bowl, toss shrimp with remaining teaspoon each oil and chili powder. Season with salt and pepper. Lay shrimp flat on a broiler pan, and cook until opaque throughout and lightly browned, turning once, 3 to 4 minutes.

3 Meanwhile, in a small bowl, whisk together mayonnaise, lime juice, Parmesan, anchovies, and 1 tablespoon water, adding more water as needed to reach desired consistency. Season with salt and pepper.

4 In a large bowl, toss lettuce with dressing. Divide among four plates, and top each with shrimp and broken tortillas. Serve with more Parmesan.

per serving: 282 calories; 12.6 g fat (1.8 g saturated fat); 23.6 g protein; 18.6 g carbohydrates; 4.3 g fiber

LIGHTER TOPPING
Here's another calorie saver: The salad is topped with baked corn tortillas, broken into pieces, instead of the usual buttery croutons.

282
CALORIES PER SERVING

82
CALORIES PER SERVING

GOOD TO KNOW Citrus fruits are excellent not just for eating out of hand, but also as substantial components of salads, particularly in the winter months, when other fresh produce can be difficult to come by. Here, orange slices are tossed with arugula and endive, and orange juice brightens the dressing.

ARUGULA, ENDIVE, AND ORANGE SALAD

SERVES 8 ■ PREP TIME: 20 MINUTES ■ **TOTAL TIME: 20 MINUTES**

2 navel oranges, peeled, quartered, and sliced (see below), plus 3 tablespoons fresh orange juice

2 tablespoons red-wine vinegar

1 tablespoon whole-grain mustard

2 tablespoons olive oil

Coarse salt and ground pepper

1½ pounds arugula (3 to 4 bunches), washed well

1 pound Belgian endive (4 to 6 heads), sliced crosswise ½ inch thick

1 In a small bowl or jar, whisk or shake orange juice, vinegar, mustard, and oil until thickened and combined; season with salt and pepper. (Dressing can be made ahead and refrigerated, covered, until ready to serve.)

2 In a large bowl, combine arugula, endive, and oranges; toss with dressing. Serve immediately.

per serving: 82 calories; 4.3 g fat (0.6 g saturated fat); 3.4 g protein; 9.9 g carbohydrates; 4 g fiber

PREPARING THE ORANGES
Slice off both ends of an orange. Following the curve of the fruit, cut away peel and white pith. Cut orange into quarters lengthwise, then, working over a bowl to catch the juice, slice sections thinly crosswise. Remove and discard seeds.

WHY IT'S LIGHT Low-fat yogurt, garlic, and vinegar are combined in a creamy, tangy dressing—without a drop of oil. Walnuts roasted with the vegetables add satisfying crunch and not much fat.

RED-LEAF SALAD WITH ROASTED SWEET POTATOES AND GREEN BEANS

SERVES 4 ■ PREP TIME: 15 MINUTES ■ **TOTAL TIME: 40 MINUTES**

2 sweet potatoes, peeled and cut into 1-inch chunks

1 medium red onion, quartered

2 tablespoons olive oil

Coarse salt and ground pepper

1 package (10 ounces) frozen cut green beans, thawed

⅓ cup walnuts

1 cup plain low-fat yogurt

2 tablespoons white-wine vinegar

1 garlic clove, crushed through a garlic press

1 head red-leaf lettuce (10 ounces), torn into bite-size pieces

1 Preheat oven to 450°F. On a large rimmed baking sheet, toss together sweet potatoes, onion, and oil; season with salt and pepper. Spread evenly and roast until sweet potatoes are browned and tender, about 20 minutes, tossing potatoes halfway through.

2 Add green beans and walnuts to sheet; toss. Roast until beans are tender, about 5 minutes.

3 Meanwhile, in a small bowl, whisk together yogurt, vinegar, and garlic; season dressing with salt and pepper.

4 Place lettuce in a large serving bowl; top with roasted vegetable mixture, and drizzle with dressing. Serve immediately.

per serving: 257 calories; 13.4 g fat (2.1 g saturated fat); 8.1 g protein; 29.2 g carbohydrates; 5.9 g fiber

257
CALORIES PER SERVING

372
CALORIES PER SERVING

FLAVOR BOOSTER Roasted vegetables are delicious—and healthful—on their own, but for variety, try tossing them with herbs or spices before cooking. Here, carrots and cauliflower are seasoned with cumin; feel free to experiment with similar ground spices. For the best flavor, lightly toast and grind the cumin seeds (or other spices) yourself.

COUSCOUS SALAD WITH ROASTED VEGETABLES AND CHICKPEAS

SERVES 4 ■ PREP TIME: 30 MINUTES ■ **TOTAL TIME: 1 HOUR**

1 pound carrots, sliced ¾ inch thick on the diagonal

1 head cauliflower (3 pounds), trimmed and cut into florets

1½ teaspoons ground cumin

3 tablespoons olive oil

Coarse salt and ground pepper

1¼ cups water

1 cup whole-wheat couscous

1 tablespoon lemon zest, plus ½ cup fresh lemon juice (from 3 lemons)

1 can (15.5 ounces) chickpeas, rinsed and drained

6 scallions, trimmed and thinly sliced

5 ounces baby arugula

1 Preheat oven to 450°F. Place carrots and cauliflower on a rimmed baking sheet; toss with cumin and 2 tablespoons oil. Season with salt and pepper. Transfer half the vegetables to a second baking sheet. Spread vegetables on both sheets in a single layer and roast until browned and tender, 25 to 30 minutes, rotating sheets and tossing vegetables halfway through. Let cool to room temperature.

2 Meanwhile, in a medium saucepan, bring the water to a boil. Stir in couscous and season with salt; cover and remove from heat. Let stand until tender, 5 minutes. Fluff with a fork; set aside to cool, uncovered.

3 Make dressing: In a small bowl, whisk together lemon zest and juice and remaining 1 tablespoon oil; season with salt and pepper.

4 In a large bowl, combine roasted vegetables with couscous, chickpeas, and scallions. Place arugula on a serving platter, and drizzle with 1 tablespoon dressing. Add remaining dressing to couscous mixture, and toss; serve with arugula.

per serving: 372 calories; 12.2 g fat (1.6 g saturated fat); 12.1 g protein; 59.8 g carbohydrates; 14.3 g fiber

WHY IT'S LIGHT This leaner take on a classic soup includes meatballs made with ground turkey instead of beef for less fat and fewer calories. To ensure the meatballs are juicy and flavorful, use dark-meat turkey with at least seven percent fat.

LIGHT ITALIAN WEDDING SOUP

SERVES 6 ■ PREP TIME: 25 MINUTES ■ **TOTAL TIME: 25 MINUTES**

1 pound ground dark-meat turkey (93% lean)

2 garlic cloves, minced

1 large egg, lightly beaten

½ cup plain dried breadcrumbs

¼ cup grated Parmesan cheese, plus more for serving

Coarse salt and ground pepper

1 tablespoon olive oil

1 medium onion, halved and thinly sliced

2 cans (14.5 ounces each) low-sodium chicken broth

2 cans (14.5 ounces each) diced tomatoes in juice

2 heads escarole (2 pounds total), trimmed and coarsely chopped

1 In a large bowl, combine turkey, garlic, egg, breadcrumbs, Parmesan, 1 teaspoon salt, and ¼ teaspoon pepper. Roll tablespoonfuls of mixture into balls.

2 In a large pot, heat oil over medium. Cook onion, stirring occasionally, until softened, 3 to 4 minutes. Add broth and tomatoes (with juice); bring to a simmer. Add meatballs; cook, without stirring, until meatballs float to surface, about 5 minutes.

3 Add as much escarole to pot as will fit. Cook, gradually adding remaining escarole, until wilted and meatballs are cooked through, about 5 minutes more. Thin soup with water if desired; season with salt and pepper. Serve soup sprinkled with more Parmesan.

per serving: 250 calories; 9.8 g fat (3 g saturated fat); 23.6 g protein; 19.3 g carbohydrates; 4.8 g fiber

ABOUT ESCAROLE
A type of chicory, escarole may look like a head of lettuce (to which it's closely related), but it's much more flavorful, and has thicker leaves and a pale yellow heart. Rich in vitamin A and folate, it's also a good source of fiber. To store escarole, refrigerate in an unsealed plastic bag lined with paper towels for up to 4 days.

250
CALORIES PER SERVING

221
CALORIES PER SERVING

WHY IT'S LIGHT For beefy taste without excess fat, use ground sirloin instead of chuck. This chili is also bulked up with extra portions of beans and tomatoes. Briefly cooking the cocoa, chili powder, and tomato paste before adding the beef helps intensify their flavors.

LIGHTER BEEF CHILI

SERVES 6 ■ PREP TIME: 25 MINUTES ■ **TOTAL TIME: 40 MINUTES**

1 tablespoon vegetable oil, such as safflower

1 medium onion, chopped

4 garlic cloves, chopped

Coarse salt and ground pepper

2 tablespoons tomato paste

2 tablespoons chili powder

2 tablespoons unsweetened cocoa powder

1 pound ground beef sirloin

2 cans (14.5 ounces each) diced tomatoes in juice

2 cans (15.5 ounces each) pinto beans, rinsed and drained

Assorted toppings, such as reduced-fat sour cream, sliced scallions, and baked tortilla chips, for serving (optional)

1 In a large, heavy-bottomed saucepan, heat oil over medium-high. Add onion and garlic, and season with salt and pepper. Cook, stirring frequently, until softened, 3 to 5 minutes.

2 Add tomato paste, chili powder, and cocoa powder. Cook, stirring, until mixture is fragrant, about 1 minute. Add beef and cook, breaking up meat with a spoon, until no longer pink, 3 to 5 minutes.

3 Add tomatoes (with their juice) and beans. Bring to a boil over high heat; reduce to a simmer, and cook until chili is slightly thickened, 10 to 15 minutes. Serve with toppings, as desired.

per serving: 221 calories; 7 g fat (1.9 g saturated fat); 20.7 g protein; 22.9 g carbohydrates; 5.5 g fiber

GOOD TO KNOW Using poached chicken keeps this Asian-style soup on the more delicate side; with this method of cooking, you get tender and moist meat as well as a tasty broth, which you can use in a variety of dishes.

ASIAN CHICKEN AND WATERCRESS SOUP

SERVES 4 ■ PREP TIME: 25 MINUTES ■ **TOTAL TIME: 25 MINUTES**

6 cups chicken broth (recipe follows)

2 red bell peppers, ribs and seeds removed, thinly sliced lengthwise, and cut crosswise into 2-inch pieces

2 tablespoons soy sauce

1 to 3 teaspoons Asian hot chili sauce

3 cups (12 ounces) diced poached chicken (recipe follows)

1 bunch watercress (6 ounces), large stems trimmed

2 scallions, trimmed, thinly sliced lengthwise, and cut crosswise into 2-inch pieces

1 In a 3-quart saucepan, bring broth, bell peppers, soy sauce, and chili sauce (to taste) to a simmer; cook until peppers are crisp-tender, stirring occasionally, about 6 minutes.

2 Add chicken and watercress; cook 1 minute. Ladle into bowls, and top with scallions.

per serving: 179 calories; 3.5 g fat (1 g saturated fat); 29.5 g protein; 9.5 g carbohydrates; 1.7 g fiber

POACHED CHICKEN BREASTS AND CHICKEN BROTH

5 pounds bone-in, skin-on chicken breasts (about 6)

1 medium onion, cut into 8 wedges

2 medium carrots, quartered crosswise

2 celery stalks, quartered crosswise

2 dried bay leaves

3 garlic cloves

6 sprigs flat-leaf parsley

3 sprigs thyme (or ¼ teaspoon dried)

1 Combine all ingredients in a 5-quart pot. Cover with water by 2 inches. Bring to a boil; reduce to a simmer, and cover. Cook chicken until no longer pink in the center and an instant-read thermometer inserted in the thickest part of the meat (avoiding bone) registers 160°F, about 15 minutes.

2 Transfer chicken to a rimmed baking sheet and arrange in a single layer. When chicken is cool enough to handle, remove and discard skin and bones. Chop or shred meat, as desired.

3 With a slotted spoon, remove and discard vegetables and herbs. Strain broth through a fine sieve lined with a damp paper towel into a large bowl. If broth is more than 8 cups (2 quarts), return to pot and reduce over medium-high heat until you have just 8 cups. (Once cooled, broth can be refrigerated in an airtight container up to 2 days, or frozen up to 3 months; thaw overnight in the refrigerator before using.) **MAKES 8 CUPS CHOPPED CHICKEN AND 8 CUPS BROTH**

349
CALORIES PER SERVING

WHY IT'S LIGHT Traditional split-pea soup is often made with ham or bacon; this version is completely meat-free, relying on a combination of vegetables, garlic, and dried thyme for flavor. It also uses water, not broth, as the base.

VEGETARIAN SPLIT-PEA SOUP

SERVES 8 ■ PREP TIME: 20 MINUTES ■ **TOTAL TIME: 1 HOUR 15 MINUTES**

3 cups dried split peas, rinsed and picked over

1½ pounds russet potatoes (about 3), peeled and cut into ½-inch pieces

7 medium carrots, sliced ½ inch thick (3 cups)

2 green bell peppers, ribs and seeds removed, cut into ¼-inch pieces (2 cups)

2 medium onions, cut into ½-inch pieces (2 cups)

2 garlic cloves, minced

1 teaspoon dried thyme

4 quarts water

Coarse salt and ground pepper

1 In a large pot, combine split peas, potatoes, carrots, peppers, onions, garlic, thyme, and the water. Bring to a boil over high heat. Reduce heat, cover partially, and simmer, stirring occasionally, until peas have broken down and liquid has thickened, about 45 minutes. Skim foam from the surface as needed.

2 Season soup with salt and pepper, and add more water if necessary to achieve a consistency that is smooth but not too thick. Serve hot.

per serving: 349 calories; 1.1 g fat (0.2 g saturated fat); 20.7 g protein; 67 g carbohydrates; 22 g fiber

FREEZING TIP
Once cooled, the soup can be frozen in single-serving microwave-safe containers. Defrost each portion at room temperature, then reheat in the microwave.

GOOD TO KNOW Puréed vegetables give soup the same sort of velvety consistency that cream does. Vegetables like sweet potatoes, because of their starch content, also lend body to soups and stews.

SWEET POTATO AND CHIPOTLE SOUP

SERVES 8 ■ PREP TIME: 15 MINUTES ■ **TOTAL TIME: 50 MINUTES**

1 tablespoon olive oil

1 medium onion, chopped

Coarse salt and ground pepper

2 teaspoons ground cumin

2 garlic cloves, minced

4 medium sweet potatoes (2 pounds total), peeled and cut into 1-inch pieces

½ to 1 canned chipotle chile in adobo, chopped

7 cups low-sodium store-bought chicken broth

Reduced-fat sour cream, for serving

Toasted flour tortilla wedges, for serving (optional)

1 In a large Dutch oven or other heavy pot, heat oil over medium-high. Add onion and season with salt and pepper; cook until beginning to brown around edges, stirring occasionally, about 7 minutes. Add cumin and garlic and cook, stirring, until fragrant, about 1 minute. Stir in sweet potatoes, chipotle chile to taste, and broth. Bring to a boil; reduce to a rapid simmer, partially cover, and cook until sweet potatoes can be mashed easily with a spoon, 20 to 25 minutes.

2 Let soup cool slightly. Working in batches, transfer soup to a blender and purée until smooth, being careful not to fill blender more than halfway each time. Return puréed soup to pot over low heat and season with salt and pepper. Divide soup among eight bowls, and top with sour cream; serve with tortilla wedges, if desired.

per serving: 156 calories; 3.2 g fat (0.7 g saturated fat); 6.3 g protein; 27 g carbohydrates; 3.8 g fiber

156
CALORIES PER SERVING

285
CALORIES PER SERVING

WHY IT'S LIGHT Because lots of Indian food entrees use high-fat ghee (clarified butter) or coconut milk as the cooking liquid, they can contain more fat and calories than you might think. For this vegetarian curry, chickpeas and spices are simmered simply in water, yet the results are still delicious. Serve with rice or warm whole-wheat pitas.

QUICK CHICKPEA CURRY

SERVES 4 ■ PREP TIME: 20 MINUTES ■ **TOTAL TIME: 40 MINUTES**

1 tablespoon olive oil

1 large yellow onion, finely chopped

3 garlic cloves, minced

1 tablespoon curry powder, preferably Madras

1 cinnamon stick (3 inches)

Pinch of ground cloves

2 cans (15 ounces each) chickpeas, rinsed and drained

3 tablespoons ketchup

2 cups water

Coarse salt and ground pepper

Chopped cilantro and lemon wedges, for serving (optional)

1 In a large straight-sided skillet, heat olive oil over medium-high. Add onion and cook, stirring occasionally, until dark brown around edges, about 6 minutes. Add garlic, curry, cinnamon, and cloves; cook, stirring, until fragrant, 30 seconds.

2 Add chickpeas, ketchup, and the water; season with salt and pepper. Bring to a boil; reduce to a simmer, cover, and cook 20 minutes.

3 Uncover and increase heat to medium-high; cook, stirring, until sauce is slightly reduced, about 5 minutes. Serve topped with cilantro, with lemon wedges alongside, if desired.

per serving: 285 calories; 5.5 g fat (0.6 g saturated fat); 12.8 g protein; 46.8 g carbohydrates; 9.7 g fiber

FLAVOR BOOSTER The carrots and tofu are both briefly marinated in a soy sauce mixture before being broiled. Scallions, rice vinegar, and toasted sesame oil lend other Asian elements. Be sure to use extra-firm tofu, as it will hold up better than other types of tofu.

SOY-GLAZED TOFU AND CARROTS

SERVES 4 ■ PREP TIME: 15 MINUTES ■ TOTAL TIME: 45 MINUTES

2 tablespoons vegetable oil, such as safflower

3 tablespoons soy sauce

1 teaspoon coarse salt

1½ pounds carrots (8 to 9 medium), cut into 2-inch lengths (thick pieces halved lengthwise)

2 packages (12 to 14 ounces each) extra-firm tofu, drained, each block cut into 16 equal pieces

4 scallions, trimmed and thinly sliced

1 to 2 tablespoons rice vinegar (unseasoned)

1 to 2 teaspoons toasted sesame oil

1 Heat broiler, with rack 4 inches from heat. In a large bowl, whisk together vegetable oil, soy sauce, and salt. Add carrots; toss to coat.

2 With a slotted spoon, transfer carrots (reserving bowl with marinade) to a rimmed baking sheet. Push carrots to one side.

3 A few pieces at a time, add tofu to marinade in bowl; turn gently to coat, then transfer to sheet, arranging in a single layer. Reserve bowl with marinade.

4 Broil until carrots and tofu are browned, turning tofu halfway through cooking time and tossing carrots occasionally (more frequently toward end of cooking time), 20 to 25 minutes.

5 Transfer tofu and carrots to reserved bowl with marinade. Add scallions along with vinegar and sesame oil to taste; toss gently to combine, and serve.

per serving: 340 calories; 20.5 g fat (0.9 g saturated fat); 22.3 g protein; 23.9 g carbohydrates; 6.2 g fiber

340

CALORIES PER SERVING

418
CALORIES PER SERVING

FLAVOR BOOSTER With its tangy flavor and crumbly texture, a little feta cheese goes a long way. Use it to add oomph to salads such as this one, which is bulked up with cucumber, cabbage, shallot, and fresh parsley.

COLD SOBA SALAD WITH FETA AND CUCUMBER

SERVES 4 ■ PREP TIME: 15 MINUTES ■ TOTAL TIME: 15 MINUTES (PLUS CHILLING)

- 1 package (8.8 ounces) soba (Japanese buckwheat noodles)
- ½ English cucumber, cut into matchsticks
- ¼ head red cabbage, thinly sliced
- 1 shallot, thinly sliced
- 1 cup fresh flat-leaf parsley leaves, coarsely chopped, plus more for garnish
- ¼ cup fresh lemon juice
- 3 tablespoons olive oil

   Coarse salt and ground pepper
- 4 ounces feta cheese, crumbled

1 In a large pot of boiling salted water, cook soba according to package instructions. Drain, then rinse under cold water to stop the cooking. Drain well.

2 In a large bowl, combine cucumber, cabbage, shallot, parsley, lemon juice, and oil. Add soba and toss to combine; season with salt and pepper. Refrigerate until chilled, about 30 minutes.

3 To serve, toss salad with feta, and garnish with parsley.

per serving: 418 calories; 16.8 g fat (5.8 g saturated fat); 15 g protein; 58.6 g carbohydrates; 1.8 g fiber

GOOD TO KNOW When tucking into heartier dishes and casseroles, such as these pillowy potato dumplings, keep portions in check by preparing individual servings in separate baking pans. Vacuum-sealed packages of gnocchi are found in the pasta aisle as well as the refrigerator or freezer section of larger grocery stores. There's no need to thaw frozen gnocchi before cooking.

BAKED GNOCCHI WITH RICOTTA AND MARINARA

SERVES 4 ■ PREP TIME: 15 MINUTES ■ TOTAL TIME: 20 MINUTES

Coarse salt and ground pepper

1 package (15 to 16 ounces) frozen gnocchi

½ cup homemade or store-bought marinara sauce

¾ cup ricotta cheese

¼ cup grated Parmesan cheese

1 Bring a large pot of water to a boil; add salt. Cook gnocchi according to package instructions (they are ready when most have floated to the top). Remove with a slotted spoon and drain in a colander.

2 Heat broiler, with rack in the top position. Divide gnocchi among four 8-ounce shallow baking dishes (or place in an 8-inch square baking dish). Season with salt and pepper. Top with marinara sauce and ricotta, then sprinkle evenly with Parmesan.

3 Broil until tops are browned in spots and gnocchi are heated through, 3 to 5 minutes (longer for 8-inch version), rotating once. Serve immediately.

per serving: 341 calories; 9.1 g fat (5.1 g saturated fat); 14.3 g protein; 50.7 g carbohydrates; 3.1 g fiber

341
CALORIES PER SERVING

269
CALORIES PER SERVING

FLAVOR BOOSTER Chicken thighs and drumsticks are not as lean as breast meat, but they have great flavor and stay juicy when cooked by long and slow methods such as braising. Here, they are braised in an oil-free liquid seasoned with soy sauce, brown sugar, fresh ginger, garlic, cilantro, balsamic vinegar, scallions, and ground spices.

SOY-GINGER CHICKEN

SERVES 4 ■ PREP TIME: 30 MINUTES ■ TOTAL TIME: 2 HOURS

⅓ cup soy sauce

2 tablespoons dark-brown sugar

5 garlic cloves, thinly sliced

⅔ cup fresh cilantro, coarsely chopped, plus whole leaves for garnish

1 piece fresh ginger (about 2 inches), peeled and cut into thin strips

5 scallions, trimmed and thinly sliced on the diagonal (1 cup packed)

1 tablespoon balsamic vinegar

1 teaspoon ground coriander

½ teaspoon ground pepper

4 chicken drumsticks and 4 thighs (about 2½ pounds total), skin removed

2 medium carrots, thinly sliced crosswise

1 cup plus 1 tablespoon water

1 tablespoon cornstarch

Cooked rice, for serving (optional)

1 Preheat oven to 350°F. In a 5-quart Dutch oven or other heavy pot, stir together soy sauce, brown sugar, garlic, cilantro, ginger, ½ cup scallions, the vinegar, coriander, and pepper. Add chicken and carrots; toss to coat, then stir in 1 cup water. Cover pot and transfer to oven; cook until chicken is tender, about 1½ hours. Using a large spoon, skim off any fat from surface of cooking liquid.

2 In a 2-cup glass measuring cup or small bowl, whisk cornstarch with remaining 1 tablespoon water. Ladle 1 cup cooking liquid into measuring cup; whisk to combine. Pour into a small saucepan, and bring to a boil; cook until thickened, about 1 minute. Stir mixture into pot to combine.

3 Serve chicken mixture with rice, if desired, garnished with cilantro leaves and remaining ½ cup scallions.

per serving (without rice): 269 calories; 8.5 g fat (2.3 g saturated fat); 29.5 g protein; 18.5 g carbohydrates; 2.1 g fiber

FLAVOR BOOSTER Fennel, tomato, and wine are common ingredients in Mediterranean cooking; in this recipe, they make a wonderful bed for chicken breast halves. Once the chicken is cooked through, the vegetables become a flavorful sauce to serve alongside.

CHICKEN WITH FENNEL AND TOMATO

SERVES 4 ■ PREP TIME: 20 MINUTES ■ **TOTAL TIME: 40 MINUTES**

6 plum tomatoes (about 1 pound), cored and cut into ¾-inch pieces

2 fennel bulbs (10 to 12 ounces each), halved, cored, and thinly sliced crosswise, fronds reserved for garnish

½ cup dry white wine

Coarse salt and ground pepper

4 boneless, skinless chicken breast halves (6 to 8 ounces each)

1 In a large, deep skillet, combine tomatoes, sliced fennel, and wine; season with salt and pepper. Place chicken breasts in a single layer on top of vegetables; season with salt and pepper. Bring to a boil; reduce heat to medium-low, cover skillet, and simmer gently until chicken is cooked through, 15 to 20 minutes.

2 Use a slotted spatula to transfer chicken to a cutting board and slice crosswise about ½ inch thick. To serve, divide vegetable mixture among shallow bowls; top each with a sliced breast. Garnish with reserved fennel fronds.

per serving: 323 calories; 3.2 g fat (0.8 g saturated fat); 54.7 g protein; 12.4 g carbohydrates; 4.7 g fiber

STEAMING THE CHICKEN
Choose a skillet that is just deep enough to hold all the ingredients (the vegetables will wilt slightly during cooking), with enough room to cover tightly with a lid. Also, allow as much space as possible between the chicken breasts to ensure even cooking.

323
CALORIES PER SERVING

372

CALORIES PER SERVING

GOOD TO KNOW Even though the chicken thighs are seared with the skin on, the extra fat is poured off from the pot before the other ingredients are added. Swapping brown rice for white adds a better dose of fiber and nutrients.

ONE-POT CHICKEN AND BROWN RICE

SERVES 4 ■ PREP TIME: 15 MINUTES ■ **TOTAL TIME: 1 HOUR 40 MINUTES**

1 tablespoon olive oil

4 bone-in, skin-on chicken thighs (6 to 8 ounces each)

Coarse salt and ground pepper

1 large yellow onion, cut into 8 wedges

2 celery stalks, cut into 1½-inch pieces

2 medium carrots, cut into 1½-inch pieces

1 dried bay leaf

1¾ cups water

1 cup brown rice

1 In a large Dutch oven or other heavy pot, heat oil over medium-high. Season chicken with salt and pepper and place, skin side down, in pot. Cook until golden brown on both sides, 10 to 12 minutes total.

2 Pour off all but 1 tablespoon fat from pot; add onion and celery. Reduce heat to low, cover, and cook 20 minutes.

3 Add carrots, bay leaf, and the water; stir in rice and season with salt and pepper. Bring to a boil, then reduce heat to low. Cover and cook until rice absorbs almost all the liquid, 40 to 45 minutes. Let stand, covered, 10 minutes before serving.

per serving: 372 calories; 13.9 g fat (3.3 g saturated fat); 18.3 g protein; 42.6 g carbohydrates; 4.6 g fiber

WHY IT'S LIGHT Baking the lightly breaded pieces on a wire rack results in "fried" chicken that is lower in fat and calories; removing the skin before cooking also helps. For spicier chicken, add a few drops of hot sauce to the buttermilk marinade.

OVEN-FRIED CHICKEN

SERVES 4 ■ PREP TIME: 10 MINUTES ■ **TOTAL TIME: 1 HOUR 20 MINUTES** (WITH MARINATING)

1 whole chicken (3½ to 4 pounds), cut into 10 pieces, wings reserved for another use

¼ cup low-fat buttermilk

1 garlic clove, minced

2 teaspoons coarse salt

¼ teaspoon ground pepper

6 slices whole-wheat sandwich bread

3 tablespoons vegetable oil, such as safflower

1 Remove skin from chicken and discard. In a large bowl, toss chicken with buttermilk, garlic, salt, and pepper. Marinate at room temperature 30 minutes (or refrigerate, covered, up to overnight).

2 Meanwhile, preheat oven to 425°F. In a food processor, pulse bread until coarse crumbs form. Transfer to a rimmed baking sheet and toss with the oil. Spread evenly and bake crumbs until golden brown, 8 to 12 minutes, tossing twice. Transfer to a large bowl.

3 Set a wire rack over the baking sheet. Working with one piece at a time, lift chicken from buttermilk mixture and dredge in breadcrumbs. Transfer chicken to rack.

4 Bake chicken, without turning, until cooked through, 30 to 40 minutes, tenting with foil if crust is browning too quickly. Serve warm.

per serving: 385 calories; 16.6 g fat (2.7 g saturated fat); 39.5 g protein; 18.3 g carbohydrates; 2.9 g fiber

COATING THE CHICKEN
When dredging the chicken in breadcrumbs, work with one piece at a time, and allow excess marinade to drip off before coating; this will prevent lumps. Turn the chicken to coat completely, and pat the crumbs firmly to adhere.

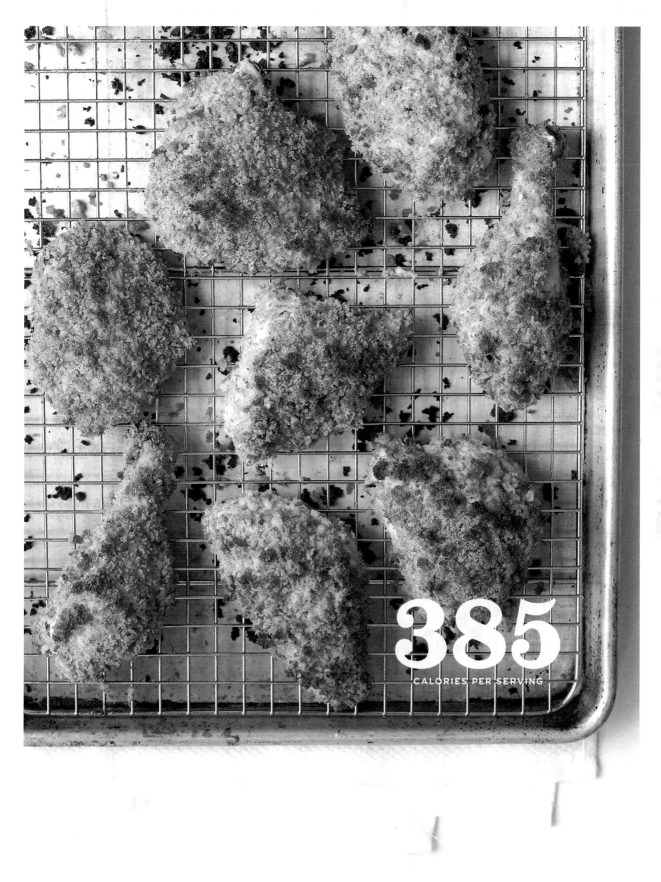

385
CALORIES PER SERVING

389

CALORIES PER SERVING

WHY IT'S LIGHT Only one side of the chicken is breaded here, and an egg white instead of a whole egg is used to bind the whole-wheat crumbs to the meat. Serve the chicken with a side of whole-wheat spaghetti tossed with olive oil and fresh herbs, or a simple salad.

LIGHT CHICKEN PARMESAN

SERVES 4 ■ PREP TIME: 20 MINUTES ■ TOTAL TIME: 35 MINUTES

2 slices whole-wheat sandwich bread, torn into pieces

1 tablespoon grated Parmesan cheese

1 teaspoon olive oil

Coarse salt and ground pepper

2 tablespoons all-purpose flour

1 large egg white

4 boneless, skinless chicken breast halves (6 to 8 ounces each)

¾ cup shredded part-skim mozzarella cheese (3 ounces)

1 can (28 ounces) whole peeled tomatoes in purée

1 garlic clove, minced

1 Preheat oven to 425°F, with rack in upper third. Line a rimmed baking sheet with foil. In a food processor, combine bread, Parmesan, oil, and a pinch each of salt and pepper. Pulse until coarse crumbs form; transfer to a shallow bowl. Place flour in a second shallow bowl; season with salt and pepper. Place egg white in a third shallow bowl, and beat with a fork until frothy.

2 Dip top side of a chicken breast half in flour, shaking off excess. Dip same side in egg white, letting excess drip off, then in breadcrumbs, pressing to adhere. (Do not bread other side.) Repeat with remaining chicken and transfer, breaded side up, to prepared baking sheet.

3 Bake until breadcrumbs are crisp and browned, 8 to 10 minutes. Remove from oven; sprinkle with mozzarella. Continue baking until chicken is cooked through and cheese is lightly browned, 2 to 4 minutes.

4 Meanwhile, place tomatoes (with purée) in a large skillet, and break them up with your fingers. Add garlic; season with salt and pepper. Bring to a boil, reduce to a simmer, and cook until sauce has thickened, 6 to 8 minutes. Serve chicken with a generous amount of tomato sauce.

per serving: 389 calories; 8.3 g fat (2.3 g saturated fat); 55.9 g protein; 18 g carbohydrates; 2.7 g fiber

WHY IT'S LIGHT Lean chicken breast replaces the more common corned beef in a hearty-yet-healthy hash. For more flavor, roast the chicken with bones and skin intact, then remove them once the chicken is cooked. Spinach is another unexpected—and fat-free—addition.

CHICKEN, SPINACH, AND POTATO HASH

SERVES 4 ■ PREP TIME: 25 MINUTES ■ **TOTAL TIME: 50 MINUTES**

2 bone-in, skin-on chicken breast halves (12 to 14 ounces each)

2 tablespoons olive oil

Coarse salt and ground pepper

2 teaspoons fresh thyme leaves

1½ pounds Yukon Gold potatoes, cut into ¾-inch pieces

2 large shallots, finely chopped

2 garlic cloves, minced

2 tablespoons water

½ pound spinach, trimmed, washed, and coarsely chopped

2 tablespoons fresh lemon juice

1 Preheat oven to 450°F. Place chicken on a rimmed baking sheet. Drizzle with 2 teaspoons oil, dividing evenly, and season with salt, pepper, and the thyme. Roast until chicken is cooked through (an instant-read thermometer inserted in thickest part, avoiding bone, should register 160°F), about 35 minutes. When cool enough to handle, discard skin and bones; cut chicken into bite-size pieces.

2 Meanwhile, in a medium saucepan, cover potatoes with water. Bring to a boil and add salt; cook until potatoes are tender when pierced with the tip of a paring knife, about 15 minutes; drain.

3 In a large skillet, heat remaining 1 tablespoon plus 1 teaspoon oil over medium-high. Add shallots and cook, stirring, until softened, about 3 minutes. Add garlic and cook, stirring, until fragrant, 30 seconds. Add potatoes and cook, stirring often, until golden brown, about 7 minutes. Add the water, scraping up browned bits from bottom of pan with a wooden spoon. Cook, stirring often, until skillet is dry and potatoes are browned, about 3 minutes more.

4 Add chicken and spinach; cook, stirring, until spinach wilts and chicken is heated through, about 2 minutes. Stir in lemon juice and season with salt and pepper. Serve immediately.

per serving: 295 calories; 8.6 g fat (1.4 g saturated fat); 20.1 g protein; 41.3 g carbohydrates; 6.4 g fiber

295
CALORIES PER SERVING

391
CALORIES PER SERVING

WHY IT'S LIGHT There's less pasta (half a package) than usual but still plenty of leaner-than-pork poultry sausage and two bunches of broccoli rabe in this satisfying main course for four. Blanching the broccoli rabe tones down its bite before it is finished in the skillet.

ORECCHIETTE WITH CHICKEN SAUSAGE AND BROCCOLI RABE

SERVES 4 ■ PREP TIME: 20 MINUTES ■ **TOTAL TIME: 35 MINUTES**

Coarse salt and ground pepper

2 bunches broccoli rabe (2 pounds total), trimmed and cut into ½-inch pieces

8 ounces orecchiette or other short pasta shapes

2 precooked Italian chicken or turkey sausages (6 ounces total), cut into ¼-inch slices

2 tablespoons white-wine vinegar

1 garlic clove, minced

1 tablespoon olive oil

1 Bring a large pot of water to a boil; add salt. Blanch broccoli rabe until bright green, about 1 minute. Using a wire skimmer or small sieve, transfer to a colander and let drain. Return water to a boil. Add pasta, and cook until al dente according to package instructions. Drain.

2 Heat a large skillet over medium-high. Add sausage; cook, without turning slices, until browned, about 4 minutes. Add broccoli rabe, vinegar, and garlic. Cook until broccoli rabe is tender, scraping up browned bits in skillet, 2 to 3 minutes. Add pasta and oil and season with salt and pepper; toss to combine. Serve immediately.

per serving: 391 calories; 8 g fat (2.2 g saturated fat); 22.2 g protein; 53 g carbohydrates; 7.5 g fiber

SUBSTITUTION
You can use 1 head broccoli, cut into small florets, in place of the broccoli rabe in this recipe. Follow recipe to blanch florets, then cook in skillet until just tender.

SMART SUBSTITUTION Next time you make a sandwich wrap, reach for lettuce leaves instead of a flatbread or tortilla. This recipe is based on a popular Korean dish (ssam bap) that has a spicy filling of beef and fresh herbs encased in lettuce. Cellophane noodles, tossed with a bit of oil and scallions, round out the meal.

BEEF AND MANGO LETTUCE WRAPS

SERVES 4 ■ PREP TIME: 10 MINUTES ■ **TOTAL TIME: 30 MINUTES**

1½ pounds flank steak

   Coarse salt and ground pepper

1 package (3.75 ounces) cellophane noodles

2 tablespoons vegetable oil, such as safflower

6 scallions, trimmed; 3 thinly sliced and 3 cut into thirds

¼ cup fresh lime juice (from about 2 limes)

¼ cup coarsely chopped fresh cilantro

1 garlic clove, minced

8 Boston lettuce leaves

1 ripe mango, peeled, pitted, and cut into strips

1 Heat broiler, with rack 4 inches from heat. Place steak on a large rimmed baking sheet; season with salt and pepper. Broil until medium-rare, 10 to 12 minutes, turning halfway through. Transfer to a cutting board. Let rest 10 minutes, tented with foil.

2 While steak rests, cook noodles until tender according to package instructions; drain and return to pot. Add 1 tablespoon oil and the sliced scallions; season with salt and pepper.

3 In a small bowl, combine lime juice, cilantro, garlic, and remaining 1 tablespoon oil; season sauce with salt and pepper.

4 Thinly slice steak against the grain. Fill lettuce leaves with beef, mango, and remaining scallion pieces; drizzle with sauce. Serve with noodles.

per serving: 482 calories; 21.3 g fat (6.7 g saturated fat); 37.1 g protein; 35 g carbohydrates; 1.8 g fiber

CUTTING A MANGO
Peel the mango with a sharp vegetable peeler or knife. Stand upright and cut both sides away from the large oblong pit in the center, then cut the flesh into thin slices (or as directed in a specific recipe).

482
CALORIES PER SERVING

327
CALORIES PER SERVING

WHY IT'S LIGHT Made with lean sirloin, and studded with chopped carrots, celery, and onion, this meatloaf is just as delicious as the diner classic, but better for you. The meat mixture is bound with an egg white, not the whole egg, as well as the flaky Japanese breadcrumbs known as panko. Even the potatoes are lighter, since they are mashed with low-fat buttermilk (rather than butter, cream, or whole milk).

LIGHTER BLUE-PLATE SPECIAL

SERVES 4 ■ PREP TIME: 30 MINUTES ■ **TOTAL TIME: 1 HOUR**

- 2 small carrots, chopped
- 2 celery stalks, chopped
- ¼ medium onion, chopped
- ¼ cup panko (Japanese breadcrumbs)
- 1 large egg white
- ¾ pound ground beef sirloin
  Coarse salt and ground pepper
- ¼ cup homemade or store-bought barbecue sauce
- 1 pound russet potatoes, peeled and sliced ½ inch thick
- ¾ cup low-fat buttermilk
- 1 pound green beans, stem ends removed
- 1 teaspoon olive oil

1 Preheat oven to 450°F. Process carrots, celery, onion, and panko with egg white in a food processor until finely chopped and combined, about 1 minute. Transfer to a large bowl; mix in beef, 1 teaspoon salt, and ⅛ teaspoon pepper.

2 On a foil-lined rimmed baking sheet, form meat mixture into a 6-inch-long loaf; brush with half the barbecue sauce. Bake until an instant-read thermometer inserted in loaf registers 160°F, 25 to 30 minutes, brushing halfway through with remaining sauce.

3 Meanwhile, in a medium saucepan, cover potatoes with cold water by 1 inch. Bring to a boil; add salt. Reduce to a simmer, and cook until potatoes are easily pierced with the tip of a paring knife, 15 to 20 minutes. Drain; return to pan. Stir over medium until a starchy film forms on bottom of pan, about 1 minute. Remove from heat; mash with buttermilk until smooth. Season with salt and pepper.

4 While potatoes cook, set a steamer basket in a pot filled with 1 inch of simmering water. Add green beans; cover, and cook until crisp-tender and bright green, 4 to 6 minutes. Transfer to a bowl; add oil, season with salt and pepper, and toss.

5 Serve meatloaf with mashed potatoes and green beans.

per serving: 327 calories; 5.9 g fat (2.2 g saturated fat); 24.7 g protein; 45.2 g carbohydrates; 7 g fiber

SMART SUBSTITUTIONS Small swap-ins can make a big difference. Whole-wheat noodles, low-fat cottage cheese, and lean ground sirloin lighten up this lasagna. Sautéed eggplant rounds out the ground-beef sauce; melted part-skim mozzarella on top (but not inside) keeps the dish feeling indulgent, but more moderately so.

HEALTHIER MEAT LASAGNA

SERVES 4 ■ PREP TIME: 40 MINUTES ■ **TOTAL TIME: 1 HOUR 20 MINUTES**

6 whole-wheat lasagna noodles (about 4 ounces total), broken in half

1 tablespoon olive oil

1 medium onion, chopped

1 small Italian eggplant (1 pound), peeled and cut into ½-inch slices

2 garlic cloves, minced

Coarse salt and ground pepper

8 ounces ground beef sirloin

1 can (10.75 ounces) tomato purée

2 cups low-fat (1%) cottage cheese

¼ cup plus 2 tablespoons grated Parmesan cheese (1 ounce)

½ cup shredded part-skim mozzarella cheese (2 ounces)

1 Preheat oven to 375°F. Place noodles in an 8-inch square baking dish, and cover with hot water; set aside to soften.

2 In a medium Dutch oven or other heavy pot, heat oil over medium-high. Add onion, eggplant, and garlic; season with salt and pepper. Cover and cook, stirring occasionally, until eggplant is very tender, 8 to 10 minutes. Add sirloin and cook, breaking up meat with a spoon, until no longer pink, 3 to 5 minutes. Add tomato purée and cook until thickened, 3 to 5 minutes. Season meat sauce with salt and pepper.

3 Meanwhile, in a medium bowl, combine cottage cheese and ¼ cup Parmesan; season with salt and pepper. Remove noodles from baking dish, discarding water (dry dish).

4 Spread about ¼ cup meat sauce in bottom of dish, and top with 4 noodle halves in a single layer. Sprinkle evenly with a third of the cheese mixture, then top with a third of the sauce. Repeat twice with remaining noodles, cheese mixture, and sauce. Sprinkle evenly with mozzarella and remaining 2 tablespoons Parmesan.

5 Bake until lasagna is bubbling and cheese topping is golden, 30 to 35 minutes. Let stand 10 minutes before cutting and serving.

per serving: 469 calories; 15.4 g fat (6 g saturated fat); 40.4 g protein; 42.4 g carbohydrates; 9.5 g fiber

469
CALORIES PER SERVING

415
CALORIES PER SERVING

WHY IT'S LIGHT Lamb is naturally tender and flavorful; shoulder meat is leaner than other cuts (such as loin or sirloin chops). You may substitute any other lean cut of meat, such as cubed beef chuck, pork shoulder, or boneless, skinless chicken thighs.

IRISH LAMB STEW

SERVES 8 ■ PREP TIME: 30 MINUTES ■ TOTAL TIME: 2 HOURS 15 MINUTES

½ cup all-purpose flour

Coarse salt and ground pepper

3 pounds boneless lamb stew meat (preferably shoulder), trimmed of excess fat and cut into 2-inch cubes

3 tablespoons vegetable oil, such as safflower

2¼ cups water

1 large onion, chopped

¾ teaspoon dried thyme

1½ cups (12 ounces) dark beer

1½ pounds medium new potatoes, peeled and quartered

1 pound carrots, cut ½ inch thick diagonally

3 tablespoons chopped fresh flat-leaf parsley

1 In a large bowl, season flour with salt and pepper. Dredge lamb in flour mixture, shaking off excess. In a large Dutch oven or other heavy pot, heat oil over medium. Working in batches, brown lamb on all sides, about 5 minutes per batch. Transfer to a plate.

2 Pour ¼ cup water into pot and scrape up browned bits from bottom with a wooden spoon. Add onion; cook, stirring occasionally, until water has evaporated and onion is beginning to soften, about 5 minutes. Return lamb to pot; stir in thyme, beer, and 1½ cups water. Cover; simmer until lamb is tender, 1 to 1½ hours.

3 Add potatoes, carrots, and remaining ½ cup water. Cover and cook until vegetables are tender and stew has thickened, about 20 minutes. Season with salt and pepper. Stir in parsley and serve immediately.

per serving: 415 calories; 16.9 g fat; 36.6 g protein; 28 g carbohydrates; 3.6 g fiber

FREEZING STEW
Let stew cool completely, then transfer to airtight containers. Freeze for up to 3 months. Thaw in the microwave or overnight in the refrigerator and reheat over low. Stir in parsley just before serving.

GOOD TO KNOW Soaking pearl and cipollini onions in warm water for just ten minutes makes their thin, tight skin easier to remove. After soaking, simply cut off the root end and peel back the skin. If you can't find pearl or cipollini onions, you can substitute one large or two small yellow onions, each cut into eight wedges.

PORK LOIN WITH ONIONS AND DRIED APRICOTS

SERVES 4 ■ PREP TIME: 25 MINUTES ■ **TOTAL TIME: 1 HOUR**

1 teaspoon olive oil

1½ pounds boneless pork loin, tied at 1-inch intervals

½ teaspoon ground coriander

Coarse salt and ground pepper

½ pound pearl or cipollini onions, peeled (see above)

⅓ cup dry white wine, such as Sauvignon Blanc

½ cup low-sodium store-bought chicken broth

½ teaspoon fennel seeds

1 strip (1 to 2 inches) fresh orange zest

¼ cup coarsely chopped dried apricots (2 ounces)

1 teaspoon red-wine vinegar

1 Preheat oven to 350°F. In a large Dutch oven or other heavy pot, heat oil over medium-high. Pat dry pork, sprinkle with coriander, and season with salt and pepper. Cook until browned on all sides, about 10 minutes total. Transfer pork to a plate. Reduce heat to medium and add onions to pot. Cook, stirring, until onions are golden brown, about 3 minutes.

2 Return pork to pot and add wine, broth, fennel seeds, orange zest, and apricots. Bring mixture to a boil. Cover and transfer to oven. Cook until an instant-read thermometer inserted in thickest part of pork registers 140°F, 25 to 30 minutes.

3 Transfer pork to a cutting board, tent loosely with foil, and let rest 10 minutes. Bring cooking liquid to a boil over medium-high heat and cook until slightly thickened, about 3 minutes. Stir in vinegar.

4 Thinly slice pork against the grain and serve with onions, apricots, and sauce.

per serving: 386 calories; 19 g fat (7 g saturated fat); 35 g protein; 15 g carbohydrates; 2 g fiber

386
CALORIES PER SERVING

368

CALORIES PER SERVING

FLAVOR BOOSTER Instead of water, the polenta is cooked in a combination of skim milk and low-sodium chicken broth. A dab of butter, stirred in at the end, adds just the right amount of richness.

PORK TENDERLOIN WITH SWISS CHARD AND POLENTA

SERVES 4 ■ PREP TIME: 35 MINUTES ■ **TOTAL TIME: 35 MINUTES**

  2 cups skim milk

3½ cups low-sodium store-bought chicken broth

  ¾ cup quick-cooking polenta

    Coarse salt and ground pepper

  1 pork tenderloin (1 pound), excess fat removed, cut crosswise into 12 equal slices

  1 tablespoon plus 1 teaspoon extra-virgin olive oil

  2 medium onions, halved and thinly sliced lengthwise

  1 bunch Swiss chard (12 ounces), stems cut into ½-inch pieces and leaves coarsely chopped

  2 to 3 teaspoons sherry vinegar

  2 teaspoons unsalted butter

1 In a 4-quart pot, bring milk and 2½ cups broth to a boil over medium-high heat. Gradually whisk in polenta. Continue to whisk until polenta thickens. Reduce heat to low, season with salt and pepper, and simmer gently, stirring occasionally to prevent sticking, until mixture is creamy and just pulls away from side of pot, about 25 minutes.

2 Meanwhile, flatten pork slices into medallions with the palms of your hands. Pat dry pork and season with salt and pepper. In a large skillet, heat 1½ teaspoons oil over medium-high. Add half the pork and cook until browned on both sides, about 3 minutes total. Transfer to a plate and tent loosely with foil. Repeat with 1½ teaspoons oil and remaining pork.

3 Return skillet to heat and add remaining 1 teaspoon oil, the onions, chard stems, and ¼ cup broth. Cook, scraping up browned bits, until vegetables begin to soften, about 5 minutes (reduce heat to prevent burning as needed). Add chard leaves and cook until wilted, about 2 minutes. Add vinegar, remaining ¾ cup broth, and pork along with any accumulated juices; cook until liquid has almost evaporated, about 4 minutes.

4 When polenta has finished cooking, stir in butter. Season pork and vegetables with salt and pepper and serve over polenta.

per serving: 368 calories; 11.1 g fat (3.3 g saturated fat); 33.3 g protein; 33 g carbohydrates; 3.5 g fiber

FLAVOR BOOSTER A potent spice blend is sprinkled over the fish before it is steamed atop rice, making up for any lack of crust the fish might get from pan-searing in butter or oil. The same mixture could also be rubbed over chicken or pork tenderloin before roasting or grilling.

SPICE-DUSTED FISH WITH LEMON RICE

SERVES 4 ■ PREP TIME: 10 MINUTES ■ TOTAL TIME: 30 MINUTES

1 tablespoon plus 1 teaspoon unsalted butter

1 small yellow onion, finely chopped

1 garlic clove, coarsely chopped

1 cup basmati rice

½ teaspoon poppy seeds (optional)

1 tablespoon finely grated lemon zest, plus 1 tablespoon fresh lemon juice

2 cups low-sodium store-bought chicken broth

1 medium zucchini, halved lengthwise and cut into 1-inch half-moons

Coarse salt and ground pepper

1 pound cod or other firm white-fleshed fish, cut into 4 fillets

2 teaspoons Coriander Spice Mix (recipe follows)

1 In a wide, medium saucepan, heat butter over medium. Add onion and garlic and cook, stirring occasionally, until onion is soft, about 4 minutes. Stir in rice and poppy seeds (if using) and cook, stirring, 1 minute. Add lemon zest and juice, broth, and zucchini; season with salt and pepper. Bring to a boil over medium-high heat. Reduce to a simmer, cover, and cook 13 minutes.

2 Pat dry fish and sprinkle spice mix over tops, dividing evenly. Arrange fish snugly in a single layer, spice side up, on top of rice; cover and cook until rice is tender and fish is opaque throughout, 5 to 7 minutes. Serve immediately.

per serving: 348 calories; 5 g fat (3 g saturated fat); 32 g protein; 41 g carbohydrates; 2 g fiber

CORIANDER SPICE MIX

¼ cup ground coriander

1 tablespoon ground ginger

1 tablespoon paprika

1 tablespoon coarse salt

1½ teaspoons ground cumin

¼ teaspoon ground pepper

Combine all ingredients in an airtight container. Store up to 3 months in a cool, dark spot.
MAKES ABOUT ½ CUP

348
CALORIES PER SERVING

344
CALORIES PER SERVING

WHY IT'S LIGHT Because they are baked, these "breaded" fish fillets are lower in fat—and much easier to prepare—than fried versions. Coating only the top of the fish with an herbed breadcrumb mixture also helps. Roasted broccoli makes the perfect seasonal side dish.

BAKED FISH WITH HERBED BREADCRUMBS AND BROCCOLI

SERVES 4 ■ PREP TIME: 10 MINUTES ■ **TOTAL TIME: 30 MINUTES**

- 1 head broccoli (about 1 pound), trimmed and cut into florets
- 3 tablespoons olive oil

  Coarse salt and ground pepper
- 1 hoagie or other sandwich roll, torn into large pieces
- 2 teaspoons finely chopped fresh thyme
- 2 tablespoons unsalted butter, melted and cooled slightly
- 4 fillets skinless firm white-fleshed fish such as haddock, cod, or halibut (each 5 ounces and ½ inch thick)

  Lemon wedges, for serving

1 Preheat oven to 425°F, with rack in upper third. On a rimmed baking sheet, drizzle broccoli with 2 tablespoons oil; season with salt and pepper. Toss to combine, then spread in a single layer. Roast until broccoli is tender and lightly browned, tossing halfway through, 15 to 20 minutes.

2 Meanwhile, in a food processor, pulse bread, thyme, ¼ teaspoon salt, and ⅛ teaspoon pepper until coarse crumbs form. Transfer breadcrumbs to a bowl and stir in butter with a fork.

3 Coat another rimmed baking sheet with remaining 1 tablespoon oil. Arrange fish on sheet and season with salt and pepper. Top each fillet with enough breadcrumbs to coat, pressing firmly to adhere. Bake until fish is opaque throughout and breadcrumbs are golden brown, about 8 minutes. Serve immediately, with broccoli and lemon wedges.

per serving: 344 calories; 18.3 g fat (5 g saturated fat); 31.5 g protein; 15.1 g carbohydrates; 3.3 g fiber

Heart-healthy olive oil
replaces butter in this garlicky
scampi. Just a drizzle of oil
is enough for broiling, rather
than sautéing, the shrimp.

BROILED SHRIMP SCAMPI

SERVES 4 ■ PREP TIME: 20 MINUTES
■ **TOTAL TIME: 20 MINUTES**

1½ pounds large shrimp, peeled and
   deveined, tails left on, patted dry

 1 tablespoon olive oil

 2 garlic cloves, minced

   Coarse salt and ground pepper

 2 tablespoons fresh lemon juice

 2 tablespoons chopped fresh
   flat-leaf parsley

   Lemon wedges, for serving

1 Heat broiler, with rack 4 inches from
heat. Place shrimp on a large rimmed
baking sheet. Drizzle with oil and sprinkle
with garlic; season generously with salt
and pepper. Toss to coat. Arrange shrimp
in a single layer.

2 Broil until shrimp are opaque throughout, 3 to 4 minutes. Sprinkle with lemon
juice and parsley; toss to combine. Serve
immediately with lemon wedges.

per serving: 215 calories; 6.3 g fat (1.1 g saturated
fat); 34.7 g protein; 2.8 g carbohydrates; 0.1 g fiber

215

CALORIES PER SERVING

362

CALORIES PER SERVING

WHY IT'S LIGHT In this version of a Southern staple, the grits are enriched with a little butter, but no cheese. The shrimp are cooked in a quick tomato sauce seasoned with smoky bacon, onion, and hot sauce.

SAUCY SHRIMP AND GRITS

SERVES 4 ■ PREP TIME: 25 MINUTES ■ TOTAL TIME: 40 MINUTES

4¾ cups water

1 cup coarse grits (not quick-cooking)

Coarse salt and ground pepper

2 tablespoons unsalted butter

2 slices bacon (2 ounces),
cut crosswise into ½-inch pieces

1 medium onion, halved
and thinly sliced

2 garlic cloves, thinly sliced

1 can (14.5 ounces) diced tomatoes
in juice

1 pound large shrimp, peeled
and deveined

¼ teaspoon hot sauce

1 In a medium saucepan, bring 4½ cups water to a boil. Whisk in grits; season with salt and pepper. Reduce heat to medium-low. Cover and cook, whisking occasionally, until grits are creamy and tender, about 30 minutes; stir in butter.

2 After grits have cooked 15 minutes, cook bacon in a large skillet over medium heat until browned, 4 to 6 minutes. Using a slotted spoon, transfer to a paper-towel-lined plate. Add onion and garlic to rendered fat in skillet; season with salt and pepper. Cook, stirring occasionally, until onion is tender and browned, 8 to 10 minutes.

3 Add tomatoes (with their juice) and remaining ¼ cup water to skillet; bring to a boil. Add shrimp; cook, stirring, until opaque throughout, 2 to 4 minutes. Stir in hot sauce. Serve immediately over grits, sprinkled with bacon.

per serving: 362 calories; 9.5 g fat (4.5 g saturated fat); 28.9 g protein; 39.4 g carbohydrates; 1.1 g fiber

FRESH VS. FROZEN
Frozen shrimp are a handy and less expensive alternative to fresh. In fact, most "fresh" shrimp have already been frozen and thawed. Look for raw "easy peel" shrimp rather than peeled. They're already deveined, and the shell helps preserve flavor and texture. Simply thaw them in a cool-water bath, then peel.

WHY IT'S LIGHT Broiling is a fat-free way to cook salmon burgers; these are perked up with lemon, horseradish, and scallions and served on toasted whole-wheat buns. Yogurt flavored with fresh dill makes a very delicious—and low-fat—topping.

SALMON BURGERS WITH YOGURT-DILL SAUCE

SERVES 4 ■ PREP TIME: 10 MINUTES ■ **TOTAL TIME: 20 MINUTES**

1 pound skinless salmon fillet, finely diced (see below)

1 tablespoon prepared horseradish

½ teaspoon grated lemon zest, plus 1 tablespoon fresh lemon juice

1 large egg, lightly beaten

3 scallions, trimmed and thinly sliced

2 tablespoons plain dried breadcrumbs

Coarse salt and ground pepper

½ cup plain low-fat yogurt

1 tablespoon coarsely chopped fresh dill

4 whole-wheat hamburger buns, split and toasted

Romaine lettuce, for serving

1 Heat broiler, with rack 4 inches from heat. In a medium bowl, combine salmon, horseradish, lemon zest and juice, egg, scallions, breadcrumbs, 1 teaspoon salt, and ⅛ teaspoon pepper; mix gently with a fork.

2 Form salmon mixture into four 3½-by-1-inch patties; place on a rimmed baking sheet. Broil without turning until browned on top and opaque throughout, 6 to 7 minutes.

3 Meanwhile, combine yogurt and dill in a small bowl; season with salt and pepper. Serve burgers on buns with yogurt-dill sauce and lettuce.

per serving: 332 calories; 11.2 g fat (2.2 g saturated fat); 30.1 g protein; 28.3 g carbohydrates; 3.8 g fiber

CAREFUL CUTTING
To finely dice salmon without crushing it, start by thinly slicing the fillet with a sharp knife. Cut the slices lengthwise into strips, then cut crosswise.

332
CALORIES PER SERVING

385

CALORIES PER SERVING

GOOD TO KNOW To impart more flavor and moistness, cook the salmon fillets with the skin intact. The skin will cook to a delightful crisp, but you can remove it before serving if desired.

SALMON WITH SPICY CUCUMBER-PINEAPPLE SALSA

SERVES 4 ■ PREP TIME: 15 MINUTES ■ **TOTAL TIME: 25 MINUTES**

2 tablespoons fresh lime juice

1 tablespoon honey

2 tablespoons vegetable oil, such as safflower

2 Kirby cucumbers, finely diced

1 cup finely diced fresh pineapple (from about ¼ pineapple)

2 scallions, trimmed and thinly sliced

1 jalapeño chile (ribs and seeds removed for less heat, if desired), minced

¼ cup fresh basil leaves, finely chopped

Coarse salt and ground pepper

4 skin-on salmon fillets (6 to 8 ounces each)

1 In a medium bowl, whisk together lime juice, honey, and 1 tablespoon oil; add cucumbers, pineapple, scallions, jalapeño, and basil. Season with salt and pepper; toss gently to combine.

2 Pat dry salmon; generously season with salt and pepper. In a large skillet, heat remaining 1 tablespoon oil over medium-high; add salmon, skin side down. Cook until skin is crisp and salmon is opaque about three-quarters of the way through, 4 to 6 minutes. Turn salmon, and continue to cook just until opaque throughout, 2 to 4 minutes. Serve salmon topped with salsa.

per serving: 385 calories; 19.7 g fat (2.7 g saturated fat); 40.1 g protein; 11.3 g carbohydrates; 1.1 g fiber

SAUTÉED COLLARDS WITH ALMONDS AND RAISINS

¼ cup slivered almonds

1 tablespoon olive oil

1¼ pounds collard greens (about 2 bunches), stalks removed, leaves sliced crosswise

½ cup raisins

2 teaspoons white-wine vinegar

1 Preheat oven to 350°F. Spread almonds on a rimmed baking sheet and toast until golden, tossing halfway through, about 8 minutes.

2 Meanwhile, in a large skillet, heat oil over medium-high. Add collard greens and raisins; cook, tossing occasionally, until collards are tender, 6 to 8 minutes. Remove from heat, and stir in vinegar. Sprinkle with almonds and serve. **SERVES 4**

per serving: **168 calories;** 8.1 g fat (0.8 g saturated fat); 4.4 g protein; 22.7 g carbohydrates; 4.5 g fiber

SPINACH WITH CARAMELIZED SHALLOTS

1 tablespoon plus 1 teaspoon olive oil

4 large shallots, minced

Coarse salt and ground pepper

1 tablespoon water

1 teaspoon whole-grain mustard

1 tablespoon red-wine vinegar

2 bags (10 ounces each) baby spinach

1 In a large skillet, heat oil over medium. Add shallots and season with salt and pepper. Cook, stirring often, until lightly browned, about 10 minutes. Add the water and cook, stirring and scraping up browned bits from skillet, until shallots are dark brown, 3 to 5 minutes.

2 Remove skillet from heat; stir in mustard and 2 teaspoons vinegar. Place spinach in a large bowl and pour warm shallot mixture over top. Add remaining 1 teaspoon vinegar, toss, and serve. **SERVES 4**

per serving: **139 calories;** 4.6 g fat (0.6 g saturated fat); 4.8 g protein; 24.8 g carbohydrates; 7.1 g fiber

SHREDDED BRUSSELS SPROUTS WITH BACON

3 slices bacon (3 ounces)

1 pound brussels sprouts, trimmed and shredded

1 cup water

Coarse salt and ground pepper

Cider vinegar, for drizzling (optional)

1 In a large nonstick skillet over medium heat, cook bacon until crisp, 4 to 5 minutes; transfer to paper towels to drain.

2 Discard all but 1 tablespoon rendered fat from skillet. Add brussels sprouts and the water; season with salt and pepper. Reduce heat to medium-low. Cover and cook, stirring occasionally, until sprouts are tender, 20 to 25 minutes (add more water if pan becomes dry).

3 To serve, crumble bacon over sprouts; drizzle with vinegar, if desired. **SERVES 4**

per serving: **76 calories;** 2.7 g fat (0.9 g saturated fat); 5.3 g protein; 10.2 g carbohydrates; 4.3 g fiber

GINGER-SESAME BOK CHOY

1 tablespoon rice vinegar (unseasoned)

1 tablespoon soy sauce

¼ teaspoon toasted sesame oil

1 cup water

5 thin slices peeled fresh ginger

4 or 5 heads baby bok choy (1 pound total), halved lengthwise

1 In a small bowl, whisk together vinegar, soy sauce, and sesame oil. In a large skillet, bring the water and ginger to a boil. Add bok choy; reduce to a simmer. Cover; cook until stems are fork-tender, 3 to 5 minutes. Drain well; discard ginger.

2 Transfer bok choy to a serving platter, drizzle with vinegar-soy mixture, and serve immediately. **SERVES 4**

per serving: **22 calories;** 0.5 g fat (0.1 g saturated fat); 2.1 g protein; 3.5 g carbohydrates; 1.1 g fiber

241
CALORIES PER SERVING

WHY IT'S LIGHT To produce onion rings that are wonderfully crisp and not at all greasy, bake them instead of deep-frying. Preheating the oiled baking sheet before adding the onion slices helps ensure a crunchy outer coat, as do crushed cornflakes in the batter.

BAKED ONION RINGS

SERVES 4 ■ PREP TIME: 15 MINUTES ■ **TOTAL TIME: 30 MINUTES**

1½ cups cornflakes

½ cup plain dried breadcrumbs

1 large egg

½ cup low-fat buttermilk

¼ cup all-purpose flour

⅛ teaspoon cayenne

Coarse salt and ground pepper

1 medium-size sweet onion, such as Vidalia, quartered crosswise and separated into rings (discard small center rings)

2 tablespoons olive oil

1 Preheat oven to 450°F. In a food processor, pulse cornflakes and breadcrumbs until fine crumbs form, then transfer to a medium bowl. In another bowl, whisk together egg, buttermilk, flour, and cayenne; season with salt and pepper.

2 Working in batches, dip onion slices in egg mixture, letting excess drip off, then dredge in cornflake mixture; place on a large plate.

3 Pour oil onto a rimmed baking sheet. Heat in oven 2 minutes. Remove sheet from oven and tilt to coat evenly with oil. Arrange coated onions on sheet in a single layer. Bake, flipping halfway through, until onion rings are golden brown, about 15 minutes. Season with salt and serve immediately.

per serving: 241 calories; 9.2 g fat (1.7 g saturated fat); 6.8 g protein; 33.7 g carbohydrates; 2.4 g fiber

BAKED FENNEL WITH PARMESAN AND THYME

3 fennel bulbs, trimmed and split lengthwise

1 tablespoon unsalted butter, room temperature, plus more for dish

Coarse salt and ground pepper

⅓ cup grated Parmesan cheese

4 sprigs thyme

1 Preheat oven to 450°F. Bring a medium pot of water to a boil, and cook fennel until tender, about 15 minutes. Transfer fennel, cut side down, to paper towels and let drain 5 minutes.

2 Place fennel, cut side up, in a buttered 8-inch square baking dish and brush with 1 tablespoon butter. Season with salt and pepper and sprinkle evenly with Parmesan and thyme. Bake until cheese is golden brown, about 20 minutes. Serve warm. **SERVES 6**

per serving: **89 calories;** 5.3 g fat (3.2 g saturated fat); 3.2 g protein; 8.8 g carbohydrates; 3.7 g fiber

CHILE-LEMON CAULIFLOWER

1 large head cauliflower (about 2 pounds), trimmed and cut into florets

1 tablespoon finely grated lemon zest, plus 2 tablespoons fresh lemon juice

¼ teaspoon red-pepper flakes

Coarse salt and ground pepper

1 Place a steamer basket in a medium saucepan with 2 inches simmering water. Add cauliflower; cover and steam until easily pierced with the tip of a paring knife, about 8 minutes.

2 Transfer to a bowl and toss with lemon zest and juice and red-pepper flakes. Season with salt and pepper. Serve warm or at room temperature. **SERVES 4**

per serving: **42 calories;** 0 g fat (0 g saturated fat); 3 g protein; 11 g carbohydrates; 5 g fiber

SESAME BROCCOLI

1 head broccoli (about 1 pound), trimmed and separated into florets

2 tablespoons olive oil

1 tablespoon soy sauce

2 teaspoons fresh lemon juice, plus lemon wedges for serving

1 teaspoon sesame seeds

1 Preheat oven to 450°F. On a rimmed baking sheet, toss broccoli with oil, and spread in a single layer. Roast until tender and lightly browned, tossing halfway through, 15 to 20 minutes.

2 Transfer to a medium bowl and toss with soy sauce, lemon juice, and sesame seeds. Serve warm with lemon wedges. **SERVES 4**

per serving: **99 calories;** 7.5 g fat (1 g saturated fat): 3.9 g protein; 6.7 g carbohydrates; 3.4 g fiber

LEMONY SMASHED POTATOES

3 pounds small red new potatoes

¼ cup extra-virgin olive oil

2 teaspoons finely grated lemon zest

Coarse salt and ground pepper

1 Place a steamer basket in a large saucepan with 2 inches simmering water. Add potatoes; cover and cook until easily pierced with the tip of a paring knife, about 25 minutes.

2 Lightly smash potatoes, toss with oil and lemon zest, and season with salt and pepper. Serve warm. **SERVES 8**

per serving: **190 calories;** 7.2 g fat (1 g saturated fat); 2.7 g protein; 29.4 g carbohydrates; 2.7 g fiber

126
CALORIES PER SERVING

WHY IT'S LIGHT Our recipe for a hearty steakhouse side tweaks the formula for greater emphasis on the spinach and less on the "cream." In fact, despite its name, there's no cream in this dish. Instead, a mixture of flour and just one tablespoon of butter thickens a silky béchamel sauce.

CREAMED SPINACH

SERVES 4 ■ PREP TIME: 20 MINUTES ■ **TOTAL TIME: 20 MINUTES**

1 tablespoon unsalted butter
2 tablespoons finely chopped onion
1 tablespoon all-purpose flour
Coarse salt and ground pepper
1¼ cups milk
¼ cup water
2 pounds baby spinach

1 In a medium saucepan, melt butter over medium heat. Add onion and cook until softened, 3 to 4 minutes. Add flour and ¼ teaspoon salt; cook, stirring frequently, until mixture is pale golden and has a slightly nutty aroma, about 2 minutes.

2 Whisking constantly, pour in milk; whisk until smooth. Cook mixture, stirring constantly and scraping bottom of pan, until boiling, about 3 minutes. Reduce heat to low. Simmer gently, stirring occasionally, until sauce thickens, about 5 minutes.

3 Meanwhile, in a large saucepan, bring the water to a simmer; add salt. Add spinach; cover and cook until spinach wilts, about 3 minutes. Transfer spinach to a colander to drain, pressing out as much liquid as possible.

4 In a large bowl, stir together spinach and warm sauce until spinach is completely coated. Season with salt and pepper. Serve immediately.

per serving: 126 calories; 5.2 g fat (3.1 g saturated fat); 5.4 g protein; 17.5 g carbohydrates; 5.4 g fiber

SECRET INGREDIENT When puréed in a food processor, nonfat cottage cheese—high in protein but low in calories—becomes a smooth, creamy base for delectable cheesecakes such as this chocolate-espresso flavored version.

MINI MOCHA CHEESECAKES

MAKES 9 ■ PREP TIME: 8 MINUTES ■ **TOTAL TIME: 3 HOURS** (WITH COOLING AND CHILLING)

2 cups nonfat cottage cheese

2 large eggs

1½ cups confectioners' sugar

⅓ cup unsweetened cocoa powder

1 tablespoon plus 1½ teaspoons all-purpose flour

1½ teaspoons instant espresso powder (not instant coffee)

1½ teaspoons pure vanilla extract

9 chocolate wafer cookies, such as Famous

Whipped cream, for serving (optional)

1 Preheat oven to 275°F. Line 9 cups of a standard muffin tin with paper liners. In a food processor, combine cottage cheese, eggs, confectioners' sugar, cocoa powder, flour, espresso powder, and vanilla. Purée until smooth, about 4 minutes, scraping down sides as needed.

2 Divide mixture among prepared cups, filling each one just below rim, and place 1 cookie on top of each. Bake until fillings are set and cookies soften, 25 to 30 minutes. Transfer to a wire rack and let cool completely in pan, then refrigerate (in pan) at least 1½ hours (or up to 3 days, covered).

3 To serve, invert cheesecakes onto plates and peel off liners. Top each with a dollop of whipped cream, if desired.

per cheesecake (without whipped cream): 196 calories; 2 g fat (1 g saturated fat); 10 g protein; 34 g carbohydrates; 1 g fiber

ABOUT COTTAGE CHEESE
Cottage cheese varieties range from nonfat to 4% milk fat and have small, medium, or large curds. We prefer nonfat cottage cheese with small curds for this recipe. For a heart-healthy diet, choose one with fewer than 400 milligrams sodium per serving.

196
CALORIES PER SERVING

213
CALORIES PER SERVING

GOOD TO KNOW There's a reason it's called angel food cake—not only is it light as air and divinely delicious, it's also virtually fat-free. The cake gets its lofty texture from a dozen whipped egg whites folded into the batter; it makes an excellent partner for fresh berries or berry sauce (see note). To make a chocolate version, see the variation below.

ANGEL FOOD CAKE

SERVES 8 ■ PREP TIME: 30 MINUTES ■ **TOTAL TIME: 70 MINUTES (PLUS COOLING)**

1 cup cake flour (not self-rising)

¼ teaspoon salt

12 large egg whites, room temperature

1 teaspoon cream of tartar

1¼ cups sugar

2 teaspoons pure vanilla extract

Whipped cream, for serving (optional)

CHOCOLATE VARIATION
Replace ¼ cup cake flour with ¼ cup unsweetened cocoa powder; reduce vanilla extract to 1 teaspoon.

BERRY SAUCE
To create a fast flourish for angel food cake, make a colorful sauce: Combine 10 ounces frozen raspberries and ½ cup sugar in a saucepan; bring to a simmer and cook, stirring occasionally, until berries have broken down and mixture has thickened, about 10 minutes. Serve warm, cold, or at room temperature.

1 Preheat oven to 350°F. Sift together flour and salt into a small bowl. With an electric mixer, beat egg whites on medium-high speed until foamy. Add cream of tartar; beat until soft peaks form. With mixer running, gradually add sugar; continue beating until stiff peaks form. Add vanilla; beat to combine.

2 Gently transfer egg white mixture to a large wide bowl. In four batches, using a fine-mesh sieve, sift flour mixture over egg white mixture. While turning the bowl, use a flexible spatula to fold in the mixture in a J motion, cutting down the center and coming up the sides.

3 Gently spoon batter into an ungreased 10-inch tube pan; smooth top. Run a small spatula or knife through batter to release air bubbles. Bake until cake is golden and springs back when lightly pressed, 35 to 40 minutes.

4 Invert pan onto its legs (or onto a wire rack); let cool completely in pan, about 1 hour. Run a knife around edge of cake to loosen from pan, and unmold onto rack. (Cake can be stored in an airtight container at room temperature up to 4 days.) Serve slices topped with whipped cream, if desired.

per serving (without whipped cream): 213 calories; 0.2 g fat (0 g saturated fat); 6.9 g protein; 45.3 g carbohydrates; 0.3 g fiber

MAXIMUM LIFT
Large bubbles in the batter will inhibit proper rising during baking. Once the batter is in the tube pan, gently run a small offset spatula or a table knife through it to release any air trapped inside.

WHY IT'S LIGHT Next time you crave a rich tasting brownie, reach for one of these lighter cookies instead. They've got just as much chocolate flavor, but far less butter—and thus less fat—per serving.

BROWNIE COOKIES

MAKES 34 ■ PREP TIME: 15 MINUTES ■ TOTAL TIME: 1 HOUR (PLUS COOLING)

12 ounces bittersweet chocolate, finely chopped

½ cup all-purpose flour

¼ teaspoon baking powder

¼ teaspoon salt

6 tablespoons unsalted butter, room temperature

½ cup granulated sugar

½ cup packed light-brown sugar

3 large eggs

1 teaspoon pure vanilla extract

1 Preheat oven to 350°F. Place chocolate in a heatproof bowl set over (not in) a saucepan of simmering water. Stir until melted, then remove bowl from heat and let cool.

2 In a small bowl, whisk together flour, baking powder, and salt. In a large bowl, using an electric mixer, beat butter and both sugars on medium-high speed until fluffy. Add eggs and vanilla and beat until combined. With mixer on low speed, add chocolate and flour mixture in alternating batches; mix just until combined after each (do not overmix; the consistency will be more like brownie batter than stiffer cookie doughs).

3 Drop dough by heaping tablespoons, about 2 inches apart, onto two parchment-lined baking sheets. Bake, rotating sheets halfway through, until a toothpick inserted in center of a cookie comes out clean, 14 to 16 minutes. Transfer cookies to a wire rack to cool completely. (Cookies can be stored in an airtight container at room temperature up to 4 days.)

per cookie: 105 calories; 6.8 g fat (3.6 g saturated fat); 1.5 g protein; 12.7 g carbohydrates; 0.8 g fiber

105
CALORIES PER SERVING

303
CALORIES PER SERVING

WHY IT'S LIGHT Made with skim rather than whole milk, this velvety rice pudding is still plenty satisfying, thanks to eggs in the custardy filling. The recipe takes well to experimentation: Try adding pistachios, substitute chopped dried apricots or figs for the raisins, or use freshly grated nutmeg in place of the cardamom or cinnamon.

LIGHTENED RICE PUDDING

SERVES 8 ■ PREP TIME: 35 MINUTES ■ **TOTAL TIME: 1 HOUR 35 MINUTES (WITH CHILLING)**

1 cup long-grain white rice

6 cups skim milk

1 cup sugar

3 large eggs

1 teaspoon pure vanilla extract

¼ teaspoon ground cardamom or cinnamon, plus more for garnish

½ cup golden raisins, plus more for garnish

1 In a large saucepan, combine rice and 5 cups milk; bring to a boil. Reduce heat to medium; simmer, stirring occasionally, until rice is tender, 15 to 17 minutes.

2 In a medium bowl, whisk together sugar, eggs, vanilla, cardamom, and remaining 1 cup milk. Stirring constantly, slowly pour egg mixture into rice mixture; cook over medium-low, stirring, until pudding coats the back of the spoon, 3 to 5 minutes.

3 Remove from heat; stir in raisins. Pour pudding into a 6-quart casserole dish or a large bowl; let cool to room temperature. Cover and refrigerate at least 1 hour (or up to 3 days). Serve pudding garnished with additional cardamom and raisins.

per serving: 303 calories; 2.2 g fat (0.7 g saturated fat); 10.6 g protein; 61.1 g carbohydrates; 0.7 g fiber

GOOD TO KNOW In this fruit-topped, vanilla-scented cake, vegetable oil stands in for butter, reducing the amount of saturated fat in each portion. Swapping out a third of the all-purpose flour with whole-wheat flour boosts the fiber content.

LIGHTER PINEAPPLE UPSIDE-DOWN CAKE

SERVES 8 ■ PREP TIME: 20 MINUTES ■ **TOTAL TIME: 1 HOUR 20 MINUTES** (PLUS COOLING)

⅓ cup vegetable oil, such as safflower, plus more for pan

1 cup packed light-brown sugar

1 firm ripe pineapple, peeled, cut into 16 thin wedges, and cored

1 cup all-purpose flour

½ cup whole-wheat flour

1½ teaspoons baking powder

½ teaspoon baking soda

½ teaspoon coarse salt

¾ cup low-fat buttermilk

2 large eggs

1 teaspoon pure vanilla extract

1 Preheat oven to 350°F. Brush a 9-inch square baking pan with oil; line with parchment, leaving an overhang on two sides. Brush parchment with oil. Sprinkle bottom of pan with ¼ cup brown sugar. Trim pineapple wedges to no more than 4 to 5 inches long; arrange in pan in groups of four, alternating direction (see opposite).

2 In a medium bowl, whisk together both flours, baking powder, baking soda, and salt. In a large bowl, whisk together buttermilk, eggs, vanilla, oil, and remaining ¾ cup brown sugar. Add flour mixture; mix just until combined. Pour batter over pineapple in pan. Tap pan firmly on counter to release any air bubbles, then smooth top.

3 Bake until a toothpick inserted in center of cake comes out clean, 50 to 60 minutes. Transfer to a wire rack and let cool 20 minutes in pan, then invert onto a serving platter (peel off and discard paper). Serve warm or at room temperature.

per serving: 343 calories; 11.1 g fat (1.6 g saturated fat); 5.5 g protein; 58.4 g carbohydrates; 2.8 g fiber

PREPARING PINEAPPLE
Slice off top and bottom so pineapple sits level on board. Slice off skin in wide strips. Then, for this cake, cut pineapple lengthwise into thin wedges, and slice off core from the tip of each wedge.

343
CALORIES PER SERVING

2

SPRING

The arrival of spring is a great time to seek out leafy greens, asparagus, and other seasonal standouts. Spring vegetables shine when simply steamed, needing little adornment, as does clean-tasting fish such as salmon.

Take full advantage of the distinctive flavors of fresh herbs like mint, cilantro, and tarragon to enhance everything from Asian-inspired dishes to sautéed chicken breasts. And don't overlook the satisfying nature of salads—incorporate a bit of lean meat and lots of garden-fresh vegetables, and a starter is suddenly elevated to a complete meal. For dessert, keep things light with crisp, lacy cookies or easy-to-assemble sorbet floats.

355

CALORIES PER SERVING

SMART SUBSTITUTION Mayonnaise—and the fat and calories that it imparts to chicken salads—is replaced by a vinaigrette in this slimmed-down version; using only poached breast meat also helps.

TARRAGON CHICKEN SALAD

SERVES 4 ■ PREP TIME: 10 MINUTES ■ **TOTAL TIME: 30 MINUTES**

4 boneless, skinless chicken breast halves (6 to 8 ounces each)

Coarse salt and ground pepper

¼ cup white-wine vinegar

¼ cup olive oil

3 celery stalks, thinly sliced

2 tablespoons chopped fresh tarragon

1 head green-leaf lettuce, leaves separated

1 Place chicken in a large, deep straight-sided skillet or heavy pot. Add enough water to just cover chicken, and bring to a boil. Season with salt, cover, and reduce to a bare simmer; cook 5 minutes. Remove skillet from heat and let chicken stand, covered, until cooked through, 12 to 14 minutes. Remove chicken from liquid and let cool completely.

2 With two forks, shred chicken. In a large bowl, whisk together vinegar and oil and season with salt and pepper. Add chicken, celery, and tarragon; toss to combine. Serve over lettuce leaves.

per serving: 355 calories; 16.2 g fat (2.6 g saturated fat); 47.3 g protein; 3 g carbohydrates; 1.4 g fiber

GOOD TO KNOW Poached salmon fillets are ultramoist. But there's just one hard-and-fast rule to follow when preparing them: Do not overcook. Poach the fish ever so gently just until the center remains slightly translucent.

SALMON SALAD WITH PARSLEY AND CAPERS

SERVES 4 ■ PREP TIME: 5 MINUTES ■ **TOTAL TIME: 15 MINUTES**

½ small red onion, thinly sliced

2 tablespoons red-wine vinegar

3 tablespoons chopped capers (rinsed and drained)

2 tablespoons olive oil

½ teaspoon coarse salt

Poached Salmon Fillets (recipe follows), flaked

½ cup fresh parsley leaves

In a large bowl, combine onion, vinegar, capers, oil, and salt. Let stand 10 minutes. Add salmon and parsley; toss gently to combine and serve.

per serving: 279 calories; 16.4 g fat (2.4 g saturated fat); 29.4 g protein; 2 g carbohydrates; 0.6 g fiber

POACHED SALMON FILLETS

2 medium carrots, cut into 1-inch pieces

1 celery stalk, cut into 1-inch pieces

1 small onion, halved

½ lemon, thinly sliced

Coarse salt

6 cups water

4 skinless salmon fillets (each about 6 ounces and 1 inch thick)

1 In a large, deep straight-sided skillet or heavy pot, combine carrots, celery, onion, lemon, 1½ teaspoons salt, and the water. Bring to a boil; reduce to a simmer, cover, and cook 8 minutes.

2 Season salmon with salt and gently lower into simmering liquid (liquid should just cover fish). Reduce to a bare simmer. Cover and cook until salmon is opaque throughout, about 5 minutes (longer for thicker fillets). With a wide slotted spatula, remove salmon from liquid. (Salmon can be refrigerated, covered, up to 3 days; let cool completely before storing.) **MAKES 4**

per serving: 277 calories; 12.3 g fat (1.9 g saturated fat); 38.5 g protein; 0.5 g carbohydrates; 0 g fiber

279
CALORIES PER SERVING

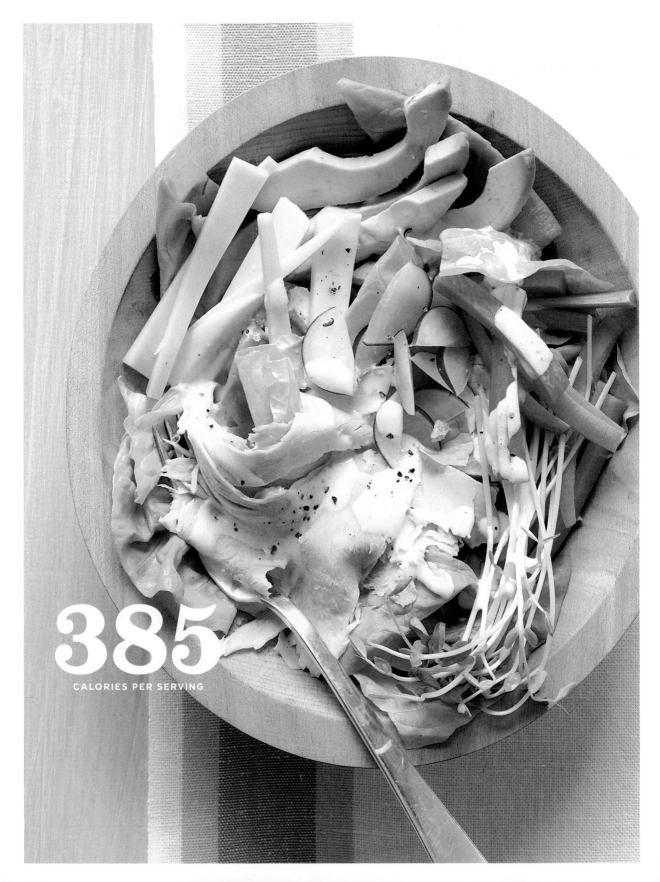

385
CALORIES PER SERVING

SMART SUBSTITUTIONS The dressing in this healthier chef's salad omits the mayonnaise and includes a combination of low-fat buttermilk and reduced-fat sour cream in its place. A mere tablespoon of honey helps to thicken it. Plus we've left out the eggs, ham, and croutons from the salad in favor of turkey, avocado, and sprouts.

LIGHTER CHEF'S SALAD

SERVES 4 ■ PREP TIME: 25 MINUTES ■ **TOTAL TIME: 25 MINUTES**

⅓ cup low-fat buttermilk

⅓ cup reduced-fat sour cream

2 tablespoons cider vinegar

1 tablespoon honey

  Coarse salt and ground pepper

1 large head Boston lettuce

1 pound sliced roasted turkey breast,
  torn into pieces

1 avocado, halved lengthwise, pitted,
  peeled, and sliced

1 cup alfalfa sprouts or pea shoots

6 radishes, halved and thinly sliced

4 medium carrots, cut into matchsticks

4 ounces Monterey Jack cheese,
  cut into thin strips (about 1 cup)

1 In a small bowl, combine buttermilk, sour cream, vinegar, and honey; season with salt and pepper.

2 Divide lettuce among four salad bowls or plates; top with turkey, avocado, sprouts, radishes, carrots, and cheese. Drizzle with dressing, and serve.

per serving: 385 calories; 20.3 g fat (9.1 g saturated fat); 30.1 g protein; 23.8 g carbohydrates; 6.2 g fiber

FLAVOR BOOSTER This modern take on velvety vichyssoise (potato-leek soup) contains no cream or even milk. Watercress adds surprising flavor—and color—to the warm soup.

WATERCRESS AND LEEK SOUP

SERVES 4 ■ PREP TIME: 20 MINUTES ■ TOTAL TIME: 35 MINUTES

2 tablespoons olive oil

2 medium leeks, pale-green parts only, chopped, washed well and dried

Coarse salt and ground pepper

1 can (14.5 ounces) low-sodium chicken broth

1 medium russet potato, peeled and chopped

4 cups water

3 bunches watercress (about 5 ounces each), thick ends trimmed, chopped

1 tablespoon fresh lemon juice

1 In a medium saucepan, heat 1 tablespoon oil over medium. Add leeks and season with salt and pepper. Cook until tender, stirring occasionally, 4 to 6 minutes. Add broth, potato, and the water. Bring to a boil; reduce to a simmer and cook, partially covered, until potato is tender, 10 to 12 minutes.

2 Add two-thirds of the watercress and cook until bright green and tender, about 3 minutes. Working in batches, purée soup until smooth in a blender, being careful not to fill jar more than halfway each time. Return to pan and season soup with salt (reheat over medium if necessary).

3 In a small bowl, whisk together remaining 1 tablespoon oil and the lemon juice; season with salt and pepper. Add remaining watercress and toss. Serve soup topped with watercress.

per serving: 161 calories; 7.2 g fat (1.2 g saturated fat); 5.8 g protein; 20.5 g carbohydrates; 2.2 g fiber

ABOUT WATERCRESS
Watercress is a dark, leafy green with thick stems and a peppery taste that mellows once it's cooked. Look for bunches with bright, glossy green leaves that haven't begun to wilt. Wrap in paper towels and refrigerate in a plastic bag up to 3 days. Always wash watercress just before using— place in a colander, and rinse well with cold water. Dry thoroughly and trim off thick stems.

161
CALORIES PER SERVING

162
CALORIES PER SERVING

FLAVOR BOOSTER Roasting maximizes the sweetness of fresh plum tomatoes (and preserves them for later use), perfect for making a delicious puréed soup that requires very little added oil or butter. Use any leftover roasted tomatoes as a topping for pasta or on sandwiches.

SPICED TOMATO SOUP

SERVES 4 ■ PREP TIME: 20 MINUTES ■ **TOTAL TIME: 25 MINUTES**

- 1 tablespoon extra-virgin olive oil
- 1 small onion, chopped
- 2 garlic cloves, smashed and peeled
  Coarse salt and ground pepper
- 1 teaspoon ground cumin
- ½ teaspoon ground coriander
- 4 cups Whole Roasted Tomatoes (recipe follows)
- ½ teaspoon sugar
- 1 cup water
- 1 tablespoon unsalted butter
  Fresh cilantro leaves and red-pepper flakes, for garnish

1 In a medium saucepan, heat oil over medium. Add onion and garlic and season with salt and pepper. Cook, stirring occasionally, until onion is soft, about 12 minutes. Add cumin and coriander; cook, stirring, until fragrant, about 30 seconds. Add roasted tomatoes, sugar, and the water; cook until warmed through, about 5 minutes.

2 Working in batches, purée soup in a blender until smooth, being careful not to fill jar more than halfway each time. Strain through a fine sieve into pan (reheat over medium if necessary). Stir in butter and season with salt and pepper. Serve soup garnished with cilantro and red-pepper flakes.

per serving: 162 calories; 10.1 g fat (2.8 g saturated fat); 3.7 g protein; 17.3 g carbohydrates; 5.1 g fiber

WHOLE ROASTED TOMATOES

- 8 pounds plum tomatoes
- 6 sprigs thyme
- 2 tablespoons extra-virgin olive oil
  Coarse salt and ground pepper

Preheat oven to 450°F. Divide tomatoes and thyme between two rimmed baking sheets. Drizzle with oil; season with salt and pepper. Toss to combine and spread in a single layer. Roast until tomatoes burst, rotating pans halfway through, about 45 minutes. Let cool, then coarsely chop. (Tomatoes can be refrigerated in airtight containers up to 3 days or frozen up to 3 months; thaw at room temperature.)
MAKES 10 CUPS

GOOD TO KNOW You won't miss the chicken in this meat-free version of the Southwestern favorite; black beans provide plenty of protein. Store-bought tortilla chips make a time-saving alternative to crisping the tortillas yourself; the chips soften in the soup, adding more heft. Save some chips for crumbling over the servings, and hold off on the cheese, sour cream, and other high-fat toppings.

TORTILLA SOUP WITH BLACK BEANS

SERVES 4 ■ PREP TIME: 15 MINUTES ■ **TOTAL TIME: 15 MINUTES**

1 tablespoon olive oil

4 garlic cloves, minced

1 teaspoon chili powder

2 cans (14.5 ounces each) diced tomatoes in juice

2 cans (15.5 ounces each) black beans, rinsed and drained

1 can (14.5 ounces) low-sodium chicken or vegetable broth

1 package (10 ounces) frozen corn kernels (do not thaw)

1 cup water

Coarse salt and ground pepper

1 cup crumbled tortilla chips, plus more for serving (optional)

1 tablespoon fresh lime juice, plus lime wedges for serving

1 In a large saucepan, heat oil over medium. Add garlic and chili powder and cook, stirring, until fragrant, about 1 minute. Add tomatoes (with their juice), beans, broth, corn, and the water; season with salt and pepper.

2 Bring soup to a boil; reduce to a simmer. Add tortilla chips; cook until softened, about 2 minutes. Remove from heat; stir in lime juice, and season with salt and pepper. Serve soup with lime wedges and, if desired, additional chips.

per serving: 277 calories; 6.3 g fat (0.8 g saturated fat); 12.8 g protein; 46.3 g carbohydrates; 8.3 g fiber

277
CALORIES PER SERVING

355
CALORIES PER SERVING

GOOD TO KNOW To release the citrusy flavor of lemongrass, pound the stalks with a meat mallet or the bottom of a heavy pot. If you can't find fresh lemongrass, look for dried in the spice aisle of your grocery store, or at Asian food markets.

ASIAN NOODLE SOUP WITH CHICKEN AND SNOW PEAS

SERVES 4 ■ PREP TIME: 10 MINUTES ■ TOTAL TIME: 35 MINUTES

Coarse salt and ground pepper

8 ounces flat, wide rice noodles

2 cans (14.5 ounces each) low-sodium chicken broth

1 piece fresh lemongrass (3 inches), smashed, or 3 sticks dried lemongrass

1 piece (1 inch) fresh ginger, peeled and cut into matchsticks

3 cups water

2 boneless, skinless chicken breast halves (6 to 8 ounces each), thinly sliced crosswise

8 ounces snow peas, trimmed and halved

2 tablespoons fresh lime juice, plus lime wedges for serving

¼ cup fresh mint leaves

Asian chili sauce, such as Sriracha, for serving (optional)

1 In a large pot of boiling salted water, cook noodles until tender according to package instructions. Drain noodles.

2 In a saucepan, combine broth, lemongrass, ginger, and the water. Bring to a boil; reduce to a simmer, cover, and cook until fragrant, 10 minutes.

3 Strain broth mixture through a fine sieve, discarding solids, and return to saucepan. Add chicken and snow peas and simmer until chicken is cooked through and snow peas are crisp-tender, 2 to 4 minutes.

4 Remove soup from heat and stir in lime juice. Season with salt and pepper. Divide noodles among bowls, and pour soup over noodles. Serve with mint, lime wedges, and, if desired, chili sauce.

per serving: 355 calories; 1.8 g fat (0.7 g saturated fat); 27.5 g protein; 55.3 g carbohydrates; 2 g fiber

SMART SUBSTITUTIONS This recipe is inspired by saag paneer, an Indian dish traditionally made with soft, fresh cheese; here, the cheese is replaced with tofu, which is lower in fat. Reduced-fat sour cream, instead of coconut milk, thickens the curry sauce.

CURRIED SPINACH AND TOFU

SERVES 4 ■ PREP TIME: 20 MINUTES ■ TOTAL TIME: 40 MINUTES

2 tablespoons vegetable oil, such as safflower

1 medium onion, minced

4 garlic cloves, minced

Coarse salt and ground pepper

1 tablespoon curry powder, preferably Madras

½ teaspoon ground ginger

2 packages (10 ounces each) frozen chopped spinach, cut into pieces (do not thaw)

1½ cups water

¾ cup reduced-fat sour cream

2 packages (12.5 ounces each) extra-firm silken tofu, drained and cut into ½-inch cubes

Cooked rice, preferably basmati, for serving (optional)

1 Heat oil in a large skillet over medium-high. Add onion and garlic, and season with salt and pepper. Cook, stirring occasionally, until onion begins to brown, 5 to 7 minutes. Add curry powder and ginger; cook, stirring, until fragrant, about 1 minute.

2 Add spinach and the water; bring to a boil, breaking up spinach with a spoon. Reduce heat to medium; simmer, stirring occasionally, until almost all liquid has evaporated, 10 to 12 minutes.

3 Stir in sour cream and tofu; cook just to heat through, 3 to 5 minutes (do not boil). Serve with rice, if desired.

per serving (without rice): 294 calories; 17.3 g fat; 21.5 g protein; 17.6 g carbohydrates; 5.6 g fiber

ABOUT TOFU
Tofu is sold in two types of packaging in grocery stores: refrigerated and shelf stable. Shelf-stable tofu can be stored at room temperature until opened, up to about 1 year (check the label for the use-by date); look for it in the Asian-food section.

294
CALORIES PER SERVING

315
CALORIES PER SERVING

GOOD TO KNOW Although this version of a classic Thai noodle dish is vegetarian, we've added a little optional protein in the form of scrambled egg. You could add thinly sliced poached chicken breast instead; add chicken to the skillet in step 3, tossing to coat with sauce.

VEGETABLE PAD THAI

SERVES 4 ■ PREP TIME: 10 MINUTES ■ **TOTAL TIME: 25 MINUTES**

8 ounces flat, wide rice noodles

2 tablespoons dark-brown sugar

2 tablespoons fresh lime juice, plus lime wedges for serving

3 tablespoons soy sauce

2 teaspoons vegetable oil, such as safflower

3 scallions, trimmed, white and green parts separated and thinly sliced

1 garlic clove, minced

2 large eggs, lightly beaten (optional)

½ cup fresh cilantro leaves, for garnish

¼ cup chopped roasted, salted peanuts, for garnish

1 Soak noodles according to package instructions, then drain. In a small bowl, whisk together brown sugar, lime juice, and soy sauce.

2 In a large nonstick skillet, heat oil over medium-high. Add scallion whites and garlic; cook, stirring constantly, until fragrant, 30 seconds. Add eggs, if using, and cook, scraping skillet with a heatproof flexible spatula, until eggs are almost set, about 30 seconds. Transfer egg mixture to a plate. (If not using eggs, leave scallion-white mixture in skillet.)

3 Add noodles and soy sauce mixture to skillet; cook, tossing constantly, until noodles are soft and coated with sauce, about 1 minute. Add egg mixture and toss to coat, breaking eggs up gently. Divide noodles among four shallow bowls; garnish with cilantro and peanuts, and serve with lime wedges.

per serving: 315 calories; 7 g fat (0.9 g saturated fat); 3.6 g protein; 60.5 g carbohydrates; 1.4 g fiber

WHY IT'S LIGHT Wedges of polenta are lightly brushed with olive oil and broiled instead of fried. The asparagus spears are broiled alongside the polenta, and a small amount of cream is all it takes to make the mushrooms taste luxurious.

POLENTA WEDGES WITH ASPARAGUS AND MUSHROOMS

SERVES 4 ■ PREP TIME: 40 MINUTES ■ TOTAL TIME: 1 HOUR 40 MINUTES

2 cups milk

3¼ cups low-sodium store-bought chicken broth

¾ cup polenta

Coarse salt and ground pepper

1 tablespoon plus 2 teaspoons vegetable oil, such as safflower, plus more for baking dish

1 pound cremini mushrooms, trimmed and sliced ¼ inch thick

2 tablespoons heavy cream

1 pound asparagus, tough ends trimmed (stalks peeled if tough)

1 In a 4-quart pot, bring milk and 2½ cups broth to a boil over medium-high heat. Gradually whisk in polenta. Continue to whisk until polenta thickens. Reduce heat to low, season with salt and pepper, and simmer gently, stirring occasionally to prevent sticking, until polenta is creamy and just pulls away from sides of pan, about 25 minutes.

2 Pour polenta into a lightly oiled 8-inch square baking dish; let cool completely. Cover with plastic wrap and refrigerate until chilled and set, about 1 hour (or up to 2 days).

3 Heat broiler, with rack 5 inches from heat. In a large skillet, heat 1 tablespoon oil over medium-high. Add mushrooms and cook, stirring occasionally, until golden brown, about 5 minutes. Season with salt and pepper. Add remaining ¾ cup broth and cook until reduced by half, about 4 minutes. Stir in cream and cook 2 minutes. Remove from heat; cover to keep warm.

4 Meanwhile, heat a rimmed baking sheet in oven, 5 minutes. Cut polenta into 8 wedges and pat wedges dry. Lightly brush both sides with 1½ teaspoons oil. Toss asparagus with remaining ½ teaspoon oil. Spread asparagus on one half of hot sheet and season with salt and pepper; arrange polenta wedges evenly on other half.

5 Broil until asparagus is crisp-tender and polenta is golden, about 6 minutes, rotating sheet and tossing asparagus halfway through. Serve polenta and asparagus with mushrooms.

per serving: 261 calories; 9.2 g fat (2.4 g saturated fat); 12.8 g protein; 32 g carbohydrates; 3.2 g fiber

261
CALORIES PER SERVING

443
CALORIES PER SERVING

WHY IT'S LIGHT A springtime pasta dish forgoes heavy sauce in favor of a toss-together topping of arugula, lemon zest and juice, and extra-virgin olive oil. A generous amount of Pecorino Romano cheese ensures the dish satisfies both appetite and palate.

LEMONY PASTA WITH WILTED ARUGULA

SERVES 4 ■ PREP TIME: 15 MINUTES ■ **TOTAL TIME: 20 MINUTES**

Coarse salt and ground pepper

¾ pound short tubular pasta

3 ounces wild or baby arugula (3 cups)

2 teaspoons grated lemon zest, plus 1 tablespoon lemon juice

2 tablespoons extra-virgin olive oil

¾ cup grated Pecorino Romano cheese, plus more for serving (optional)

1 In a large pot of boiling salted water, cook pasta until al dente according to package instructions.

2 Meanwhile, in a large bowl, combine arugula with lemon zest and juice; season with salt and pepper.

3 Drain pasta and immediately add to arugula along with oil and cheese. Toss and season with salt and pepper. Serve topped with more cheese if desired.

per serving: 443 calories; 12.6 g fat (3.9 g saturated fat); 17.9 g protein; 64.9 g carbohydrates; 3.1 g fiber

SECRET INGREDIENT Each of these little pies has a "crust" made from polenta, a whole-grain, low-fat alternative to buttery doughs. This recipe calls for prepared polenta in a vacuum-wrapped tube, sold at most supermarkets; if you can't find it, follow the recipe on page 134 to make your own, and cut into small rounds (instead of wedges) with a cookie cutter the same size as the baking dishes.

INDIVIDUAL PINTO AND BLACK BEAN TAMALE PIES

MAKES 8 ■ PREP TIME: 35 MINUTES ■ **TOTAL TIME: 1 HOUR**

2 tablespoons vegetable oil, such as safflower

2 bunches scallions, trimmed, white and green parts separated and thinly sliced

4 garlic cloves, minced

Coarse salt and ground pepper

2 cans (15.5 ounces each) pinto beans, rinsed and drained

2 cans (15.5 ounces each) black beans, rinsed and drained

1 can (14.5 ounces) diced tomatoes in juice

½ cup water

1 tube (16 ounces) prepared plain polenta, sliced into 8 equal rounds and patted dry

1 packed cup fresh cilantro leaves, coarsely chopped, plus more for garnish (optional)

½ teaspoon hot sauce, such as Tabasco

1½ cups shredded pepper Jack cheese (6 ounces)

Salsa, for serving (optional)

1 Preheat oven to 400°F. In a large saucepan, heat 1 tablespoon oil over medium; add white parts of scallions and garlic and season with salt and pepper. Cook until softened, stirring constantly, 2 to 3 minutes. Add both beans, tomatoes (with their juice), and the water and bring to a boil, mashing about one-quarter of the beans with the back of a spoon against side of pan. Reduce to a simmer; cook until mixture has thickened, 10 to 15 minutes.

2 Meanwhile, brush eight 10- to 12-ounce ramekins or custard cups with remaining tablespoon oil (if using pie plates, see below). Place a polenta round in each ramekin.

3 Remove bean mixture from heat. Stir in green parts of scallions, cilantro, and hot sauce; season with salt and pepper. Spoon bean mixture into ramekins, dividing evenly, then top with cheese. Bake until cheese is melted and filling is bubbling, 15 to 20 minutes. Let stand 10 minutes before serving. If desired, garnish with additional cilantro, and serve with salsa.

per serving: 332 calories; 11 g fat (4.3 g saturated fat); 17.3 g protein; 42.8 g carbohydrates; 11.6 g fiber

LARGE PIE VARIATION
Brush each of two deep-dish pie plates with 1½ teaspoons oil. Slice polenta crosswise into 16 equal rounds; place 8 rounds in each pie plate. Dividing evenly, top with bean mixture, then cheese. Bake and let stand as directed.

332

362
CALORIES PER SERVING

GOOD TO KNOW It takes only a tablespoon (or two) of olive oil to sauté chicken cutlets to a golden finish. Dredging the chicken in flour first encourages browning, but the temperature of the pan is the real key: Start with a hot skillet, and let the chicken form a crust before turning. After you remove the chicken from the pan, incorporate the browned bits into a quick sauce with wine, herbs, and some butter.

CHICKEN CUTLETS WITH HERB BUTTER

SERVES 4 ■ PREP TIME: 25 MINUTES ■ TOTAL TIME: 25 MINUTES

¼ cup all-purpose flour

8 thin chicken cutlets (1½ pounds total)

Coarse salt and ground pepper

2 tablespoons olive oil

¾ cup dry white wine

2 tablespoons cold unsalted butter, cut into small pieces

3 tablespoons finely chopped fresh flat-leaf parsley or mint (or a combination)

1 Place flour in a shallow dish. Pat dry chicken, then season with salt and pepper and dredge in flour to coat. In a large skillet, heat 1 tablespoon oil over medium-high. Working in batches, cook chicken until browned, 1 to 3 minutes per side, adding more oil to skillet as needed. Transfer each batch of chicken to a plate and tent loosely with foil to keep warm.

2 Add wine and accumulated juices from chicken to skillet and bring to a boil. Cook until liquid has reduced by half, about 4 minutes. Return chicken to skillet and turn to coat. Remove skillet from heat and swirl in butter and herbs. Season with salt and pepper. Serve immediately.

per serving: 362 calories; 14.6 g fat (5.1 g saturated fat); 40.3 g protein; 7 g carbohydrates; 0.3 g fiber

GOOD TO KNOW   Rotisserie chicken is a good shortcut (use only the breast meat) if you don't have time to poach your own. Corn tortillas—crisped in the oven instead of fried—provide a crunchy base for a filling salad packed with Mexican flavors. We've started with tomato, avocado, red onion, and cilantro, but you can add other favorite ingredients such as sliced radishes or corn—and perhaps a little reduced-fat sour cream in place of Mexican crema.

CHICKEN TOSTADA SALAD

SERVES 4 ■ PREP TIME: 20 MINUTES ■ TOTAL TIME: 25 MINUTES

- 2 boneless, skinless chicken breast halves (6 to 8 ounces each)
- Coarse salt and ground pepper
- 4 corn tortillas (6-inch)
- 1 tablespoon extra-virgin olive oil
- ¾ cup grated Monterey Jack cheese (3 ounces)
- ½ small red onion, finely diced
- ½ teaspoon chili powder
- 1 garlic clove, minced
- ¼ cup water
- 1 tablespoon plus 1 teaspoon fresh lime juice
- ½ head romaine lettuce (6 ounces), shredded
- 1 tomato, seeded and chopped
- 1 avocado, halved lengthwise, pitted, peeled, and diced
- Fresh cilantro, for serving

1 Preheat oven to 400°F. Place chicken in a medium pot. Add water to cover, and bring to a boil. Season with salt, cover, and reduce to a bare simmer; cook 5 minutes. Remove pan from heat and let chicken stand, covered, until cooked through, 12 to 14 minutes. Remove chicken from liquid. When cool enough to handle, shred into bite-size pieces.

2 Meanwhile, lightly brush both sides of tortillas with a total of 2 teaspoons oil and place in a single layer on a rimmed baking sheet. Bake until golden and crisp, rotating sheet halfway through, about 10 minutes. Divide cheese evenly among tortillas and bake until cheese is bubbling, about 3 minutes. Remove from oven.

3 In a large skillet, heat remaining teaspoon oil over medium-high. Add half the onion and cook until softened, about 3 minutes. Add chili powder and garlic and cook, stirring, until fragrant, about 30 seconds. Add chicken and the water and season with salt and pepper. Cook, stirring frequently, until chicken is warmed through and water is almost evaporated, about 2 minutes. Stir in 1 teaspoon lime juice and remove from heat.

4 In a large bowl, combine lettuce and remaining tablespoon lime juice; season with salt and pepper. Toss well to coat and divide among tortillas; top each with chicken mixture, tomato, avocado, remaining onion, and cilantro.

per serving: 326 calories; 17.5 g fat (4.8 g saturated fat); 24.3 g protein; 19.6 g carbohydrates; 6 g fiber

326
CALORIES PER SERVING

265
CALORIES PER SERVING

GOOD TO KNOW Like chickpeas and other legumes, lentils are high in fiber and protein and have very little fat. Adding them to main dishes allows you to cut back on the amount of animal-based proteins such as poultry and beef.

SHREDDED CHICKEN WITH KALE AND LENTILS

SERVES 4 ■ PREP TIME: 15 MINUTES ■ **TOTAL TIME: 35 MINUTES**

1 boneless, skinless chicken breast half (6 to 8 ounces)

Coarse salt and ground pepper

2 tablespoons extra-virgin olive oil

1 small onion, finely chopped

1 teaspoon fresh thyme leaves

2 bunches kale, tough stems removed, leaves torn into bite-size pieces

1 can (15.5 ounces) lentils, rinsed and drained

Lemon wedges, for serving

1 Place chicken in a medium saucepan and cover with water. Bring to a boil, season with salt, and reduce to a bare simmer. Cover and cook 5 minutes. Remove pan from heat and let chicken stand, covered, until cooked through, 12 to 14 minutes more. Remove chicken from liquid. When cool enough to handle, shred into bite-size pieces.

2 Meanwhile, in a large skillet, heat 1 tablespoon oil over medium. Add onion and thyme; season with salt and pepper. Cook, stirring occasionally, until onion is softened, about 5 minutes. Add kale and cook, stirring occasionally, until wilted and tender, 4 to 6 minutes. Transfer to a medium bowl.

3 Add remaining tablespoon oil and the lentils to skillet; season with salt and pepper. Cook, stirring, until warmed through, about 20 seconds. Transfer to bowl with kale and add chicken; toss to combine. Divide evenly among four bowls, squeeze lemon wedge over each, and serve.

per serving: 265 calories; 9 g fat (2 g saturated fat); 25 g protein; 20 g carbohydrates; 9 g fiber

FLAVOR BOOSTER A spicy dry rub is a great, no-calorie way to flavor skinless chicken breasts. Combined with red onion and lime juice, heart-healthy avocado creates a soothing salsa for a nice balance of hot and cool.

CAYENNE-RUBBED CHICKEN WITH AVOCADO SALSA

SERVES 4 ■ PREP TIME: 10 MINUTES ■ **TOTAL TIME: 30 MINUTES**

4 boneless, skinless chicken breast halves (6 to 8 ounces each)

1 medium red onion, finely diced

2 tablespoons fresh lime juice

Coarse salt and ground pepper

¼ teaspoon cayenne pepper

2 tablespoons olive oil

1 avocado, halved lengthwise, pitted, peeled, and cut into medium dice

1 Pat dry chicken. In a medium bowl, combine onion and lime juice. In a small bowl, combine 1 teaspoon salt, ¼ teaspoon pepper, and the cayenne; rub mixture all over chicken.

2 In a large skillet, heat oil over medium. Add chicken, and cook until browned on the outside and cooked through, 8 to 10 minutes per side.

3 Just before serving, fold avocado into onion mixture; season with salt and pepper. Serve chicken topped with salsa.

per serving: 344 calories; 13.7 g fat (2.2 g saturated fat); 47 g protein; 7 g carbohydrates; 3.5 g fiber

344
CALORIES PER SERVING

377
CALORIES PER SERVING

FLAVOR BOOSTERS This one-dish meal is a great example of how the bright notes of lemon (zest and juice) and parsley can help reduce the need for unwanted fat. The recipe is very adaptable; if you have other vegetables such as fresh spinach or snap peas on hand, add them to the couscous at the end. You can also substitute the leg and thigh meat from a rotisserie chicken.

SPRING-VEGETABLE COUSCOUS WITH CHICKEN

SERVES 4 ■ PREP TIME: 15 MINUTES ■ **TOTAL TIME: 35 MINUTES**

3 bone-in, skin-on chicken thighs (6 to 8 ounces each)

Coarse salt and ground pepper

3 tablespoons unsalted butter

4 scallions, trimmed, white and green parts separated and thinly sliced crosswise

2 strips (1 to 2 inches each) lemon zest, plus 1 tablespoon fresh lemon juice

1¼ cups water

1 pound asparagus, tough ends trimmed, cut into ½-inch pieces

½ cup frozen peas (do not thaw)

1 cup couscous

2 tablespoons finely chopped fresh flat-leaf parsley

1 Preheat oven to 450°F. Heat a large ovenproof skillet over medium-high. Season chicken with salt and pepper. Cook chicken, skin side down, until skin is browned, 5 to 7 minutes. Flip chicken and cook until browned, about 3 minutes. Transfer skillet to oven and roast until chicken is cooked through, about 20 minutes. Remove from oven and let cool, then shred into bite-size pieces.

2 In a medium saucepan, melt butter over medium-high heat. Add scallion whites and cook, stirring constantly, until softened, about 3 minutes. Add lemon zest and the water, and season with salt and pepper. Cover and bring to a boil, then add asparagus and peas. Return to a boil, stir in couscous, then add chicken and remove from heat. Cover and let stand 7 minutes.

3 Add lemon juice and parsley and season with salt and pepper. Fluff couscous with a fork and serve.

per serving: 377 calories; 13 g fat (6.6 g saturated fat); 22.2 g protein; 42 g carbohydrates; 5.8 g fiber

GOOD TO KNOW The full-flavored traditional Mexican sauce called mole is made from dried chile, garlic, tomatoes, chocolate, and spices. Serve the leftover sauce with pork or use it to make enchiladas. Here, a salad of romaine and radish plus rice flecked with scallion completes the meal.

TURKEY WITH MOLE SAUCE

SERVES 6 ■ PREP TIME: 10 MINUTES ■ **TOTAL TIME: 1 HOUR**

¾ cup Mole Sauce (recipe follows)

½ cup water

1 tablespoon olive oil

1 boneless, skinless turkey breast half (about 2 pounds)

Coarse salt and ground pepper

½ teaspoon sesame seeds, for garnish (optional)

1 Preheat oven to 325°F. Whisk together mole sauce and the water until smooth. In a large heavy ovenproof saucepan, heat oil over medium-high. Pat dry turkey and season with salt and pepper. Cook, rounded side down, until browned, about 5 minutes. Turn breast; pour mole mixture over turkey.

2 Cover pan tightly; bake until an instant-read thermometer inserted in the thickest part of turkey registers 145°F, about 40 minutes. Transfer to a cutting board; let rest 10 minutes before thinly slicing against the grain.

3 Stir sauce in pan to combine and serve with turkey. Garnish with sesame seeds, if desired.

per serving (without rice and salad): 246 calories; 8.4 g fat (1.3 g saturated fat); 34.2 g protein; 7.8 g carbohydrates; 1.3 g fiber

MOLE SAUCE

2 tablespoons olive oil

1 dried ancho chile

⅓ cup blanched almonds

2 garlic cloves

2 corn tortillas (6-inch), cut into ½-inch-wide strips

1 small onion, halved and thinly sliced

2 plum tomatoes

¼ cup raisins

1 teaspoon red-pepper flakes

1 ounce semisweet chocolate, chopped

¼ teaspoon ground cinnamon

¼ cup water

Coarse salt and ground pepper

1 In a large heavy saucepan, heat oil over medium-high. Add ancho; cook until soft (do not brown), 30 to 60 seconds. Remove with a slotted spoon; discard stem.

2 Add almonds, garlic, and tortillas to pan; cook, stirring, until toasted, 2 to 3 minutes; transfer to food processor with slotted spoon.

3 Add onion and tomatoes to pan; cook until tomatoes begin to blacken, 8 to 10 minutes (reduce heat if necessary). Add raisins and pepper flakes; transfer mixture to food processor.

4 Add chocolate, cinnamon, and ancho to food processor; purée to a coarse paste, about 3 minutes. Add the water; purée until smooth, about 7 minutes. Season with salt and pepper. (Sauce can be refrigerated up to 1 week or frozen up to 3 months in an airtight container. Thaw over low heat or in the microwave.) **MAKES 1½ CUPS**

246
CALORIES PER SERVING

441

CALORIES PER SERVING

WHY IT'S LIGHT In this recipe, the steak and vegetables are cooked on the stove, with just one tablespoon of oil for the whole dish. Because flank steak is one of the leanest cuts of beef, be careful not to overcook it, and slice the meat thinly against the grain for the most tender results.

FLANK STEAK, SNAP-PEA, AND ASPARAGUS STIR-FRY

SERVES 4 ■ PREP TIME: 35 MINUTES ■ **TOTAL TIME: 35 MINUTES**

1 cup long-grain white rice

1 tablespoon vegetable oil, such as safflower

1 pound flank steak

Coarse salt and ground pepper

8 ounces sugar snap peas, trimmed (see below)

1 bunch asparagus (1 pound), tough ends removed, cut into 2-inch lengths

4 garlic cloves, thinly sliced

½ teaspoon red-pepper flakes

¼ cup water

2 tablespoons soy sauce

2 tablespoons rice vinegar (unseasoned)

1 Cook rice according to package instructions. Meanwhile, in a large skillet, heat oil over medium-high. Pat dry steak and season with salt and pepper. Add to skillet and cook 4 to 6 minutes per side for medium-rare. Transfer to a plate, and tent loosely with foil.

2 Combine snap peas, asparagus, garlic, red-pepper flakes, and the water in same skillet. Cook, tossing, until vegetables are crisp-tender, 3 to 5 minutes. Add soy sauce and vinegar; toss to combine.

3 Slice steak thinly across the grain. To serve, divide steak, vegetables, and rice among four plates, and drizzle with pan juices.

per serving: 441 calories; 13.3 g fat (4.4 g saturated fat); 30.9 g protein; 46.8 g carbohydrates; 3.2 g fiber

TRIMMING SNAPS
To trim snap peas, cut off stem end with a knife. Or, if the string is especially tough, snap off stem end with fingers, and pull string down the pod.

WHY IT'S LIGHT Just three-quarters of a pound of beef serves four as a main course when rolled around a filling of peppers and cheese and accompanied by a leafy salad. This dish is just as delicious (and even leaner) with chicken or turkey cutlets instead of beef.

BEEF ROLLS WITH SPRING SALAD

SERVES 4 ■ PREP TIME: 20 MINUTES ■ TOTAL TIME: 20 MINUTES

1 tablespoon plus 2 teaspoons olive oil

2 medium onions, halved and sliced ¼ inch thick

3 red or orange bell peppers, ribs and seeds removed, sliced ¼ inch thick

Coarse salt and ground pepper

¾ cup water

¾ pound thinly sliced top round beef, cut into 4 equal pieces

2 ounces pepper Jack cheese, thinly sliced

2 teaspoons olive oil

1 package (7 ounces) spring lettuce mix

1½ teaspoons sherry vinegar

1 In a large skillet, heat 1 tablespoon oil over medium-high. Add onions and peppers; cook, stirring occasionally, until beginning to brown, about 7 minutes. Season with salt and pepper and add the water; cover and simmer 3 minutes. Uncover and cook, stirring occasionally, until vegetables are soft and liquid has evaporated, about 2 minutes.

2 Pat meat dry with paper towels and season with salt and pepper. Place cheese and onion-pepper mixture in center of beef pieces. Beginning with narrow end of meat, roll filling up tightly. Carefully flip meat seam side up and secure with toothpicks.

3 Heat a medium skillet over medium-high; brush with 1 teaspoon oil. Place meat rolls, seam side down, in skillet; cook, turning occasionally, until beef browns and cheese melts, about 8 minutes (reduce heat if beef is browning too quickly). Transfer beef rolls to a plate.

4 Toss lettuce with vinegar and remaining teaspoon oil; season with salt and pepper. Remove toothpicks from beef rolls; serve with salad.

per serving: 227 calories; 11.2 g fat (4.1 g saturated fat); 24.5 g protein; 7.7 g carbohydrates; 2.8 g fiber

227
CALORIES PER SERVING

412
CALORIES PER SERVING

GOOD TO KNOW Lamb needs few additional ingredients to make it flavorful. In this recipe, the meat is rubbed with salt, pepper, and olive oil, then studded with garlic slivers before being roasted. A sauce made from fresh mint is a vibrant alternative to the traditional mint jelly as an accompaniment. Serve the lamb with roasted new pototoes and a sprig of watercress.

LEG OF LAMB WITH MINT SAUCE

SERVES 10 ■ PREP TIME: 30 MINUTES ■ **TOTAL TIME: 2 HOURS 15 MINUTES**

1 whole bone-in leg of lamb (7 to 8 pounds), trimmed of excess fat and membrane

Coarse salt and ground pepper

1 tablespoon olive oil

4 large garlic cloves, cut into 20 slivers total

Mint Sauce (recipe follows)

1 Preheat oven to 450°F, with rack in lower third. Rub lamb with a generous amount of salt and pepper, then rub with oil. With the tip of a sharp paring knife, cut twenty ½-inch-deep slits all over lamb; insert a garlic sliver into each opening.

2 Place lamb on a roasting rack set on a rimmed baking sheet or roasting pan; transfer to oven. Immediately reduce oven to 325°F. Roast lamb until an instant-read thermometer inserted in the thickest part (avoiding bone) registers 125°F to 135°F for rare, or 135°F to 140°F for medium, 1¼ to 1¾ hours. Remove from oven; tent with foil and let rest 10 to 15 minutes before carving. Serve with mint sauce.

per serving: 412 calories; 14.1 g fat; 46.7 g protein; 22 g carbohydrates; 0.7 g fiber

MINT SAUCE

½ cup white-wine vinegar

1 cup sugar

½ cup water

1 cup packed fresh mint leaves, coarsely chopped

In a small saucepan, bring vinegar, sugar, and the water to a boil. Reduce heat; simmer until liquid is syrupy and reduced to 1 cup, 10 to 15 minutes. Remove from heat, stir in mint, and let cool completely. (Sauce can be refrigerated up to 1 week in an airtight container.) **MAKES ABOUT 1½ CUPS**

FLAVOR BOOSTER Toasted sesame oil, used in many Asian dishes, has a robust and nutty taste. Combined with rice vinegar, lime juice, garlic, and red-pepper flakes, it multitasks in this recipe as both marinade and salad dressing.

ASIAN STEAK SALAD WITH CUCUMBER AND NAPA CABBAGE

SERVES 4 ■ PREP TIME: 25 MINUTES ■ **TOTAL TIME: 40 MINUTES**

¼ cup fresh lime juice (from about 2 limes)

¼ cup rice vinegar (unseasoned)

2 tablespoons vegetable oil, such as safflower

1 tablespoon toasted sesame oil

½ teaspoon red-pepper flakes

1 garlic clove, smashed and peeled

1 pound flank steak

¼ cup soy sauce

½ head napa cabbage (1 pound), thinly sliced crosswise

1 English cucumber, halved lengthwise and thinly sliced on the diagonal

¼ cup coarsely chopped unsalted roasted peanuts

1 Heat broiler, with rack 4 inches from heat. In a small bowl, whisk together lime juice, vinegar, both oils, red-pepper flakes, and garlic.

2 Pierce steak all over with a fork; place in a shallow dish or resealable plastic bag. Pour soy sauce and half of lime-juice mixture over steak (reserve remaining half for dressing), and marinate at room temperature, 10 minutes (or up to 1 day, covered, in the refrigerator).

3 Lift steak from marinade (discard marinade), and place on a foil-lined rimmed baking sheet. Broil, without turning, 8 to 10 minutes for medium-rare. Remove from broiler; tent with foil and let rest 5 to 10 minutes before slicing thinly on the diagonal, against the grain.

4 In a large bowl, toss cabbage and cucumber with reserved dressing. To serve, divide salad among four plates; top with steak and peanuts.

per serving: 317 calories; 17.7 g fat (4.5 g saturated fat); 27.9 g protein; 11.5 g carbohydrates; 2.7 g fiber

317
CALORIES PER SERVING

241

CALORIES PER SERVING

FLAVOR BOOSTER Although the crimson glaze contains only a few ingredients, it tastes surprisingly rich, thanks to molasses and tart pomegranate juice. Here the pork is served with couscous and a salad of Bibb lettuce, celery, and parsley.

SEARED PORK TENDERLOIN WITH POMEGRANATE GLAZE

SERVES 4 ■ PREP TIME: 15 MINUTES ■ **TOTAL TIME: 25 MINUTES**

1 tablespoon olive oil

1 pork tenderloin (about 1 pound)
    Coarse salt and ground pepper

1 cup unsweetened pomegranate juice

1 tablespoon unsulfured molasses

¼ cup dried currants

1 Preheat oven to 350°F. In a large ovenproof skillet, heat oil over medium-high. Pat dry pork and generously season with salt and pepper; cook until browned on all sides, 6 to 8 minutes. Transfer skillet to oven, and roast until an instant-read thermometer inserted in thickest part of tenderloin registers 140°F, 10 to 15 minutes. Remove pork from oven, place it on a plate, and tent with foil.

2 Add pomegranate juice, molasses, and currants to skillet and bring to a boil over medium-high heat. Cook until sauce is thickened to a glaze (it should coat the back of a spoon and hold a line drawn through it with your finger), 5 to 6 minutes. To serve, slice pork against the grain, and drizzle with glaze.

per serving: 241 calories; 7.3 g fat (1.8 g saturated fat); 24.4 g protein; 19.3 g carbohydrates; 0.6 g fiber

ABOUT POMEGRANATE JUICE
You'll find bottled pomegranate juice in most supermarkets and health-food stores. Check the ingredients list, and select one without added sugar, other juices, or preservatives.

WHY IT'S LIGHT Many versions of North Carolina pulled pork are made with pork shoulder, but this one uses tenderloin for less fat. Use light or dark brown sugar depending on your taste preference; dark offers a more pronounced molasses flavor. Plenty of light cabbage slaw on top brings the sandwich into balance.

LIGHTER PULLED-PORK SANDWICHES

SERVES 4 ■ PREP TIME: 20 MINUTES ■ **TOTAL TIME: 1 HOUR**

1 can (15 ounces) crushed tomatoes in purée

1 tablespoon light- or dark-brown sugar

2 garlic cloves, finely chopped

1 tablespoon spicy brown mustard

½ cup plus 1 tablespoon water

Coarse salt and ground pepper

1 pork tenderloin (about 1 pound), cut into 4 pieces

¼ cup light mayonnaise

1 tablespoon plus 1 teaspoon cider vinegar

¼ teaspoon celery seeds

¼ small head green cabbage, shredded

4 whole-wheat rolls, split

1 In a medium saucepan, stir together tomatoes (with purée), sugar, garlic, mustard, and ½ cup water; season with salt and pepper. Bring to a boil; add pork, cover, and simmer until tender, 18 to 20 minutes. Transfer pork to a plate to cool. Continue to simmer sauce (uncovered) over medium heat until reduced by half, about 20 minutes.

2 Meanwhile, in a small bowl, whisk together mayonnaise, 1 tablespoon vinegar, the celery seeds, and remaining 1 tablespoon water; season with salt and pepper. Add cabbage, and toss to coat.

3 Shred pork with two forks, and return to sauce; stir in remaining teaspoon vinegar. Serve pork on rolls, topped with cabbage mixture.

per serving: 369 calories; 11.2 g fat (2.5 g saturated fat); 30.2 g protein; 38.2 g carbohydrates; 6.7 g fiber

369
CALORIES PER SERVING

405
CALORIES PER SERVING

WHY IT'S LIGHT The beloved combination of spaghetti, bacon, and eggs (as in spaghetti carbonara) can still fit within a low-fat diet by replacing some of the pasta with wilted frisée. Top each serving with some crisped bacon pieces and a fried egg.

SPAGHETTI WITH FRISÉE AND FRIED EGG

SERVES 4 ■ PREP TIME: 20 MINUTES ■ **TOTAL TIME: 20 MINUTES**

Coarse salt and ground pepper

8 ounces spaghetti

8 ounces bacon (8 strips), cut into 1-inch pieces

1 large head frisée, coarsely chopped

2 tablespoons sherry vinegar

4 large eggs

Grated Parmesan cheese, for serving (optional)

1 In a large pot of boiling salted water, cook pasta until al dente according to package instructions. Reserve ¼ cup pasta water; drain pasta and transfer to a large bowl.

2 Meanwhile, cook bacon in a large nonstick skillet over medium-high heat until browned, about 7 minutes, pouring off and reserving rendered fat halfway through. With a slotted spoon, transfer bacon to paper towels to drain.

3 Add frisée to skillet and season with salt and pepper. Cook, stirring, until frisée just begins to wilt, 1½ to 2 minutes. Stir in vinegar and transfer to bowl with pasta. Add reserved pasta water and toss to combine.

4 Return skillet to medium heat and add reserved bacon fat. Working in two batches, fry eggs until whites are just set and edges are golden brown, about 2 minutes. Season with salt and pepper. Serve pasta topped with bacon, Parmesan (if desired), and a fried egg.

per serving: 405 calories; 13.9 g fat (4.3 g saturated fat); 22.2 g protein; 47.3 g carbohydrates; 5.8 g fiber

WHY IT'S LIGHT A very thin pork cutlet is a healthful main course meat, even after sautéing in olive oil; the secret is to only dredge in flour and skip the more traditional bread-crumb coatings. Fill out the plate with vegetables such as leafy greens and sautéed cherry tomatoes.

PORK CUTLETS WITH ARUGULA SALAD AND SAUTÉED TOMATOES

SERVES 4 ■ PREP TIME: 30 MINUTES ■ TOTAL TIME: 40 MINUTES

2 tablespoons fresh lemon juice, plus wedges for serving

2 tablespoons olive oil

Coarse salt and ground pepper

4 boneless pork loin chops (5 ounces each), excess fat removed

¼ cup all-purpose flour

1 pint cherry tomatoes, halved

4 bunches arugula (about 1 pound total), thick stems trimmed, washed well and dried

Shaved Parmesan cheese, for serving (optional)

1 In a large bowl, combine lemon juice and 1 teaspoon oil. Season dressing with salt and pepper.

2 Place pork on a work surface; to butterfly chops, slice each one in half horizontally, stopping before cutting all the way through. Open up like a book. Then, one at a time, place opened chops between two large pieces of plastic wrap. Using a meat mallet or the bottom of a small heavy pan, pound until an even ¼ inch thickness. On a plate, combine flour, 1 teaspoon salt, and ¼ teaspoon pepper. Dredge each cutlet in flour mixture to coat completely, then shake off excess.

3 In a medium skillet, heat 1 teaspoon oil over medium-high. Add tomatoes, and cook until softened, about 5 minutes. Remove tomatoes.

4 In same skillet, heat 2 teaspoons oil over medium-high. Add 2 cutlets; cook until browned, 1 to 2 minutes. Turn over; cook until cooked through, about 30 seconds more. Transfer to a plate; tent with foil to keep warm. Repeat with remaining 2 teaspoons oil and 2 cutlets.

5. Add arugula to bowl with dressing; toss to coat. Divide tomatoes among plates; add 1 cutlet to each. Top pork with arugula and, if desired, Parmesan. Serve with lemon wedges.

per serving: 351 calories; 14.1 g fat (3.7 g saturated fat); 26.2 g protein; 14.3 g carbohydrates; 2.9 g fiber

351

CALORIES PER SERVING

346
CALORIES PER SERVING

WHY IT'S LIGHT The salmon and green beans—along with capers and strips of lemon zest—are steamed in parchment (see page 18), with only one teaspoon olive oil per packet.

SALMON IN PARCHMENT WITH GREEN BEANS AND LEMON ZEST

SERVES 4 ■ PREP TIME: 15 MINUTES ■ **TOTAL TIME: 30 MINUTES**

4 skinless salmon fillets (about 6 ounces each)

¾ pound green beans, trimmed

12 wide strips (1 to 2 inches) lemon zest (from 2 lemons)

1 tablespoon plus 1 teaspoon capers, rinsed and drained

Coarse salt and ground pepper

1 tablespoon plus 1 teaspoon olive oil

1 Preheat oven to 400°F. Place salmon fillets in center of four 16-inch-long pieces of parchment. Top with green beans, lemon zest, and capers. Season with salt and pepper and drizzle each with 1 teaspoon oil. Fold parchment into a "twist" or "envelope" shape (see page 19).

2 Place packets on a rimmed baking sheet and transfer to oven. Cook until packets are puffed up (salmon will be opaque throughout), 12 to 15 minutes. Serve immediately.

per serving: 346 calories; 17.1 g fat (2.6 g saturated fat); 40.3 g protein; 6.6 g carbohydrates; 3.2 g fiber

GOOD TO KNOW Cod and other lean, firm-fleshed fish are good choices for steaming, since they stay moist after cooking. To steam in the oven, combine fillets in a baking dish with rice vinegar (or another flavorful liquid, such as lemon juice or wine), oil, and aromatics, then cover the dish tightly to trap in moisture as the fish cooks.

STEAMED COD WITH GINGER

SERVES 4 ■ PREP TIME: 15 MINUTES ■ **TOTAL TIME: 50 MINUTES**

- 4 scallions, trimmed, white and green parts separated and thinly sliced
- 2 tablespoons minced peeled fresh ginger
- 2 tablespoons rice vinegar (unseasoned)
- 2 tablespoons vegetable oil, such as safflower
- ¼ teaspoon red-pepper flakes
- 1 teaspoon sugar

  Coarse salt
- 4 skinless cod fillets (about 6 ounces each)

1 Preheat oven to 375°F. In a shallow nonreactive 2-quart baking dish, stir together scallion whites, ginger, vinegar, oil, red-pepper flakes, and sugar. Season with salt. Add cod and let marinate at room temperature 20 minutes, turning once.

2 Cover tightly with parchment, then foil. Transfer to oven and cook until fish is opaque throughout, 30 to 35 minutes. Remove from oven, garnish with scallion greens, and serve.

per serving: 215 calories; 8.2 g fat (1 g saturated fat); 30.7 g protein; 3.8 g carbohydrates; 0.5 g fiber

215

298
CALORIES PER SERVING

FLAVOR BOOSTER Salmon fillets are dressed with a sweet-and-sour glaze that combines dark-brown sugar with pungent whole-grain mustard. Arrange the fish on a platter with watercress and lemon wedges for an impressive presentation fit for a dinner party.

SALMON WITH BROWN SUGAR–MUSTARD GLAZE

SERVES 8 ▪ PREP TIME: 15 MINUTES ▪ TOTAL TIME: 20 MINUTES

1 tablespoon extra-virgin olive oil

1 large shallot, minced

¼ cup red-wine vinegar

¼ cup whole-grain mustard

¼ cup packed dark-brown sugar

Coarse salt and ground pepper

1 side salmon (about 3 pounds), skin removed, cut into 8 fillets

1 bunch watercress (about ¾ pound), thick stems trimmed

Lemon wedges, for serving

1 Heat broiler, with rack in top position. In a small saucepan, heat oil over medium-high. Add shallot and cook, stirring often, until softened, about 3 minutes. Add vinegar and cook until almost evaporated, about 1 minute. Add mustard and brown sugar; stir until warm and combined, about 1 minute. Season with salt and pepper and remove from heat. (To store, refrigerate cooled glaze in an airtight container, up to 1 day.)

2 Line a rimmed baking sheet with parchment, if desired (for easy cleanup). Place salmon fillets on baking sheet and season with salt and pepper. Transfer ½ cup glaze to a small dish and brush on top of salmon. Broil salmon until glaze is bubbling and fish is opaque throughout, 5 to 10 minutes, depending on thickness. Remove from broiler; brush remaining glaze over fillets. Serve salmon with watercress and lemon wedges.

per serving: 298 calories; 13 g fat (2 g saturated fat); 35 g protein; 12 g carbohydrates; 1 g fiber

SECRET INGREDIENT Cracker crumbs help bind the fish mixture so it holds together when cooked; they also lend a crunchy coating to the cakes, which are dredged in the crumbs before baking. Put the crackers in a resealable plastic bag and crush with a rolling pin or small heavy skillet, or pulse in a food processor until coarsely ground.

LEMON-HORSERADISH FISH CAKES

SERVES 8 ■ PREP TIME: 20 MINUTES ■ **TOTAL TIME: 45 MINUTES**

3 tablespoons olive oil

2 pounds tilapia fillets (about 6)

Coarse salt and ground pepper

2 large eggs, lightly beaten

½ cup light mayonnaise

½ cup coarsely chopped fresh flat-leaf parsley, plus sprigs for garnish (optional)

¼ cup fresh lemon juice (from about 2 lemons)

3 tablespoons prepared horseradish

1½ cups coarse cracker crumbs (from about 36 crackers)

Tartar sauce, for serving (optional)

1 Preheat oven to 400°F. Brush each of two rimmed baking sheets with 1½ teaspoons oil. Place fillets on sheets; season with salt and pepper. Roast until cooked through, 10 to 15 minutes. Let cool completely; pat dry with paper towels. With a fork, flake fish into small pieces.

2 In a large bowl, combine eggs, mayonnaise, parsley, lemon juice, and horseradish. Fold in fish and ½ cup cracker crumbs; season with salt and pepper. Place remaining 1 cup crumbs on a plate. Form 16 cakes, using about ¼ cup fish mixture for each. Gently dredge cakes in crumbs, pressing to help adhere.

3 In a large skillet, heat 1 tablespoon oil over medium-high. Place 8 cakes in skillet; cook until golden brown, 4 to 6 minutes per side. Transfer to a platter. Repeat with remaining tablespoon oil and cakes. Serve with tartar sauce and parsley sprigs, if desired.

per serving: 286 calories; 14.8 g fat (2.7 g saturated fat); 25.9 g protein; 12.5 g carbohydrates; 0.8 g fiber

FREEZING FISH CAKES
Place uncooked cakes on a baking sheet, and freeze until firm. Wrap each in plastic; transfer to resealable freezer bags. Freeze up to 3 months. Defrost overnight in refrigerator before cooking.

286
CALORIES PER SERVING

425

CALORIES PER SERVING

WHY IT'S LIGHT Cut strips of sliced cabbage to resemble long, thin noodles and you can reduce the amount of real noodles by half. Cooked briefly, the cabbage wilts slightly but retains some of its characteristic crunch. Linguine stands in for the usual wheat-flour noodles (called lo mein) in this version of the Chinese take-out favorite, but you can use Asian noodles if you have them.

SHRIMP AND CABBAGE LO MEIN

SERVES 4 ■ PREP TIME: 20 MINUTES ■ TOTAL TIME: 20 MINUTES

Coarse salt and ground pepper

8 ounces linguine or Asian noodles

¼ cup soy sauce

¼ cup rice vinegar (unseasoned)

2 teaspoons grated peeled fresh ginger

½ teaspoon sugar

½ teaspoon red-pepper flakes

1 tablespoon vegetable oil, such as safflower

1 pound large shrimp, peeled and deveined

2 garlic cloves, minced

1 head green cabbage (about 2 pounds), halved, cored, and thinly sliced

½ cup water

¼ cup fresh cilantro, for serving (optional)

1 In a large pot of boiling salted water, cook pasta until al dente according to package instructions. Drain and return to pot.

2 While pasta is cooking, combine soy sauce, vinegar, ginger, sugar, and red-pepper flakes in a small bowl. Heat oil in a large skillet over medium. Add shrimp and half the garlic; season with salt and pepper. Cook, tossing frequently, until shrimp are opaque throughout, 2 to 3 minutes. Transfer to a plate.

3 In the same skillet, combine cabbage, remaining garlic, and the water. Cook, stirring occasionally, until cabbage is crisp-tender, 6 to 7 minutes. Transfer to pot with pasta. Add soy sauce mixture and shrimp; toss to combine. Serve immediately, garnished with cilantro if desired.

per serving: 425 calories; 6.5 g fat (1 g saturated fat); 34.6 g protein; 58.6 g carbohydrates; 6.4 g fiber

ASPARAGUS WITH CREAMY MUSTARD SAUCE

  1 pound asparagus, tough ends trimmed
  2 tablespoons mayonnaise
  1 tablespoon olive oil
  1 tablespoon white-wine vinegar
  1 tablespoon Dijon mustard
    Coarse salt and ground pepper

1 Prepare a large ice-water bath. Set a steamer basket in a large pot filled with 1 inch boiling water. Add asparagus, cover, and cook until crisp-tender, 2 to 6 minutes (depending on thickness). Immediately plunge asparagus into the ice bath and let cool. Drain and pat dry with paper towels and transfer to a serving platter.

2 Stir together mayonnaise, oil, vinegar, and mustard. Season with salt and pepper. Drizzle over asparagus and serve immediately. **SERVES 4**

per serving: **110 calories;** 9 g fat (1.3 g saturated fat); 2.5 g protein; 4.7 g carbohydrates; 2.4 g fiber

MINTED PEA MASH

  1 tablespoon unsalted butter
  2 bags (10 ounces each) frozen peas, thawed
  ⅓ cup lightly packed fresh mint leaves, coarsely chopped
    Coarse salt and ground pepper

In a large skillet, melt butter over medium-high heat. Add peas and cook, stirring constantly, until warmed through, about 5 minutes. Transfer to a food processor and pulse until coarsely puréed. Stir in mint and season with salt and pepper. Serve warm. **SERVES 4**

per serving: **138 calories;** 3.4 g fat (1.9 g saturated fat); 7.7 g protein; 20.1 g carbohydrates; 6.5 g fiber

CILANTRO-LIME RICE

  1½ cups plus 2 tablespoons water
  1 cup long-grain white rice
    Coarse salt
  ½ cup fresh cilantro leaves
  2 tablespoons fresh lime juice
  1 tablespoon olive oil
  1 garlic clove

1 In a medium saucepan, bring 1½ cups water to a boil. Add rice and ¼ teaspoon salt; cover and reduce to a simmer. Cook until water is absorbed and rice is just tender, 16 to 18 minutes.

2 Meanwhile, in a blender, purée cilantro, lime juice, oil, garlic, and remaining 2 tablespoons water until smooth. Stir into cooked rice and fluff with a fork. Serve immediately. **SERVES 4**

per serving: **202 calories;** 3.7 g fat (0.6 g saturated fat); 3.4 g protein; 38 g carbohydrates; 0.7 g fiber

ASPARAGUS, PEAS, AND RADISHES WITH TARRAGON

  3 pounds asparagus, tough ends trimmed, cut into 2-inch pieces
    Coarse salt and ground pepper
  3 tablespoons unsalted butter
  1 package (10 ounces) frozen peas, thawed
  1 pound radishes, halved and thinly sliced
  ⅓ cup fresh tarragon, coarsely chopped

1 Prepare a large ice-water bath, and line a baking sheet with a double thickness of paper towels.

2 Cook asparagus in a pot of boiling salted water until crisp-tender, 3 to 4 minutes. With a slotted spoon, transfer to the ice bath. Let cool completely, then transfer to lined baking sheet and pat dry.

3 Heat butter in same pot over medium. Add asparagus and peas. Cover and cook, stirring occasionally, until heated through, 6 to 8 minutes. Remove from heat; stir in radishes and tarragon. Season with salt and pepper; serve. **SERVES 8**

per serving: **93 calories;** 4.6 g fat (2.8 g saturated fat); 4.4 g protein; 10.3 g carbohydrates; 4.1 g fiber

ICEBERG SLAW

- 3 tablespoons low-fat buttermilk
- 3 tablespoons plain low-fat yogurt
- ½ small shallot, minced

  Coarse salt and ground pepper
- 1 head iceberg lettuce (1 pound), quartered, cored, and shredded
- 1 tablespoon finely chopped fresh dill
- 1 tablespoon finely chopped fresh flat-leaf parsley

1 In a large bowl, whisk together buttermilk, yogurt, and shallot; season with salt and pepper. Add lettuce and toss to coat with dressing. Cover and refrigerate at least 1 hour (or up to 1 day).

2 Just before serving, stir in dill and parsley; season with more salt and pepper to taste. **SERVES 4**

per serving: **36 calories;** 0.5 g fat (0.2 g saturated fat); 2.4 g protein; 6.6 g carbohydrates; 1.7 g fiber

BEET AND CARROT SLAW

- ¼ cup fresh orange juice
- 2 tablespoons olive oil
- 2 teaspoons red-wine vinegar
- 1½ teaspoons Dijon mustard

  Coarse salt and ground pepper
- 1 medium bunch beets with greens (about 1 pound)
- 2 medium carrots, grated

In a large bowl, whisk together orange juice, oil, vinegar, and mustard; season with salt and pepper. Cut greens off beets; discard stems and cut leaves crosswise into ¼-inch-wide strips, then wash well and dry. Peel and grate beets; place in a sieve and rinse until water runs clear, then squeeze dry with paper towels. Add to bowl along with beet leaves and carrots. Toss to combine. Let stand 15 minutes before serving. **SERVES 4**

per serving: **136 calories;** 7.3 g fat (1 g saturated fat); 2.3 g protein; 16.3 g carbohydrates; 4.2 g fiber

RED CABBAGE SLAW

- ¼ cup light mayonnaise
- 2 tablespoons white-wine vinegar
- 2 teaspoons sugar

  Coarse salt and ground pepper
- ½ small head red cabbage, quartered, cored, and shredded
- 2 tablespoons finely chopped fresh cilantro

1 In a large bowl, whisk together mayonnaise, vinegar, and sugar; season with salt and pepper. Add cabbage and toss to coat with dressing. Cover and refrigerate at least 1 hour (or up to 1 day).

2 Just before serving, stir in cilantro; season with more salt and pepper. **SERVES 4**

per serving: **93 calories;** 5.2 g fat; 1.9 g protein; 12.1 g carbohydrates; 3 g fiber

ASIAN SLAW

- 2 tablespoons fresh lime juice
- 2 tablespoons rice vinegar (unseasoned)
- 1 tablespoon vegetable oil, such as safflower
- 2 teaspoons sugar

  Coarse salt
- ½ small head Savoy or green cabbage quartered, cored, and shredded
- 1 cup fresh cilantro leaves
- 4 scallions, trimmed and cut into matchsticks
- 1 medium carrot, grated
- ½ jalapeño chile, minced (ribs and seeds removed for less heat, if desired)

In a large bowl, whisk together lime juice, vinegar, oil, and sugar; season with salt. Add cabbage, cilantro, scallions, carrot, and jalapeño. Toss to combine. Let stand 15 minutes before serving. **SERVES 4**

per serving: **116 calories;** 3.6 g fat (0.4 g saturated fat); 2.9 g protein; 18.5 g carbohydrates; 5.8 g fiber

FLAVOR BOOSTERS Mexican-inspired flavors make these hardy sides hard to resist. Black beans are enlivened by chili powder and lime; peppery watercress is topped with crunchy toasted pepitas and a cumin-scented dressing.

BLACK BEANS WITH LIME AND SCALLIONS

- 1 tablespoon olive oil
- 2 scallions, trimmed, white and green parts separated and thinly sliced

  Coarse salt and ground pepper
- 2 cans (19 ounces each) black beans, rinsed and drained
- 1 teaspoon chili powder
- ¼ cup water
- 1 tablespoon fresh lime juice

1 In a medium saucepan, heat oil over medium. Add white parts of scallions, and season with salt and pepper. Cook until softened, stirring frequently, about 3 minutes.

2 Add beans, chili powder, and the water. Cook until warmed through, stirring occasionally, about 5 minutes. Remove from heat, and stir in lime juice; season with more salt and pepper. Serve immediately, garnished with scallion greens. **SERVES 6**

per serving: **157 calories;** 2.9 g fat (0.5 g saturated fat); 9.1 g protein; 24.8 g carbohydrates; 9.1 g fiber

WATERCRESS AND PEPITA SALAD

- ⅓ cup pepitas (hulled pumpkin seeds)
- 2 tablespoons white-wine vinegar
- ½ teaspoon ground cumin

  Coarse salt and ground pepper
- 3 tablespoons olive oil
- 1½ pounds watercress, tough stems removed

1 Preheat oven to 350°F. Spread pepitas on a rimmed baking sheet; toast until golden brown, tossing occasionally, 10 to 15 minutes.

2 In a large bowl, whisk together vinegar and cumin; season with salt and pepper. Whisk in oil. Add watercress; toss to combine. Serve immediately, garnished with pepitas. **SERVES 6**

per serving: **116 calories;** 10.4 g fat (1.6 g saturated fat); 4.5 g protein; 3.2 g carbohydrates; 0.9 g fiber

ABOUT PEPITAS

Remove the white hull from pumpkin seeds, and you're left with a Mexican favorite: delicately flavored green pepitas. Look for them next to nuts at your supermarket, in Mexican specialty shops, or in health-food stores. Toast them and try in a salad or as a healthy snack.

GOOD TO KNOW Cooking vegetables in parchment is a great way to highlight their flavor while preserving their nutrients (and low-calorie profiles). Group vegetables with similar cooking times so they'll be ready at once.

BROCCOLI, SNAP PEAS, AND ASPARAGUS IN PARCHMENT

1½ cups small broccoli florets (from 1 head broccoli)

½ bunch asparagus (6 ounces), tough ends trimmed, cut into 2-inch lengths

1¼ cups sugar snap peas, trimmed

1 tablespoon unsalted butter (optional)

Coarse salt and ground pepper

1 Preheat oven to 400°F. Place broccoli, asparagus, snap peas, and butter (if using) in center of a 24-inch-long piece of parchment. Season with salt and pepper. Fold into a "twist" or "envelope" shape (page 19).

2 Place packet on a rimmed baking sheet and bake until packet is puffed up and vegetables are just tender, 10 to 12 minutes. **SERVES 4**

per serving (without butter): **76 calories;** 0.6 g fat (0.1 g sat fat); 5.9 g protein; 14.1 g carbohydrates; 5.5 g fiber

POTATOES, LEEKS, AND CARROTS IN PARCHMENT

¾ pound small potatoes, scrubbed and halved or quartered

2 medium leeks, white parts only, halved lengthwise, cut into 3-inch pieces, and washed well and dried

8 ounces small carrots, halved crosswise if long, or large carrots, cut into thin 3-inch sticks

10 sprigs thyme

1 tablespoon unsalted butter (optional), cut into small pieces

Coarse salt and ground pepper

1 Preheat oven to 400°F. Place potatoes, leeks, carrots, thyme, and butter (if using) in center of a 24-inch-long piece of parchment. Season with salt and pepper. Fold into a "twist" or "envelope" shape (page 19).

2 Place packet on a rimmed baking sheet and bake until packet is puffed up and potatoes are tender, 25 to 30 minutes. **SERVES 4**

per serving (without butter): **117 calories;** 0.4 g fat (0.1 g sat fat); 3 g protein; 26.8 g carbohydrates; 4.3 g fiber

GOOD TO KNOW Sparkling Prosecco adds effervescence—and not an ounce of fat—to grown-up sorbet floats; tequila combines with orange and lime in a granita that tastes like a frozen margarita, salted glass rims and all.

SPARKLING SORBET FLOATS

½ cup raspberry sorbet

½ cup lemon sorbet

½ cup chilled dry sparkling wine, such as Prosecco

Fresh mint leaves, for garnish

Place two small glass bowls in the freezer until chilled, at least 5 minutes. Meanwhile, let sorbets sit at room temperature until slightly softened. Divide raspberry and lemon sorbet evenly between bowls. Pour sparkling wine over sorbets, and garnish with mint; serve immediately.

SERVES 2

per serving: **162 calories;** 0 g fat; 0.1 g protein; 30.9 g carbohydrates; 1.4 g fiber

MARGARITA GRANITA

3¾ cups water

1 cup plus 2 tablespoons sugar

1 tablespoon finely grated lime zest, plus ¼ cup plus 2 tablespoons fresh lime juice (from about 3 limes)

3 tablespoons tequila

2 tablespoons fresh orange juice

¼ teaspoon coarse salt

Lime wedges, for serving (optional)

1 In a medium saucepan, bring the water and sugar to a boil over medium-high heat, stirring, until sugar has dissolved, about 1 minute. Remove from heat. Stir in lime zest and juice, tequila, orange juice, and salt.

2 Pour mixture into a 2-quart shallow nonreactive baking dish; let cool, then cover tightly with plastic wrap. Freeze until set, about 6 hours (or up to 1 day). Using the tines of a fork, scrape mixture until flakes form. Granita is best served immediately, but can be covered and frozen up to several hours. Serve with lime wedges, if desired.

SERVES 6

per serving: **117 calories;** 0 g fat; 0.1 g protein; 29 g carbohydrates; 0.1 g fiber

FAST FREEZE
Chilling the dish in the freezer before pouring in the lime mixture will help the granita freeze faster.

SERVING SUGGESTION
Spoon granita into salt-rimmed glasses, cocktail style: Rub rims with a lime wedge (or dip in water), then dip in a shallow bowl of coarse salt.

152
CALORIES PER SERVING

GOOD TO KNOW Made by beating egg whites—no yolks—with sugar until stiff peaks form, meringue provides a versatile, fat-free base for all kinds of desserts. Here, scoops of meringue are poached until just firm, then chilled and served with raspberry purée.

SOFT MERINGUE PILLOWS WITH RASPBERRY SAUCE

SERVES 4 ■ PREP TIME: 25 MINUTES ■ **TOTAL TIME: 40 MINUTES**

3 large egg whites

¼ teaspoon pure vanilla extract

⅓ cup plus 3 tablespoons sugar

1½ cups frozen raspberries, thawed

2 tablespoons sliced almonds

1 Line a plate with plastic wrap. In a large bowl, using an electric mixer, beat egg whites and vanilla on medium-high speed until mixture forms soft peaks. With mixer running, add ⅓ cup sugar, about 1 tablespoon at a time; continue to beat until mixture forms stiff peaks. Using a flexible spatula, divide egg white mixture into quarters in mixing bowl.

2 Fill a large skillet with 1 inch water and bring to a simmer over high heat. Reduce heat to medium-low so water is steaming but not simmering. Dip a large slotted spoon in cool water, then scoop up a quarter of the egg white mixture; with a flexible spatula, round the top and slide meringue off spoon into skillet. Repeat with remaining egg white mixture. Poach 4 minutes on one side. Gently flip over with slotted spoon, and poach meringues until firm to the touch, about 3 minutes more. With slotted spoon, transfer to prepared plate. Cover with another piece of plastic, sealing around the edge of plate, and refrigerate at least 15 minutes (or up to 1 day).

3 Meanwhile, in a blender, combine raspberries and remaining 3 tablespoons sugar. Blend on high speed until smooth. Strain mixture through a fine-mesh sieve into a bowl, pressing on solids with a flexible spatula; discard solids. (Sauce can be covered and refrigerated up to 2 days.)

4 To serve, divide raspberry sauce among four plates, top each with a meringue, and sprinkle with almonds.

per meringue: 152 calories; 1.6 g fat (0.1 g saturated fat); 4 g protein; 31.2 g carbohydrates; 1.6 g fiber

WHY IT'S LIGHT You can have your cupcake and eat it too when you prepare smaller portions and finish them with glazes and syrups rather than buttery, creamy frostings and other high-calorie toppings. Here, the little cakes are drizzled with a lemon syrup to complement the lemon (and lime) zest and juice in the batter

LEMON-LIME TEA CAKES

MAKES 24 ■ PREP TIME: 30 MINUTES ■ **TOTAL TIME: 30 MINUTES**

½ cup (1 stick) unsalted butter, room temperature, plus more for pan

1⅓ cups sugar

1 teaspoon finely grated lemon zest, plus 1 teaspoon fresh lemon juice

1 teaspoon finely grated lime zest, plus 1 teaspoon fresh lime juice

2 large eggs

1 cup all-purpose flour

¼ teaspoon coarse salt

⅔ cup water

1 to 2 lemons, ends cut off, very thinly sliced (for a total of 24 slices), and seeds removed (optional)

1 Preheat oven to 350°F. Lightly butter a 24-cup mini-muffin tin. In a large bowl, using an electric mixer, beat butter, ⅔ cup sugar, and both citrus zests on medium speed until light and creamy (not fluffy). Add citrus juices along with eggs and beat to combine, scraping down bowl. With mixer on low, gradually add flour and salt and beat until combined. Divide batter among prepared cups (about 1 tablespoon each). Bake until cakes are golden around edges and a toothpick inserted in centers comes out clean, about 15 minutes.

2 Meanwhile, in a small saucepan, combine the water and remaining ⅔ cup sugar; cook over medium heat, stirring occasionally, until sugar dissolves, about 5 minutes. Add lemon slices (if using) and simmer rapidly until peel turns translucent and syrup thickens slightly, 5 minutes.

3 With a toothpick, poke holes all over tops of warm tea cakes in pan. Drizzle ½ teaspoon syrup over each cake. Let cakes cool slightly in pan; transfer to a wire rack to cool completely. Top each with a lemon slice, if desired.

per 2 tea cakes: 205 calories; 8.5 g fat (5.1 g saturated fat); 2.3 g protein; 31.3 g carbohydrates; 0.7 g fiber

205
CALORIES PER SERVING

231
CALORIES PER SERVING

SMART SUBSTITUTION To make this popular Italian dessert lighter, use reduced-fat cream cheese and skim milk in place of the traditional heavy cream. Thanks to the semisweet chocolate, it still tastes rich.

CHOCOLATE PANNA COTTA

SERVES 4 ■ PREP TIME: 20 MINUTES
■ **TOTAL TIME: 2 HOURS 20 MINUTES**

1½ teaspoons unflavored powdered gelatin
1½ cups cold skim milk
 3 tablespoons sugar
 3 ounces semisweet chocolate, broken into pieces
 3 ounces reduced-fat bar cream cheese, room temperature
  Pinch of salt
  Reduced-fat sour cream, for serving (optional)

1 In a small saucepan, sprinkle gelatin over ½ cup cold milk. Let soften, about 5 minutes. Cook over low heat, stirring until gelatin has dissolved (mixture will feel smooth when rubbed between fingers), about 3 minutes. Add sugar; stir until dissolved. Add remaining 1 cup milk; heat over low until warm (do not boil), about 2 minutes. Remove from heat.

2 Place chocolate in a microwave-safe bowl; heat on high in 20-second increments, stirring between each, until melted. Add cream cheese to chocolate; using a flexible spatula, stir until combined. Pour ¼ cup gelatin mixture into chocolate mixture; stir until smooth. Gradually add remaining gelatin mixture, then salt, stirring until smooth. Divide among four 6-ounce glasses or custard cups; refrigerate until firm, at least 2 hours (or up to 2 days).

3 Serve panna cottas topped with sour cream, if desired.

per serving (without sour cream): 231 calories; 11.1 g fat (7 g saturated fat); 7.5 g protein; 28.1 g carbohydrates; 1.1 g fiber

GOOD TO KNOW A mix of sugar and honey in these citrusy cookies satisfies a sweet tooth, yet each thin, delicate cookie has only forty-four calories. Go ahead, have two.

LACY ALMOND-ORANGE COOKIES

MAKES 24 ■ PREP TIME: 10 MINUTES ■ **TOTAL TIME: 20 MINUTES (PLUS COOLING)**

½ cup slivered almonds

¾ teaspoon anise or fennel seeds

4 tablespoons (½ stick) unsalted butter

¼ cup sugar

3 tablespoons honey

½ teaspoon coarse salt

¼ cup all-purpose flour

1 tablespoon finely grated orange zest

1 Preheat oven to 375°F, with racks in middle and lower thirds. In a food processor, pulse almonds and anise seeds until coarsely ground. Transfer mixture to a small saucepan. Add butter, sugar, honey, and salt. Bring to a boil over medium-high heat, stirring once to combine ingredients as butter melts. Boil 1 minute; remove from heat. Stir in flour and zest.

2 Working quickly, drop batter by teaspoonfuls, 2½ inches apart, onto parchment-lined baking sheets. Bake until golden brown, 6 to 8 minutes, rotating sheets halfway through. Let cool completely on sheets on wire racks. (Cookies can be stored between sheets of parchment in airtight containers up to 2 days at room temperature.)

per 2 cookies: 88 calories; 7 g fat (3 g saturated fat); 2 g protein; 6 g carbohydrates; 1 g fiber

88
CALORIES PER SERVING

3

SUMMER

Summer is the easiest time of year to cook light, fuss-free meals, thanks to an abundance of corn, tomatoes, zucchini, and peppers. Dress them simply and serve them as nearly effortless sides, or toss them into colorful salads and pastas.

Grilling is a quick way to prepare full-flavored meat and vegetables that are great on their own, without the need for high-fat additions. Whether it's for a backyard barbecue or a casual weeknight dinner, fire up the grill to cook healthy burgers, fish, kebabs, and even steak.

Desserts this time of year take their cues from seasonal fruit like berries and stone fruits. Think frozen ice pops made with fresh fruit and yogurt or a rustic—and relaxed—nectarine tart.

GOOD TO KNOW Here a low-fat, yogurt-based chicken salad is served over lightly dressed mixed greens; it would also make a light—and packable—lunch when used as a sandwich filling, between slices of whole-wheat bread.

CHICKEN SALAD WITH LEMON-YOGURT DRESSING

SERVES 4 ■ PREP TIME: 15 MINUTES ■ TOTAL TIME: 45 MINUTES

1½ teaspoons dried tarragon

2 teaspoons grated lemon zest, plus 1 tablespoon fresh lemon juice

Coarse salt and ground pepper

4 bone-in, skin-on chicken breast halves (12 to 14 ounces each)

⅓ cup plain low-fat yogurt

1 tablespoon plus 2 teaspoons olive oil

3 plum tomatoes, coarsely chopped

4 scallions, trimmed and thinly sliced

6 ounces mesclun (about 6 cups)

1 Preheat oven to 425°F. Rub tarragon, 1 teaspoon zest, ¾ teaspoon salt, and ¼ teaspoon pepper under skin of chicken. Place chicken on a rimmed baking sheet; roast until cooked through, about 30 minutes. Remove from oven and let cool.

2 In a large bowl, whisk together yogurt, 2 teaspoons oil, remaining 1 teaspoon zest, and 1 teaspoon lemon juice; season with salt.

3 When chicken is cool enough to handle, remove and discard skin and bones; thinly slice meat lengthwise. Add to bowl along with tomatoes and scallions; toss to combine.

4 In a separate bowl, whisk together remaining 2 teaspoons lemon juice and 1 tablespoon oil. Add mesclun; toss to coat. Divide among four plates and top with chicken salad.

per serving: 236 calories; 9.4 g fat; 29.9 g protein; 8 g carbohydrates; 2.9 g fiber

236
CALORIES PER SERVING

295
CALORIES PER SERVING

WHY IT'S LIGHT How do you trim the fat and calories from a beloved salad? Scale back on the bacon, use only the whites of hard-cooked eggs, and make the dressing with low-fat buttermilk and light mayonnaise. Then, fold a modest amount of blue cheese into the dressing, instead of crumbling it over the salad.

LIGHTER COBB SALAD

SERVES 4 ■ PREP TIME: 20 MINUTES ■ **TOTAL TIME: 20 MINUTES**

4 large eggs

3 slices bacon (3 ounces)

1 cup low-fat buttermilk

¼ cup light mayonnaise

1 tablespoon red-wine vinegar

½ cup crumbled blue cheese (2 ounces)

Coarse salt

2 heads Boston lettuce (about 1 pound total), torn into bite-size pieces

6 ounces deli turkey, diced

4 plum tomatoes, halved, seeded, and diced

1 avocado, halved lengthwise, pitted, peeled, and diced

1 Place eggs in a medium saucepan; add cold water to cover by 1 inch, and bring to a boil. Cover pan; remove from heat. Let stand 12 minutes, then drain and rinse under cool water. Let cool completely. (Unpeeled eggs can be refrigerated up to 4 days.) Peel under running water. Separate yolks and reserve for another use. Cut egg whites into ½-inch pieces.

2 Meanwhile, in a medium skillet, cook bacon over medium heat, turning occasionally, until crisp, 5 to 8 minutes. Transfer to a paper towel–lined plate to drain. Break into bite-size pieces.

3 In a medium bowl, whisk together buttermilk, mayonnaise, and vinegar. Gently fold in blue cheese; season dressing with salt.

4 Place lettuce in a large bowl; arrange egg whites, bacon, turkey, tomatoes, and avocado on top. Serve salad with dressing alongside.

per serving: 295 calories; 18.8 g fat (5.6 g saturated fat); 19.5 g protein; 14.3 g carbohydrates; 4.6 g fiber

SECRET INGREDIENT Loaded with fiber, barley provides a filling, low-calorie base for this whole-grain salad, so all you need to add is a single chicken breast—and plenty of vegetables—to turn it into a satisfying meal for four.

BARLEY SALAD WITH CHICKEN, CORN, AND SCALLIONS

SERVES 4 ■ PREP TIME: 20 MINUTES ■ TOTAL TIME: 45 MINUTES

2 boneless, skinless chicken breast halves (6 to 8 ounces each)

Coarse salt and ground pepper

1 cup pearl barley

2 bunches scallions, trimmed and cut into thirds crosswise, white parts halved lengthwise

2½ cups fresh (from about 3 ears) or frozen corn kernels (do not thaw)

3 tablespoons olive oil

1 pint grape tomatoes, halved

¼ cup fresh flat-leaf parsley leaves

1 tablespoon plus 2 teaspoons fresh lime juice

5 ounces baby spinach

1 Place chicken in a medium saucepan and cover with water. Bring to a boil, season with salt, and reduce to a bare simmer. Cover and cook 5 minutes. Remove from heat and let chicken stand, covered, until cooked through, 12 to 14 minutes more. Using tongs, remove chicken from liquid. When cool enough to handle, shred meat into bite-size pieces.

2 In a medium pot of boiling salted water, cook barley according to package instructions. Drain and let cool.

3 Meanwhile, preheat oven to 450°F. Place scallions and corn on a rimmed baking sheet. Toss with 1 tablespoon oil and season with salt and pepper. Spread in a single layer and roast, stirring halfway through, until tender and golden, about 25 minutes.

4 In a large bowl, combine chicken, barley, scallion mixture, tomatoes, parsley, 1 tablespoon oil, and 1 tablespoon lime juice; season with salt and pepper. In a medium bowl, toss spinach with remaining 1 tablespoon oil and 2 teaspoons lime juice; season with salt and pepper. Serve spinach with chicken-barley mixture.

per serving: 409 calories; 13 g fat (2 g saturated fat); 16.1 g protein; 62.4 g carbohydrates; 13.2 g fiber

409
CALORIES PER SERVING

182

CALORIES PER SERVING

WHY IT'S LIGHT Packed with seasonal vegetables, this soup needs little added fat—just two tablespoons olive oil—and just a half cup orzo to feel hearty. The soup freezes well, so you may want to double the recipe and save a batch to eat during cooler months.

LATE-SUMMER VEGETABLE SOUP

SERVES 6 ■ PREP TIME: 35 MINUTES ■ **TOTAL TIME: 35 MINUTES**

2 tablespoons olive oil

1 medium onion, finely chopped
   Coarse salt and ground pepper

2 cans (14.5 ounces each) low-sodium vegetable or chicken broth

2 cups water

2 large zucchini, halved lengthwise and thinly sliced crosswise

8 ounces green beans, trimmed and cut into thirds

3 cups fresh (from about 4 ears) or frozen corn kernels (do not thaw)

1 can (14.5 ounces) diced tomatoes in juice

½ cup orzo

1 In a 5-quart Dutch oven or other heavy pot, heat oil over medium. Add onion; season with salt and pepper. Cook, stirring frequently, until onion is translucent, 3 to 5 minutes.

2 Add broth and the water; bring to a boil. Add zucchini, green beans, corn, tomatoes (with their juice), and orzo; stir to combine. Cook, uncovered, until orzo is tender, 8 to 11 minutes. Season with salt and pepper and serve.

per serving: 182 calories; 5.6 g fat (0.8 g saturated fat); 6 g protein; 31.1 g carbohydrates; 4.7 g fiber

SMART SUBSTITUTION This seemingly rich summer chowder leaves out the cream; instead, it's thickened with the starch from a russet potato as well as some flour, and just one cup of milk.

BROCCOLI CHOWDER WITH CORN AND BACON

SERVES 4 ■ PREP TIME: 20 MINUTES ■ **TOTAL TIME: 40 MINUTES**

- 4 slices bacon (4 ounces), cut into 1-inch pieces
- 1 medium onion, finely chopped
- ¼ cup all-purpose flour
- 2 cans (14.5 ounces each) low-sodium chicken broth
- 1 large russet potato, peeled and diced
- 1 head broccoli (about 1 pound), cut into bite-size florets, stalks peeled and thinly sliced
- 2 cups fresh (from about 3 ears) or frozen corn kernels (do not thaw)
- ½ teaspoon dried thyme
- 1 cup milk
  Coarse salt and ground pepper

1 In a 5-quart Dutch oven or other heavy pot, cook bacon over medium-low heat, stirring occasionally, until crisp, 8 to 10 minutes. Using a slotted spoon, transfer to a paper towel–lined plate to drain. Increase heat to medium. Add onion and cook, stirring, until it begins to soften, 6 to 8 minutes.

2 Add flour; cook, stirring constantly, 30 seconds (do not let brown). Add broth and potato; bring to a boil. Reduce to a simmer; cook until potato is tender, about 10 minutes.

3 Add broccoli, corn, thyme, and milk; cook until broccoli is crisp-tender, 8 to 10 minutes. Season with salt and pepper. Serve immediately, topped with bacon.

per serving: 264 calories; 6.1 g fat (2.6 g saturated fat); 14.4 g protein; 42 g carbohydrates; 5 g fiber

264
CALORIES PER SERVING

182
CALORIES PER SERVING

WHY IT'S LIGHT Gazpacho is traditionally made with pieces of stale bread as a thickener. In this lightened version, vegetables alone contribute heft, and toasted bread is offered as an optional side.

GAZPACHO

SERVES 4 ■ PREP TIME: 15 MINUTES ■ **TOTAL TIME: 45 MINUTES (WITH CHILLING)**

4 large tomatoes, chopped

1 medium cucumber, peeled, seeded, and chopped

1 red bell pepper, ribs and seeds removed, chopped

2 garlic cloves, finely chopped

1 teaspoon sherry vinegar

1 teaspoon red-wine vinegar

¼ cup olive oil, plus more for serving

Coarse salt and ground pepper

Toasted country bread, for serving (optional)

Shaved Manchego or Parmesan cheese, for serving

1 In a food processor, purée tomatoes until almost smooth. Add cucumber, bell pepper, garlic, both vinegars, and oil; season with salt and pepper. Pulse until mostly smooth.

2 Transfer soup to a large bowl; cover and refrigerate until chilled, at least 30 minutes or up to 8 hours. Season with more salt and pepper, and thin with water if necessary. Brush bread, if using, with oil. Divide soup among four bowls, drizzle with oil, and top with cheese; serve bread alongside.

per serving (without bread): 182 calories; 14.8 g fat (2.1 g saturated fat); 2.3 g protein; 12.1 g carbohydrates; 3 g fiber

SMART SUBSTITUTION Instead of toting a pasta salad along to the next potluck, try a salad that features a whole grain such as bulgur (precooked wheat that's been dried and cracked). Most grains work well when tossed and seasoned with the same ingredients used in pasta salads, and they are definitely better for you.

MEDITERRANEAN GRAIN SALAD

SERVES 4 ■ PREP TIME: 5 MINUTES ■ **TOTAL TIME: 35 MINUTES**

1⅓ cups medium-grind bulgur
　　Coarse salt and ground pepper
2⅔ cups boiling water
　1 pint grape tomatoes, halved
1½ cups loosely packed fresh flat-leaf
　　parsley, coarsely chopped
　2 small shallots, minced
　¼ cup red-wine vinegar
　2 tablespoons plus 2 teaspoons
　　olive oil
　4 ounces fresh goat cheese, crumbled

1 In a heatproof bowl, combine bulgur, 1 teaspoon salt, and the boiling water. Cover and let stand until tender but slightly chewy, about 30 minutes.

2 Drain bulgur in a fine sieve, pressing to remove liquid; return to bowl. Add tomatoes, parsley, shallots, vinegar, and oil. Season with salt and pepper, and toss. Serve topped with cheese.

per serving: 358 calories; 16.2 g fat (5.6 g saturated fat); 12.9 g protein; 44.9 g carbohydrates; 10.7 g fiber

358
CALORIES PER SERVING

268

CALORIES PER SERVING

GOOD TO KNOW When pressed to remove excess moisture, extra-firm tofu does a better job of soaking up marinades and holding its shape as it cooks, especially on the grill. If using wooden skewers, soak them in water for thirty minutes before grilling.

TOFU AND SQUASH KEBABS WITH CILANTRO SAUCE

SERVES 4 ■ PREP TIME: 30 MINUTES ■ **TOTAL TIME: 30 MINUTES**

2 cups fresh cilantro leaves

¼ cup plus 1 tablespoon vegetable oil, such as safflower, plus more for grill

½ jalapeño chile, chopped (ribs and seeds removed for less heat, if desired)

1 teaspoon grated peeled fresh ginger

2 tablespoons fresh lime juice

3 scallions, trimmed, white and green parts separated and cut into 1-inch lengths

Coarse salt and ground pepper

1 package (14 ounces) extra-firm tofu, pressed (see below) and cut into 12 pieces

2 summer squash, halved lengthwise and cut into 1-inch pieces

1 Heat grill to medium. In a food processor, combine cilantro, ¼ cup oil, the jalapeño, ginger, lime juice, and scallion greens. Blend until smooth; season with salt and pepper. In a medium bowl, combine tofu, scallion whites, and 1 tablespoon oil; season with salt and pepper. Thread tofu and scallion whites onto four skewers, then thread squash onto four skewers.

2 Clean and lightly oil hot grates. Grill squash kebabs, covered, until tender, 11 to 13 minutes, turning occasionally. Transfer to a platter. Grill tofu kebabs, uncovered, until scallions are soft, 4 to 6 minutes, turning occasionally; brush with ¼ cup cilantro sauce and grill 30 seconds more. Transfer to platter. Serve kebabs with remaining cilantro sauce.

per serving: 268 calories; 23.6 g fat (3.1 g saturated fat); 13.3 g protein; 6.7 g carbohydrates; 2.8 g fiber

PRESSING TOFU
Place tofu (firm or extra-firm) on a plate lined with paper towels. Cover with more paper towels and another plate and weight with canned goods or a heavy pan. Let drain for at least 2 hours (or up to 8), replacing paper towels as necessary.

SMART SUBSTITUTION Using part-skim cheeses—such as the ricotta and mozzarella in this recipe—in place of full-fat versions is one easy way to make a favorite pasta dish healthier. And before they are filled and rolled, the eggplant slices are baked, without any oil, instead of being breaded and fried.

EGGPLANT ROLLATINI

SERVES 4 ■ PREP TIME: 15 MINUTES ■ **TOTAL TIME: 1 HOUR 25 MINUTES**

1 or 2 large Italian eggplants, cut lengthwise into eight total ½-inch-thick slices

Coarse salt and ground pepper

1 cup homemade or store-bought marinara sauce

½ cup part-skim ricotta cheese

½ cup grated Parmesan cheese, plus more for serving

1 large egg

1 garlic clove, minced

1 cup shredded part-skim mozzarella cheese (4 ounces)

Crusty bread, for serving (optional)

1 Preheat oven to 375°F. Season eggplant with salt and pepper; arrange on a parchment-lined baking sheet. Cover baking sheet securely with parchment, then foil, and bake until eggplant is tender and pliable but not fully cooked, 10 to 12 minutes.

2 Spread ¼ cup marinara sauce on the bottom of a 2-quart baking dish. In a small bowl, mix together ricotta, Parmesan, egg, garlic, ¼ teaspoon salt, and ⅛ teaspoon pepper.

3 Pat eggplant dry with paper towels. Dividing evenly, spoon ricotta mixture onto short end of eggplant slices, leaving a 1-inch border on the end and a ¼-inch border on either side. Starting at the short end, roll up slices; arrange in prepared dish, seam side down. Top with remaining ¾ cup marinara sauce.

4 Cover dish with foil, and bake until eggplant is very tender, 50 to 60 minutes. Uncover and sprinkle with mozzarella; bake until cheese is melted, 3 to 5 minutes. Remove from oven and let cool 5 minutes before serving with bread, if desired, and topped with additional Parmesan.

per serving: 267 calories; 12.8 g fat (6.8 g saturated fat); 19 g protein; 21.2 g carbohydrates; 8.7 g fiber

FILLING THE DISH
Precooking the eggplant slices makes them pliable enough to roll around the filling. Arranging the stuffed eggplant slices in a single snug layer, seam side down, ensures that each rollatino cooks through evenly.

267
CALORIES PER SERVING

310
CALORIES PER SERVING

SMART SUBSTITUTION Whole-wheat tortillas contain fewer calories than traditional pizza crusts, and they crisp quickly in the oven. Topping each round with just a sprinkle of part-skim mozzarella and a few shavings of pecorino cheese also results in a lighter pizza. Complete the low-calorie meal with an arugula salad.

TWO-CHEESE TORTILLA PIZZA WITH ARUGULA SALAD

SERVES 4 ▪ PREP TIME: 15 MINUTES ▪ **TOTAL TIME: 15 MINUTES**

- 4 whole-wheat tortillas (8-inch)
- 1 tablespoon olive oil
- 2 cans (14.5 ounces each) diced tomatoes, drained
- 3 ounces part-skim mozzarella cheese, coarsely grated
- 1 ounce Pecorino Romano cheese, shaved with a vegetable peeler
- ¼ cup pitted Kalamata olives, halved lengthwise
- ¼ teaspoon red-pepper flakes
- 2 teaspoons balsamic vinegar

  Coarse salt and ground pepper
- 2 bunches arugula (about 8 ounces total), thick stems removed, washed well and dried
- ½ cup fresh basil leaves, torn

1 Preheat oven to 450°F, with racks in upper and lower thirds. Arrange tortillas on two rimmed baking sheets; brush tops with a total of 1 teaspoon oil. Dividing evenly, layer tortillas with tomatoes, cheeses, olives, and red-pepper flakes. Bake until crust is crisp and edges are browned, 13 to 15 minutes, rotating sheets from top to bottom and front to back halfway through.

2 Meanwhile, in a medium bowl, whisk together remaining 2 teaspoons oil and the vinegar; season vinaigrette with salt and pepper.

3 When pizzas are finished baking, toss arugula with vinaigrette. Top pizzas with basil, and cut into wedges; serve with arugula salad.

per serving: 310 calories; 13.9 g fat (4.2 g saturated fat); 14 g protein; 33 g carbohydrates; 4.9 g fiber

WHY IT'S LIGHT Unlike traditional versions of lasagna, which are filled and topped with cheese and meat sauce before baking, this seasonal, no-bake variation relies on fresh vegetables for the filling. For an even lighter preparation, use part-skim ricotta cheese.

NO-BAKE SUMMER LASAGNA

SERVES 4 ■ PREP TIME: 25 MINUTES ■ **TOTAL TIME: 25 MINUTES**

½ cup ricotta cheese

3 tablespoons grated Parmesan cheese

3 tablespoons plus 2 teaspoons extra-virgin olive oil

Coarse salt and ground pepper

8 lasagna noodles, broken in half crosswise

1 garlic clove, minced

2 pints grape tomatoes, halved

2 medium zucchini, thinly sliced

2 tablespoons torn fresh basil leaves, plus more for garnish

1 In a small bowl, combine ricotta, Parmesan, and 2 teaspoons oil; season with salt and pepper. In a large pot of boiling salted water, cook noodles until al dente according to package instructions; drain.

2 Meanwhile, in a large skillet, heat 2 tablespoons oil over medium-high. Add garlic and tomatoes; season with salt and pepper. Cook, stirring, until beginning to soften, about 3 minutes. Transfer tomatoes to a bowl. Add remaining 1 tablespoon oil and the zucchini to skillet; season with salt and pepper. Cook, stirring, until zucchini are tender, about 5 minutes. Transfer to another bowl and stir in basil.

3 Divide one-third of the tomatoes among four plates; top each with a noodle half and small spoonfuls of ricotta, zucchini, and more tomatoes. Repeat with remaining noodles and tomatoes. Garnish with additional basil and serve.

per serving: 376 calories; 19.3 g fat (5.1 g saturated fat); 12.3 g protein; 40.1 g carbohydrates; 4.3 g fiber

376

CALORIES PER SERVING

258
CALORIES PER SERVING

FLAVOR BOOSTERS The bracing combination of fresh lime juice and mint adds minimal calories and not a trace of fat, yet tastes out of this world. Scallions, cucumber, and chopped peanuts up the flavor ante while also adding crunch. Soba noodles, made from buckwheat, are nuttier than those made from wheat.

ASIAN NOODLE SALAD WITH PEANUTS AND MINT

SERVES 6 ■ PREP TIME: 10 MINUTES ■ TOTAL TIME: 20 MINUTES

Coarse salt

12 ounces soba (Japanese buckwheat noodles)

2 tablespoons soy sauce

2 tablespoons fresh lime juice

1 tablespoon vegetable oil, such as safflower

2 scallions, trimmed and thinly sliced

½ English cucumber, halved lengthwise and thinly sliced

¼ cup unsalted peanuts, coarsely chopped

¼ cup fresh mint leaves, plus more for garnish

1 In a large pot of boiling salted water, cook noodles until tender according to package instructions. Drain, then rinse under cold water to stop the cooking. Drain well.

2 In a small bowl, whisk together soy sauce, lime juice, and oil. In a large bowl, combine noodles, scallions, cucumber, peanuts, and mint. Toss noodle mixture with sauce, garnish with additional mint, and serve.

MAKE AHEAD
The soy-sauce mixture and noodle mixture can be refrigerated in separate covered containers up to 1 day. Add mint just before serving.

per serving: 258 calories; 5.8 g fat (0.8 g saturated fat); 10.5 g protein; 46.2 g carbohydrates; 1 g fiber

GRILLED LEMON CHICKEN WITH TABBOULEH

SERVES 4 ■ PREP TIME: 25 MINUTES ■ **TOTAL TIME: 25 MINUTES**

¾ cup water

½ cup medium-grain bulgur

Coarse salt and ground pepper

1½ cups coarsely chopped fresh
flat-leaf parsley

½ English cucumber, halved lengthwise
and cut into ½-inch dice

1 large tomato, cut into ½-inch dice

2 tablespoons fresh lemon juice

2 tablespoons olive oil, plus more
for grill

1 garlic clove, minced

8 boneless, skinless chicken thighs
(about 2 pounds total)

1 Heat grill (or grill pan) to high. In a small saucepan, bring the water to a simmer. Add bulgur, season with salt and pepper, and cook 1 minute. Remove from heat, cover, and let stand 10 minutes; fluff with a fork. In a medium bowl, combine bulgur, parsley, cucumber, tomato, 1 tablespoon lemon juice, and 1 tablespoon oil; toss tabbouleh to combine.

2 In a small bowl, stir garlic with remaining 1 tablespoon each lemon juice and oil; season with salt and pepper.

3 Clean and lightly oil hot grates. Season chicken with salt and pepper; grill until cooked through, about 4 minutes per side. Brush chicken with lemon mixture and serve with tabbouleh.

per serving: 363 calories; 18.8 g fat (4.2 g saturated fat);
30.6 g protein; 18 g carbohydrates; 4.8 g fiber

363

CALORIES PER SERVING

337
CALORIES PER SERVING

FLAVOR BOOSTER A ginger-and-lime yogurt marinade spiked with chopped jalapeños adds tang and a little heat to skinless chicken thighs. Peach chutney makes a tart-sweet, low-fat accompaniment. If using wooden skewers, soak them in water for thirty minutes before grilling.

TANDOORI CHICKEN KEBABS

SERVES 4 ▪ PREP TIME: 20 MINUTES ▪ **TOTAL TIME: 2 HOURS 20 MINUTES (WITH MARINATING)**

2 tablespoons fresh lime juice

4 garlic cloves

1 piece fresh ginger (2 inches), peeled and chopped

2 jalapeño chiles, chopped (ribs and seeds removed for less heat if desired)

1 cup plain yogurt

8 boneless, skinless chicken thighs (about 2 pounds total)

Vegetable oil, for grill

Peach Chutney, for serving (optional; recipe follows)

1 In a blender, purée lime juice, garlic, ginger, and chiles. Add yogurt and blend until smooth.

2 Trim chicken thighs; halve each lengthwise. Thread 4 chicken pieces on each of four long skewers. Arrange skewers in a nonreactive dish; pour marinade over, and turn to coat. Cover; refrigerate at least 2 hours (or up to 24 hours), turning occasionally.

3 Heat grill to high; clean and lightly oil hot grates. Place skewers on grill; cook, covered, until grill marks are visible and chicken is cooked through, turning occasionally, 8 to 10 minutes. Serve with chutney.

per serving (without chutney): 337 calories; 17 g fat (3.3 g saturated fat); 38.1 g protein; 6 g carbohydrates; 0.4 g fiber

PEACH CHUTNEY

1 tablespoon olive oil

½ cup finely chopped onion

2 garlic cloves, minced

⅛ to ¼ teaspoon red-pepper flakes

¼ cup cider vinegar

¼ cup sugar

⅓ cup dried cherries

Coarse salt and ground pepper

1½ pounds ripe peaches, peeled, pitted, and cut into ½-inch chunks

2 to 4 tablespoons water (optional)

1 Heat oil in a small saucepan over medium. Add onion and cook, stirring occasionally, until soft, about 5 minutes. Add garlic and red-pepper flakes to taste; cook 1 minute.

2 Stir in vinegar, sugar, and dried cherries; season with salt and pepper. Bring to a boil; reduce heat, and simmer until syrupy, about 5 minutes.

3 Add peaches; simmer until soft, 5 to 10 minutes. With a wooden spoon, mash some peaches against side of pan; thin with the water, if needed. Let cool completely. **MAKES 2½ CUPS**

per serving (1 tablespoon): 20 calories; 0.4 g fat (0 g saturated fat); 0.2 g protein; 4.3 g carbohydrates; 0.5 g fiber

FLAVOR BOOSTERS Lean ground turkey is just the start when preparing lower-calorie burgers; these are made supermoist and juicy with the somewhat unexpected addition of reduced-fat sour cream, mango chutney, Dijon, and chili powder; torn pieces of whole-wheat bread help bind the meat as it cooks.

OPEN-FACE TURKEY BURGERS

SERVES 4 ■ PREP TIME: 20 MINUTES ■ **TOTAL TIME: 30 MINUTES**

6 slices whole-wheat sandwich bread

1 pound ground dark-meat turkey (93% lean)

½ cup reduced-fat sour cream

¼ cup prepared mango chutney, preferably Major Grey's, finely chopped

2 tablespoons Dijon mustard

1 tablespoon chili powder

1 teaspoon coarse salt

2 ounces mesclun

1 medium tomato, sliced

1 Heat broiler, with rack 4 inches from heat. In a medium bowl, tear 2 slices bread into small pieces. Add turkey, sour cream, 3 tablespoons chutney, 1 tablespoon mustard, the chili powder, and coarse salt. Shape into 4 firmly packed 5-inch round patties.

2 Place burgers on a rimmed baking sheet; broil until firm and cooked through, 4 to 5 minutes per side. Lightly toast remaining 4 bread slices.

3 Layer each bread slice with mesclun, burger, and tomato. Stir together 1 tablespoon each chutney and mustard, and serve alongside burgers.

per serving: 365 calories; 13.6 g fat (2.7 g saturated fat); 28.7 g protein; 34.1 g carbohydrates; 4.3 g fiber

MAKE AHEAD
Freeze uncooked patties on a baking sheet until firm, about 30 minutes, then wrap each one in plastic; place patties in a resealable freezer bag, label, and date. Freeze up to 2 months. Thaw burgers overnight in the refrigerator before broiling.

365
CALORIES PER SERVING

370
CALORIES PER SERVING

FLAVOR BOOSTER A fragrant sauce made from a handful of pantry standbys—including soy sauce, garlic, vinegar, and red-pepper flakes—serves as a marinade for the chicken and a dressing for the finished salad. Feel free to substitute pork or beef for the chicken.

THAI CHICKEN AND NOODLE SALAD

SERVES 4 ■ PREP TIME: 20 MINUTES ■ **TOTAL TIME: 50 MINUTES**

1¼ pounds boneless, skinless chicken breasts, thinly sliced crosswise

Spicy Asian Dressing (recipe follows)

Coarse salt

3½ ounces Chinese rice noodles, broken in half if long

1 tablespoon vegetable oil, such as safflower

2 medium carrots, shaved into ribbons with a vegetable peeler

1 English cucumber, halved lengthwise and thinly sliced crosswise

¼ cup fresh basil leaves, torn

Assorted garnishes, such as bean sprouts, chopped peanuts, fresh mint leaves, red-pepper flakes, and sliced scallion greens (optional)

1 Place chicken and half of Spicy Asian Dressing in a resealable plastic bag (reserve remaining dressing). Marinate at room temperature 30 minutes (or refrigerate up to 1 day).

2 In a large pot of boiling salted water, cook noodles until tender according to package instructions. Drain, then rinse under cold water to stop the cooking. Drain well and transfer to a platter.

3 In a large skillet, heat oil over medium-high. Working in batches (do not crowd skillet), sauté chicken until cooked through, 1 to 2 minutes; transfer to platter on top of noodles.

4 Add carrots, cucumber, and basil. Drizzle with reserved dressing, and serve with garnishes, as desired.

per serving: 370 calories; 6 g fat (1.1 g saturated fat); 38 g protein; 40.8 g carbohydrates; 2.3 g fiber

SPICY ASIAN DRESSING

4 scallions, white parts only, thinly sliced

2 garlic cloves, minced

½ cup soy sauce

¼ cup rice vinegar (unseasoned)

2 tablespoons light-brown sugar

1 tablespoon fresh lime juice

½ teaspoon anchovy paste (or 1 minced canned anchovy)

½ teaspoon red-pepper flakes

Combine all ingredients in a medium bowl. (Dressing can be covered and refrigerated up to 1 day; bring to room temperature before using.)
MAKES ABOUT 1 CUP

SMART SUBSTITUTION Try a mix of yogurt and lemon juice for a tart, creamy pasta sauce without a lot of fat. This satisfying pasta salad, made with whole-wheat penne, makes a great summer supper; pack any leftovers for a workday lunch.

PASTA SALAD WITH CHICKEN, RAISINS, AND ALMONDS

SERVES 4 ■ PREP TIME: 15 MINUTES ■ TOTAL TIME: 25 MINUTES

2 tablespoons unblanched almonds

1 pound boneless, skinless chicken breast halves

Coarse salt and ground pepper

8 ounces whole-wheat penne rigate or other short pasta shape

1 cup plain low-fat yogurt

½ cup golden raisins (optional)

½ cup coarsely chopped fresh flat-leaf parsley

1 tablespoon finely grated lemon zest, plus 2 tablespoons fresh lemon juice

1 Preheat oven to 350°F. Spread almonds on a rimmed baking sheet; toast in oven until darkened, tossing once or twice, 10 to 12 minutes. Let cool, then coarsely chop.

2 Place chicken in a large saucepan and cover with water. Bring to a boil, season with salt, and reduce to a bare simmer. Cover and cook 5 minutes. Remove pan from heat and let chicken stand, covered, until cooked through, 12 to 14 minutes more. Remove chicken from liquid. When cool enough to handle, shred into bite-size pieces.

3 Meanwhile, in a large pot of boiling salted water, cook pasta until al dente according to package directions. Reserve ¼ cup pasta water. Drain pasta, then rinse under cold water to stop the cooking. Drain well.

4 In a large bowl, stir together pasta, chicken, yogurt, raisins (if using), parsley, almonds, and lemon zest and juice. Thin sauce with reserved pasta water if necessary. Season with salt and pepper. Salad can be covered and refrigerated up to 1 day. Serve chilled or at room temperature.

per serving: 484 calories; 9.9 g fat (2.3 g saturated fat); 56.4 g protein; 41.3 g carbohydrates; 7.8 g fiber

484
CALORIES PER SERVING

325
CALORIES PER SERVING

GOOD TO KNOW Thinly pounded chicken breasts, known as paillards in French cuisine, cook through in just a couple of minutes—perfect for a quick, low-calorie midweek dinner.

CHICKEN WITH WATERCRESS SALAD

SERVES 4 ■ PREP TIME: 30 MINUTES ■ **TOTAL TIME: 30 MINUTES**

¼ cup olive oil, plus more for grill

¼ cup fresh lemon juice (from about 2 lemons)

Coarse salt and ground pepper

2 boneless, skinless chicken breast halves (6 to 8 ounces each)

¼ teaspoon ground cumin

2 bunches watercress (about 12 ounces total), thick stems trimmed

1 bunch radishes, trimmed and thinly sliced

1 avocado, halved lengthwise, pitted, peeled, and diced

1 Heat grill to medium-high. In a large bowl, whisk together oil and lemon juice; season dressing with salt and pepper.

2 Place chicken on a work surface. Split each chicken breast in half horizontally. Cover with plastic wrap and pound each piece with the flat side of a meat mallet or the bottom of a small heavy pan until ¼ inch thick. Drizzle with 2 tablespoons dressing and sprinkle with cumin.

3 Clean and lightly oil hot grates. Grill chicken until cooked through, 1 to 2 minutes per side. Add watercress, radishes, and avocado to bowl with dressing, and toss to combine. Serve chicken topped with watercress salad.

per serving: 325 calories; 21.6 g fat (3.2 g saturated fat); 27.9 g protein; 5.7 g carbohydrates; 3.3 g fiber

SECRET INGREDIENT A tangy marinade sweetened with apple juice instead of sugar does double-duty when reduced to a sauce for grilled steak. In addition to Worcestershire sauce, mustard, and hot sauce, the marinade is further enlivened by an optional splash of whiskey.

GRILLED MARINATED FLANK STEAK

SERVES 8 ■ PREP TIME: 45 MINUTES ■ TOTAL TIME: 2 HOURS (WITH MARINATING)

6 garlic cloves, minced

Coarse salt and ground pepper

1 quart unsweetened apple juice

2 tablespoons whole-grain mustard

2 tablespoons olive oil, plus more for grill

1 tablespoon Worcestershire sauce

2 teaspoons hot sauce, such as Tabasco

¼ cup whiskey (optional)

2 flank steaks (about 1½ pounds each), pierced all over with a fork

1 In a 9-by-13-inch baking dish, whisk together garlic, ½ teaspoon each salt and pepper, the apple juice, mustard, oil, Worcestershire, hot sauce, and whiskey, if desired. Add steaks and turn to coat; marinate at room temperature 1 hour, turning occasionally (or cover with plastic wrap and refrigerate up to 1 day).

2 Transfer steaks from marinade to a platter, letting excess drip off. Pour marinade into a large saucepan. Bring to a boil over high heat; cook until thickened and reduced to about 1 cup, 20 to 25 minutes. Season sauce with salt and pepper.

3 Meanwhile, heat grill to high; clean and lightly oil grates. Grill steaks, turning once, until well browned and cooked to desired doneness, 6 to 8 minutes per side for medium-rare. Transfer steaks to a cutting board, and tent with foil. Let rest 10 minutes before thinly slicing against the grain. Serve with sauce.

per serving: 363 calories; 15.3 g fat (6 g saturated fat); 35.1 g protein; 16.5 g carbohydrates; 0.1 g fiber

363
CALORIES PER SERVING

454
CALORIES PER SERVING

GOOD TO KNOW When only a grilled steak will do, choose a leaner cut like top blade over more marbled porterhouse or rib-eye. Blade steaks have a rich flavor and are very tender; tri tip, sirloin, and strip steaks also take well to grilling without marinating. If only larger steaks are available, purchase fewer and cut them into six-ounce servings, for portion control.

GRILLED STEAK WITH TOMATOES AND SCALLIONS

SERVES 4 ■ PREP TIME: 20 MINUTES ■ **TOTAL TIME: 20 MINUTES**

1 tablespoon olive oil, plus more for grill

4 flat iron steaks (about 6 ounces each)

Coarse salt and ground pepper

2 pints cherry tomatoes

2 bunches scallions, trimmed and cut into 2-inch lengths

2 tablespoons balsamic vinegar

1 Heat grill to high; clean and lightly oil grates. Pat dry steaks and season with salt and pepper. Cook about 4 minutes per side for medium-rare. Transfer steaks to a plate, tent with foil, and let rest 10 minutes.

2 Meanwhile, place a double layer of foil on grill. Place tomatoes and scallions on foil; drizzle with the oil. Grill until tender and lightly charred, 6 to 8 minutes.

3 Transfer vegetables to a bowl, toss with vinegar, and season with salt and pepper. To serve, top steaks with vegetables.

per serving: 454 calories; 25.5 g fat (9.2 g saturated fat); 44.6 g protein; 10.3 g carbohydrates; 3 g fiber

GOOD TO KNOW Kebabs are a good way to incorporate vegetables into from-the-grill dinners. They also allow you to use a small amount of a high-fat food, such as the chorizo in the pork kebabs, to maximum effect. If using wooden skewers, soak them in water for thirty minutes before grilling.

SCALLOP, ORANGE, AND CUCUMBER KEBABS

    Vegetable oil, for grill
  2 tablespoons honey
  ½ navel orange, halved and cut into eight wedges, plus ¼ cup fresh orange juice
  8 very thin slices peeled fresh ginger
  ½ Kirby cucumber, halved lengthwise and cut into ½-inch slices
  1 pound scallops, tough muscle removed
    Coarse salt and ground pepper

1 Heat grill to medium; clean and lightly oil hot grates. In a small bowl, combine honey and orange juice.

2 Dividing ingredients evenly, thread orange wedges (through skin), ginger, cucumber, and scallops onto four skewers, beginning and ending with orange wedges; season with salt and pepper. Grill kebabs, covered, until scallops are opaque throughout, 4 to 6 minutes, turning and basting with honey mixture halfway through. **SERVES 4**

per serving: **155 calories;** 1 g fat (0.1 g saturated fat); 19.6 g protein; 17 g carbohydrates; 0.7 g fiber

PORK AND CHORIZO KEBABS

  2 boneless pork loin chops (6 to 8 ounces each), cut into 16 pieces
  1 small onion, quartered and layers separated
  2 tablespoons olive oil, plus more for grill
  1 tablespoon red-wine vinegar
    Coarse salt and ground pepper
  4 ounces dried chorizo sausage, halved lengthwise and cut into ½-inch pieces

1 In a large bowl, combine pork, onion, oil, and vinegar; season with salt and pepper. Marinate at room temperature 1 hour (or cover with plastic wrap and refrigerate up to overnight).

2 Heat grill to medium; clean and lightly oil hot grates. Dividing ingredients evenly, thread pork, onion, and chorizo onto four skewers, beginning and ending with pork; season with salt and pepper. Grill kebabs, covered, until pork is cooked through, about 13 minutes, turning occasionally. **SERVES 4**

per serving: **270 calories;** 22 g fat (6.6 g saturated fat); 15 g protein; 2.2 g carbohydrates; 0.3 g fiber

LAMB, TOMATO, AND MINT KEBABS

    Vegetable oil, for grill
  1 pound boneless leg of lamb, trimmed of excess fat and cut into 1-inch pieces
  2 teaspoons finely grated lemon zest, plus lemon wedges for serving
  ½ teaspoon ground coriander
  ¼ teaspoon ground cinnamon
    Coarse salt and ground pepper
  1 pint grape tomatoes
 12 fresh mint leaves

1 Heat grill to medium-high; clean and lightly oil hot grates. In a large bowl, combine lamb, zest, coriander, and cinnamon; season with salt and pepper.

2 Dividing ingredients evenly, thread lamb, tomatoes, and mint onto four skewers, beginning and ending with lamb. Grill kebabs, covered, until lamb is medium-rare, 5 to 6 minutes, turning occasionally. Serve with lemon wedges. **SERVES 4**

per serving: **184 calories;** 9.2 g fat (2.5 g saturated fat); 21.4 g protein; 3.4 g carbohydrates; 1.2 g fiber

390
CALORIES PER SERVING

WHY IT'S LIGHT This low-calorie Tex-Mex meal uses top round steak, a very lean cut of beef; you can also use other lean cuts such as eye of round or top sirloin. Corn tortillas have fewer calories and more nutrients than flour tortillas.

SEARED STEAK FAJITAS

SERVES 4 ■ PREP TIME: 20 MINUTES ■ **TOTAL TIME: 1 HOUR 20 MINUTES** (WITH MARINATING)

¾ pound top round steak

1 tablespoon soy sauce

¼ cup plus 1 tablespoon fresh lime juice (from 3 limes), plus lime wedges for serving

1 tablespoon extra-virgin olive oil

1 garlic clove, minced

   Coarse salt and ground pepper

2 medium green bell peppers, ribs and seeds removed, thinly sliced

1 large onion, halved and thinly sliced

8 corn tortillas (6-inch), warmed (see note)

½ cup grated white cheddar cheese (2 ounces)

1 large tomato, chopped

   Cilantro sprigs, for serving

1 In a shallow dish or bowl, combine steak, soy sauce, and ¼ cup lime juice. Refrigerate 1 hour, turning steak occasionally. Meanwhile, in a small saucepan, heat 2 teaspoons oil over medium. Add garlic and cook until fragrant, 30 seconds. Remove from heat. Stir in remaining 1 tablespoon lime juice. Set garlic oil aside.

2 Remove steak from marinade and blot dry with paper towels. Season with salt and pepper. In a large cast-iron or other heavy skillet, heat remaining 1 teaspoon oil over medium-high. Cook steak, about 2 minutes per side for medium-rare. Transfer to a cutting board, tent with foil and let rest.

3 Add bell peppers and onion to pan; season with salt and pepper. Cook, stirring, until vegetables are crisp-tender, 4 to 6 minutes. Stir in reserved garlic oil. Thinly slice steak against the grain and serve with vegetables, tortillas, cheese, tomato, and cilantro.

per serving: 390 calories; 16.5 g fat (6.1 g saturated fat); 28.3 g protein; 34.1 g carbohydrates; 5.6 g fiber

NOTE
To warm the corn tortillas, use tongs to toast them on a gas-stove burner for about 30 seconds per side. Or wrap them (stacked) in damp paper towels and microwave for 30 to 60 seconds, just until softened.

GOOD TO KNOW When planning meals with calorie and fat counts in mind, balance higher-fat proteins with low-fat sides, so the totals still fall within the target range. Here, simply seasoned pork chops—grilled on the bone for flavor and tenderness—are served with a spicy-sweet relish made from peaches, red onion, honey, and lemon juice. The relish is far better tasting and healthier than store-bought barbecue sauces.

GRILLED PORK CHOPS WITH PEACH AND RED-ONION RELISH

SERVES 4 ■ PREP TIME: 10 MINUTES ■ **TOTAL TIME: 25 MINUTES**

Vegetable oil, for grill

4 bone-in pork chops (10 to 12 ounces each)

Coarse salt and ground pepper

Peach and Red-Onion Relish, for serving (recipe follows)

Heat grill to medium-high; clean and lightly oil hot grates. Season pork chops with salt and pepper. Grill, turning once, until cooked through, 10 to 12 minutes. Serve with peach relish.

per serving: 322 calories; 11.5 g fat (4.2 g saturated fat); 42.9 g protein; 9.8 g carbohydrates; 0.9 g fiber

PEACH AND RED-ONION RELISH

¼ small red onion, very thinly sliced

2 ripe peaches, quartered and very thinly sliced

1 tablespoon honey

1 tablespoon fresh lemon juice

⅛ teaspoon cayenne

Coarse salt and ground pepper

In a small bowl of ice water, soak onion 10 minutes; drain, blot dry, and return to bowl. Add peaches, honey, lemon juice, and cayenne; season with salt and pepper. Let stand 15 minutes before serving. (Relish can be refrigerated, covered, up to 1 day. Bring to room temperature before serving.) **SERVES 4**

322
CALORIES PER SERVING

358
CALORIES PER SERVING

WHY IT'S LIGHT For a shore dinner you can make anywhere, wrap shrimp, cod, pototoes, and corn in "hobo packs" and cook them on the grill. The food steams inside, with only a half tablespoon butter per serving.

GRILLED NEW ENGLAND SEAFOOD "BAKE"

SERVES 4 ▪ PREP TIME: 25 MINUTES ▪ TOTAL TIME: 25 MINUTES

2 tablespoons unsalted butter, room temperature

2 tablespoons finely chopped fresh dill, plus more for garnish

1 small garlic clove, minced

Coarse salt and ground pepper

8 ounces new potatoes, scrubbed and thinly sliced

1 pound skinless cod fillets or other firm white-fleshed fish, such as halibut or snapper, cut into 4 equal pieces

8 ounces medium shrimp, peeled and deveined

2 ears corn, quartered

1 lemon, thinly sliced

2 hard rolls, halved

1 Heat grill to medium. In a bowl, combine butter, dill, and garlic; season with salt and pepper.

2 Fold four 14-inch squares of heavy-duty foil in half, forming four rectangles. Dividing ingredients evenly, arrange potatoes in a single layer on one half of folded foil; top with cod, then shrimp. Place 2 pieces of corn on the side. Season with salt and pepper. Add a dollop of the butter mixture and 2 lemon slices. Fold foil over ingredients, and crimp edges tightly to seal.

3 Place packets on grill, with potato layer on the bottom. Cook, rotating (but not flipping) packets occasionally, until fish and shrimp are just cooked through and potatoes are tender, 12 to 14 minutes.

4 Remove from grill. Slit packets open, and transfer contents to bowls. Garnish with dill sprigs; serve with rolls.

per serving: 358 calories; 9.1 g fat (4.2 g saturated fat); 34.7 g protein; 34.5 g carbohydrates; 2.7 g fiber

GOOD TO KNOW Often served raw in salads, peppery arugula can also be heated briefly until wilted, just like spinach. It pairs nicely not only with shrimp, as in this quick sauté, but also with chicken, steak, and sharp cheeses, such as Parmesan and Pecorino Romano.

SAUTÉED SHRIMP WITH ARUGULA AND TOMATOES

SERVES 4 ■ PREP TIME: 15 MINUTES ■ **TOTAL TIME: 15 MINUTES**

1 tablespoon plus 1 teaspoon olive oil

1 cup cherry or grape tomatoes

1 garlic clove, minced

1 pound large shrimp, peeled and deveined

4 ounces wild or baby arugula (4 cups)

Coarse salt and ground pepper

1 tablespoon fresh lemon juice

1 In a large skillet, heat oil over medium-high. Add tomatoes and cook, stirring often, until blistered, about 2 minutes. Add garlic and cook until fragrant, about 30 seconds. Add shrimp and cook, stirring often, until almost opaque throughout, about 4 minutes.

2 Add arugula, season with salt and pepper, and toss until wilted, about 1 minute. Add lemon juice and toss to combine.

per serving: 144 calories; 5.9 g fat (0.9 g saturated fat); 19.1 g protein; 3.3 g carbohydrates; 0.9 g fiber

ABOUT ARUGULA

Cultivated arugula is widely available year-round, but it's at its very best in spring and early summer. Mature arugula is sold in bunches, while baby and wild arugula come loose or prepackaged. Look for perky green leaves without blemishes or spots. Arugula can be sandy, so submerge it in a bowl of cold water, then drain and spin dry. Wrap leaves in paper towels, and refrigerate in a plastic bag, up to 3 days. Refresh limp arugula by plunging it into ice water.

144
CALORIES PER SERVING

WHY IT'S LIGHT This dish only sounds indulgent. It stays trim by combining a modest piece of bacon-wrapped fish with a generous salad. Thick fillets of any firm, flaky, and mild fish, such as halibut, haddock, or striped bass, would work well here.

BACON-WRAPPED COD WITH FRISÉE

SERVES 4 ■ PREP TIME: 25 MINUTES ■ TOTAL TIME: 25 MINUTES

1 pink grapefruit

1 skinless cod fillet (1¼ pounds and 1½ inches thick)

Coarse salt and ground pepper

12 slices bacon (12 ounces)

1½ teaspoons Dijon mustard

1½ teaspoons honey

1 tablespoon sherry vinegar

¼ cup olive oil

1 large head frisée, cut into 1-inch pieces

1 Cut off both ends of grapefruit. Working from top to bottom, cut away peel and white pith with a paring knife. Holding grapefruit over a bowl, cut along both sides of each membrane to release segments. Squeeze membrane over bowl to extract juice. Reserve ¼ cup juice.

2 Cut fish into 4 equal pieces and season with salt and pepper. On a work surface, arrange 3 slices bacon so they overlap slightly. Place a piece of fish at one short end and wrap tightly with bacon, trimming off any excess bacon. Repeat with remaining fish and bacon.

3 Whisk together mustard, honey, vinegar, and grapefruit juice; season with salt and pepper. Gradually whisk in oil.

4 Heat a large nonstick skillet over medium-high. Cook fish, seam side down, turning occasionally, until bacon is deep golden brown on all sides, and fish is opaque throughout, about 9 minutes. Toss frisée with dressing and grapefruit segments and serve with fish.

per serving: 286 calories; 22.3 g fat (4.7 g saturated fat); 10.4 g protein; 11.8 g carbohydrates; 4.7 g fiber

GOOD TO KNOW A favorite sandwich, redux: Instead of battering and deep-frying, fish fillets are cooked on the grill, with a mere brush of oil. Top with a tangy slaw and serve on toasted bread, and you won't miss the original in the least.

GRILLED FISH SANDWICH WITH CABBAGE SLAW

SERVES 4 ■ PREP TIME: 15 MINUTES ■ **TOTAL TIME: 30 MINUTES**

4 cups shredded green cabbage (from ¼ head)

Coarse salt and ground pepper

1 celery stalk, thinly sliced

½ small red onion, thinly sliced

3 tablespoons mayonnaise

1 tablespoon red-wine vinegar

¼ teaspoon caraway seed

Vegetable oil, for grilling

4 striped bass fillets or other firm-fleshed fish, such as tilapia or flounder (4 to 6 ounces each)

8 thick slices sandwich bread, such as brioche or country-style white

1 Heat grill to medium-high. In a medium bowl, toss cabbage with 2 teaspoons salt; let stand 20 minutes, then press between layers of paper towels to remove excess liquid.

2 In a clean bowl, toss cabbage with celery, onion, mayonnaise, vinegar, and caraway seed, and season with pepper.

3 Clean and lightly oil hot grates. Pat fish dry with paper towels; season with salt and pepper, and brush with oil. Grill fish until opaque around the edges and underside releases easily from grill, 2 to 4 minutes. Using a thin metal spatula, flip fish and cook until opaque throughout, 1 to 5 minutes. Transfer to a plate.

4 Grill bread until lightly toasted, 5 to 10 seconds per side. Assemble sandwiches with fish and cabbage slaw.

per serving: 420 calories; 10.7 g fat (2 g saturated fat); 41.8 g protein; 40.7 g carbohydrates; 8.5 g fiber

420
CALORIES PER SERVING

208

CALORIES PER SERVING

GOOD TO KNOW A cherry pitter makes quick work of removing the pits, but you can also use frozen pitted cherries in place of fresh; just be sure to thaw them according to package instructions and drain thoroughly before using.

GRILLED TILAPIA WITH CHERRY SALSA

SERVES 4 ■ PREP TIME: 15 MINUTES ■ **TOTAL TIME: 20 MINUTES**

- 8 ounces Bing cherries (2 cups), pitted and coarsely chopped
- ½ small red onion, finely chopped
- ¼ cup fresh cilantro leaves, chopped
- 1 jalapeño chile, minced (ribs and seeds removed for less heat, if desired)
- 1 tablespoon fresh lime juice
  Coarse salt and ground pepper
- ½ teaspoon ground coriander
- 1 tablespoon olive oil, plus more for grill
- 4 tilapia fillets (4 to 6 ounces each)

1 Heat grill (or grill pan) to high. In a medium bowl, combine cherries, onion, cilantro, jalapeño, and lime juice. Season with salt and pepper and toss to combine; set salsa aside.

2 In a small bowl, stir together coriander, 1 teaspoon salt, and ¼ teaspoon pepper. Pat fish dry with paper towels. Rub fillets all over with oil; season with spice mixture.

3 Clean and lightly oil hot grates. Grill tilapia until opaque around the edges and underside loosens easily from grill, 2 to 3 minutes. Using a thin metal spatula, flip fish; continue to cook until opaque throughout, 2 to 3 minutes. Serve tilapia topped with cherry salsa.

per serving: 208 calories; 6 g fat (1.3 g saturated fat); 29.3 g protein; 10.6 g carbohydrates; 1.6 g fiber

ROASTED PEPPERS WITH GARLIC AND HERBS

- 4 red or yellow bell peppers (or a mix), halved and seeded
- 2 tablespoons olive oil
- 2 garlic cloves, thinly sliced
- ¼ teaspoon dried oregano
- Coarse salt and ground pepper
- Fresh basil leaves, torn, for garnish

Preheat oven to 450°F. Place bell peppers, cut side up, on a rimmed baking sheet. Drizzle with oil. Divide garlic among peppers. Sprinkle with oregano and season with salt and pepper. Roast until flesh is tender and skin is blistered in spots, about 35 minutes. Transfer peppers to a platter, garnish with basil, and serve. **SERVES 4**

per serving: **97 calories;** 7.4 g fat (1.1 g saturated fat); 1.3 g protein; 7.7 g carbohydrates; 2.5 g fiber

MARINATED ZUCCHINI WITH MINT

- 3 zucchini, thinly sliced lengthwise
- ¼ cup olive oil
- Coarse salt and ground pepper
- 1 garlic clove, minced
- 1 tablespoon white-wine vinegar
- 2 tablespoons fresh mint leaves, torn

1 Preheat oven to 475°F. On two large rimmed baking sheets, toss zucchini with 2 tablespoons oil; season with salt and pepper. Roast in a single layer until tender and undersides are browned, 10 to 15 minutes.

2 Transfer zucchini to a serving plate. Sprinkle with garlic, and drizzle with remaining 2 table-spoons oil and the vinegar. Let stand 1 hour (or refrigerate, covered, up to overnight). Serve at room temperature, topped with mint. **SERVES 4**

per serving: **151 calories;** 14.3 g fat (2 g saturated fat); 1.9 g protein; 5.3 g carbohydrates; 1.7 g fiber

STEAMED EGGPLANT WITH PEANUTS

- 2 tablespoons cider vinegar
- 2 tablespoons soy sauce
- 2 teaspoons light-brown sugar
- 1 teaspoon finely grated peeled fresh ginger
- 1 garlic clove, smashed and peeled
- 1 teaspoon toasted sesame oil
- 2 small eggplants, quartered lengthwise and cut into 4-inch lengths
- ¼ cup finely chopped unsalted roasted peanuts
- 2 scallions, trimmed and thinly sliced

1 In a small saucepan, combine vinegar, soy sauce, brown sugar, ginger, garlic, and oil. Bring to a boil and cook until reduced by half, about 3 minutes.

2 Set a steamer basket in a pan filled with 1 inch simmering water. Add eggplant, cover, and steam until tender, 5 to 7 minutes. Serve warm, topped with dressing, peanuts, and scallions. **SERVES 4**

per serving: **104 calories;** 6 g fat (0.8 g saturated fat); 3.9 g protein; 11 g carbohydrates; 3.8 g fiber

GRILLED CARROTS WITH GINGER

- 1 tablespoon vegetable oil, plus more for wok
- 2 pounds carrots, cut into 1½-inch pieces
- Coarse salt and ground pepper
- 4 garlic cloves, thinly sliced
- 1 piece (1 inch) fresh ginger, peeled and sliced
- 2 tablespoons soy sauce

1 Coat a grill wok with oil; preheat on grill over high heat. Toss carrots with 2 teaspoons oil; season with salt and pepper. Add to wok, cover grill, and cook until tender, shaking wok frequently, 20 minutes. If carrots brown too quickly, move wok to cooler part of grill.

2 Toss garlic and ginger with remaining 1 tea-spoon oil. Add to hot wok; cook until garlic is golden, 3 minutes. Toss with soy sauce. Transfer to serving dish. **SERVES 4**

per serving: **129 calories;** 3.9 g fat (0.3 g saturated fat); 2.8 g protein; 22.7 g carbohydrates; 6.5 g fiber

MIXED TOMATO SALAD WITH OLIVES AND LEMON ZEST

2 pounds mixed tomatoes, such as red or yellow beefsteak, plum, and heirloom varieties, sliced

¼ cup mixed olives

1 lemon

2 tablespoons olive oil

Coarse salt and ground pepper

Arrange tomatoes and olives on a serving plate. Grate lemon zest over salad. Drizzle with oil, season with salt and pepper, and serve. **SERVES 6**

per serving: **101 calories;** 7.7 g fat (1 g saturated fat); 1.4 g protein; 8 g carbohydrates; 1.8 g fiber

WHITE BEAN SALAD WITH ZUCCHINI AND PARMESAN

2 cans (15.5 ounces each) cannellini beans, rinsed and drained

¾ pound zucchini (about 2 small), trimmed, quartered lengthwise, and thinly sliced on the diagonal

4 ounces green beans, trimmed and thinly sliced on the diagonal (¾ cup)

2 ounces Parmesan cheese, crumbled (½ cup)

½ cup fresh basil leaves, torn

Grated zest and juice of 2 lemons

1 tablespoon olive oil

Coarse salt and ground pepper

In a medium bowl, combine cannellini beans, zucchini, green beans, Parmesan, basil, lemon zest and juice, and oil. Season with salt and pepper, and serve. **SERVES 4**

per serving: **205 calories;** 7.7 g fat (3 g saturated fat); 11.2 g protein; 24 g carbohydrates; 6.7 g fiber

SESAME GREEN BEANS

1 pound green beans, trimmed

2 teaspoons rice vinegar (unseasoned)

½ teaspoon toasted sesame oil

Coarse salt and ground pepper

1 teaspoon sesame seeds

1 Set a steamer basket in a large pot filled with 1 inch simmering water. Add green beans to basket; cover and cook until crisp-tender, about 5 minutes.

2 Meanwhile, in a medium bowl, whisk together vinegar and oil; season with salt and pepper. Add green beans and sesame seeds, and season with salt and pepper. Toss. **SERVES 4**

per serving: **46 calories;** 1.1 g fat (0.1 g saturated fat); 2.2 g protein; 8.5 g carbohydrates; 3.9 g fiber

15-MINUTE ROSEMARY-GARLIC POTATOES

1 tablespoon olive oil

2 garlic cloves, sliced

2 sprigs rosemary (or ¼ teaspoon dried)

1½ pounds new potatoes, scrubbed and thinly sliced

Coarse salt and ground pepper

Combine oil, garlic, and rosemary in a 2-quart microwave-safe baking dish with a lid. Cover and microwave on high until garlic is fragrant, 1 minute. Stir in potatoes. Cover and microwave on high until potatoes are tender, 13 to 15 minutes. Season with salt and pepper. **SERVES 4**

per serving: **151 calories;** 3.6 g fat (0.5 g saturated fat); 3.3 g protein; 27.6 g carbohydrates; 3 g fiber

WHY THEY'RE LIGHT Waxy new potatoes, tossed in a flavorful mustard vinaigrette, easily outdo heavy, mayonnaise-based potato salads, while low-fat yogurt and dill dress up sliced cucumbers. Pack either low-calorie side for a picnic.

POTATOES VINAIGRETTE

1½ pounds new potatoes, scrubbed
     Coarse salt and ground pepper
¼ cup white-wine vinegar
1 tablespoon Dijon mustard
1 tablespoon whole-grain mustard
3 tablespoons olive oil
1 celery stalk, thinly sliced crosswise, plus ½ cup celery leaves

1 Place potatoes in a medium saucepan and cover with cold water. Bring to a boil, and add salt. Reduce to a simmer, and cook until just tender, 12 to 14 minutes. Drain; set aside to cool slightly.

2 Meanwhile, in a medium bowl, combine vinegar and both mustards; season with salt and pepper.

3 When potatoes are cool enough to handle, quarter and toss with mustard-vinegar mixture. Cover and refrigerate until chilled, about 2 hours or up to overnight. Add oil and celery stalk leaves to potatoes; toss and serve. **SERVES 4**

per serving: **220 calories;** 10.7 g fat (1.5 g saturated fat); 3.2 g protein; 29.2 g carbohydrates; 4.3 g fiber

DILLED CUCUMBER SALAD

2 English cucumbers
2 teaspoons coarse salt
⅓ cup plain low-fat yogurt
¼ cup loosely packed fresh dill, finely chopped, plus dill sprigs for garnish (optional)
1 teaspoon red-wine vinegar
¼ teaspoon ground pepper

1 Halve cucumbers lengthwise. With a spoon, scoop out and discard any seeds. Cut crosswise into ⅛-inch-thick slices. Place in a colander set over a bowl, and toss with 2 teaspoons salt; let stand 15 minutes.

2 Meanwhile, in a medium bowl, combine yogurt, chopped dill, vinegar, and ¼ teaspoon pepper.

3 Remove cucumbers from colander, and pat dry with paper towels. Add to bowl with yogurt dressing; toss to combine. Garnish with dill sprigs, if desired, and serve. **SERVES 4**

per serving: **30 calories;** 0.6 g fat (0.3 g saturated fat); 1.9 g protein; 4.6 g carbohydrates; 1 g fiber

SECRET INGREDIENTS This cheesecake has a velvety texture but less fat than more familiar versions, thanks to reduced-fat versions of cream cheese and sour cream—plus the unexpected addition of low-fat cottage cheese. With its delectable cherry topping, this dessert will please everyone, even those not counting calories.

LIGHT CHERRY CHEESECAKE

SERVES 10 ■ PREP TIME: 30 MINUTES ■ **TOTAL TIME: 1 HOUR 45 MINUTES (PLUS CHILLING)**

Nonstick cooking spray

8 graham crackers (3-by-5-inch size)

1 tablespoon vegetable oil, such as safflower

3 cups low-fat (1%) cottage cheese

8 ounces reduced-fat bar cream cheese, room temperature

¾ cup plus 2 tablespoons sugar

½ cup reduced-fat sour cream

4 large eggs

2 tablespoons all-purpose flour

1 teaspoon pure vanilla extract

½ teaspoon coarse salt

2 bags (12 ounces each) frozen cherries

1 Preheat oven to 325°F, with rack in lower third. Assemble a 9-inch springform pan with the rimmed side of the pan's bottom facing down. Coat pan with cooking spray; line side with a long strip of waxed or parchment paper.

2 In a food processor, grind graham crackers until fine crumbs form. Add oil and pulse to moisten. Transfer crumbs to prepared pan, and press firmly into the bottom. Place pan on a rimmed baking sheet; bake until crust is lightly browned, about 15 minutes.

3 Meanwhile, clean bowl and blade of food processor. Blend cottage cheese and cream cheese until very smooth and glossy, scraping down bowl as necessary, 4 to 5 minutes. Add ¾ cup sugar, the sour cream, eggs, flour, vanilla, and salt; blend just until filling is smooth.

4 Pour filling into crust (crust can be hot or warm). Bake until barely set in center, about 1 hour. Turn oven off; let cake cool in oven 1 hour. Transfer cake in pan to a wire rack, and let cool completely, about 2 hours. Cover and refrigerate until firm, at least 3 hours or up to 2 days.

5. While cake is baking, in a large skillet, combine cherries and remaining 2 tablespoons sugar. Boil until liquid is thick and syrupy, 10 to 15 minutes. Let cool, then transfer to a bowl, cover, and refrigerate at least 2 hours or up to 2 days.

6. To serve, unmold cheesecake (peel off and discard paper lining). Transfer to a serving platter; top with cherry topping.

per serving: 263 calories; 9.7 g fat (4.7 g saturated fat); 14.9 g protein; 30.9 g carbohydrates; 1.6 g fiber

333

CALORIES PER SERVING

BLUEBERRY POPS

5 cups fresh blueberries

½ cup water, plus more if needed

½ cup sugar

1 tablespoon fresh lemon juice

1 In a blender, purée blueberries with the water, sugar, and lemon juice. Strain mixture through a fine sieve into a bowl, pressing to release as much liquid as possible; discard solids. Add water if needed to yield 3 cups.

2 Divide among ten 2½-ounce ice pop molds. Insert wooden sticks and freeze until solid, about 4 hours (or up to 1 week). To remove, dip bottom of molds in warm water 2 to 3 seconds. **MAKES 10**

per serving: **58 calories;** 0.2 g fat; 0.4 g protein; 14.9 g carbohydrates; 1.6 g fiber

STRAWBERRY AND NECTARINE POPS

2 cups fresh strawberries, rinsed and hulled

4 nectarines, halved, pitted, and cut into chunks

½ cup sugar

1 In a blender, purée strawberries, nectarines, and sugar until smooth. Strain mixture through a fine sieve into a bowl, pressing to release as much liquid as possible; discard solids.

2 Divide mixture among eight 3-ounce molds. Insert wooden sticks, and freeze until solid, about 4 hours (or up to 1 week). To remove, dip bottom of molds in warm water 2 to 3 seconds. **MAKES 8**

per serving: **86 calories;** 0.3 g fat (0 g saturated fat); 0.9 g protein; 21.5 g carbohydrates; 1.7 g fiber

RASPBERRY-YOGURT POPS

2 cups plain low-fat yogurt

½ cup sugar

½ cup frozen raspberries (about 3 ounces)

1 In a medium bowl, whisk yogurt and sugar to combine. Transfer 1 cup to a blender and add raspberries; purée until well blended. Strain mixture through a fine sieve into another bowl, pressing to release as much liquid as possible; discard solids.

2 Dividing evenly, layer plain and raspberry yogurt mixtures in six 3-ounce ice-pop molds. Insert wooden sticks and freeze until solid, about 4 hours (or up to 1 week). To remove, dip bottom of molds in warm water 2 to 3 seconds. **MAKES 6**

per serving: **122 calories;** 1.4 g fat (0.8 g saturated fat); 4.4 g protein; 23.8 g carbohydrates; 0.5 g fiber

PINEAPPLE POPS

3 cups fresh pineapple chunks (or two 14.5-ounce cans chunk pineapple in juice, drained)

⅓ cup milk

¼ cup sugar

1 In a food processor, combine pineapple with milk and sugar; pulse until almost smooth, with some chunks of pineapple remaining.

2 Pour half the mixture into a medium bowl (or a glass measuring cup for easy pouring). Pulse remaining mixture until completely smooth; add to mixture in bowl.

3 Divide among eight 3-ounce ice pop molds or paper cups. Insert wooden sticks, and freeze until solid, about 4 hours (or up to 1 week). To remove, dip bottom of molds in warm water 2 to 3 seconds. **MAKES 8**

per serving: **58 calories;** 0.4 g fat (0.2 g saturated fat); 0.6 g protein; 14.1 g carbohydrates; 0.8 g fiber

It will come as no surprise that gelatin desserts are a calorie-counter's dream. What you may not know is that there are elegant ways of preparing—and presenting—the nostalgic desserts. Form the gelatins in pretty single-serve glasses or in a loaf pan for unmolding and slicing.

GRAPE GELATIN WITH BLUEBERRIES

1 envelope (¼ ounce) unflavored powdered gelatin

½ cup cold water

1 cup 100% white grape juice

2 cups fresh blueberries

1 In a large bowl, sprinkle gelatin over ¼ cup cold water; let soften, 5 minutes.

2 In a small saucepan, bring remaining ¼ cup water to a boil over medium-high heat. Pour over gelatin mixture; stir in grape juice.

3 Divide blueberries evenly among four 6-ounce serving glasses; pour in gelatin mixture, pressing blueberries to submerge them completely.

4 Refrigerate until set, at least 1 hour (or up to 5 days, covered with plastic wrap). **SERVES 4**

per serving: **84 calories;** 0.3 g fat (0.1 g saturated fat); 2.3 g protein; 19.3 g carbohydrates; 1.8 g fiber

MIXED BERRY TERRINE

2 envelopes (¼ ounce each) unflavored powdered gelatin

2 cups 100% white grape juice

½ cup sugar

5½ to 6 cups mixed fresh berries (about 2 pounds), such as strawberries (rinsed, hulled, and halved), raspberries, blackberries, and blueberries

1 In a small bowl, sprinkle gelatin over ¼ cup grape juice; let soften, 5 minutes.

2 Meanwhile, heat sugar with ¼ cup grape juice in a small saucepan over medium-high, stirring, until dissolved. Remove from heat; stir in softened gelatin until dissolved, then stir in remaining 1½ cups grape juice.

3 Place berries in a 4-by-8-inch (6-cup) loaf pan; pour gelatin mixture over, pressing berries gently to submerge completely (remove a few berries if necessary). Refrigerate until firm, at least 3 hours (or up to 2 days, covered with plastic wrap).

4 To unmold, dip bottom of pan in hot water about 5 seconds. Invert onto a serving platter, and shake firmly to release. Slice to serve. **SERVES 8**

per serving: **147 calories;** 0.5 g fat (0.1 g saturated fat); 2.6 g protein; 35.1 g carbohydrates; 4.9 g fiber

194
CALORIES PER SERVING

WHY IT'S LIGHT One crust makes this tart less fattening than a more traditional (read: double-crust) summer pie. It has a higher proportion of peak-season fruit, another bonus for the calorie conscious. Nectarines are featured, but plums, peaches, apricots, or any mixture of stone fruits would work beautifully here.

RUSTIC NECTARINE TART

SERVES 8 ■ PREP TIME: 30 MINUTES ■ TOTAL TIME: 1 HOUR 20 MINUTES (WITH COOLING)

1 sheet frozen puff pastry (from a 17.3-ounce package), thawed according to package instructions

1 tablespoon all-purpose flour, plus more for dusting

⅓ cup plus 2 teaspoons sugar

5 large ripe nectarines (about 1¾ pounds), halved, pitted, and sliced ¼ inch thick

Pinch of coarse salt

2 tablespoons seedless red-currant jelly, warmed until liquefied

1 Preheat oven to 425°F. Place folded pastry on a lightly floured work surface; roll out to a 12-by-14-inch rectangle. Trim edges to make even.

2 Place pastry on a parchment-lined baking sheet. With a sharp paring knife, lightly score dough to form a 1-inch border. Using a fork, prick dough inside the border every ½ inch. Sprinkle the border with 2 teaspoons sugar. Refrigerate until slightly firm, about 10 minutes (or up to 1 day, covered with plastic wrap).

3 Bake chilled dough until puffed and golden brown, 10 to 15 minutes. Meanwhile, in a large bowl, gently toss sliced nectarines with flour, remaining ⅓ cup sugar, and the salt.

4 With a fork, press dough inside border to make level; arrange nectarines in rows on top (or pile nectarines on top and then spread evenly). Bake, tented with foil, until nectarines have softened, about 10 minutes. Remove from oven and brush nectarines with warm jelly. Let cool completely, about 20 minutes, before cutting and serving.

per serving: 194 calories; 8.6 g fat (2.2 g saturated fat); 3.2 g protein; 29.6 g carbohydrates; 1.7 g fiber

4

FALL

Now is the time to savor the warmth of slow-cooked meats, richly flavored stews, and oven-roasted vegetables. In fact, roasting may just become your go-to technique, rewarding you with tender meats and vegetables with sweet, caramelized edges—and minimal added fat. Autumn squashes, broccoli, brussels sprouts, and root vegetables such as sweet potatoes and carrots all take well to roasting, as do chicken, pork, and even fish (for a one-dish meal, roast meat and vegetables in the same pan).

For a comforting, no-fuss dinner, try a simmering pot of soup, including a brothy one with turkey meatballs or a velvety vegetable purée. Apples and pears are easily incorporated into sweet, homespun—yet surprisingly lean—desserts.

267
CALORIES PER SERVING

FLAVOR BOOSTER Boiling the dressing—made with soy sauce, lemon juice, and toasted sesame oil—gives it depth and balance. Because the chicken and vegetables are all either shredded or thinly sliced, they mingle with the cooled dressing and readily soak up its flavors.

CHICKEN, MUSHROOM, AND CABBAGE SALAD

SERVES 4 ■ PREP TIME: 20 MINUTES ■ **TOTAL TIME: 40 MINUTES**

1 boneless, skinless chicken breast (6 to 8 ounces)

Coarse salt

3 tablespoons soy sauce

2 tablespoons fresh lemon juice

2 tablespoons vegetable oil, such as safflower

1½ teaspoons sugar

½ teaspoon toasted sesame oil

½ pound white or cremini mushrooms, trimmed and thinly sliced

½ head napa cabbage (about 1 pound), cored and shredded

6 radishes, trimmed and thinly sliced

1 carrot, shaved into ribbons with a vegetable peeler

1 celery stalk, thinly sliced

¼ cup fresh mint leaves

1 scallion, trimmed and sliced into thin strips, for serving

1 Place chicken in a medium saucepan and cover with water. Bring to a boil, season with salt, and reduce to a bare simmer. Cover and cook 5 minutes. Remove pan from heat and let chicken stand, covered, until cooked through, 12 to 14 minutes more. Remove chicken from liquid. When cool enough to handle, shred into bite-size pieces.

2 In a small saucepan, combine soy sauce, lemon juice, vegetable oil, sugar, and sesame oil. Bring to a boil, then let cool to room temperature.

3 Transfer soy mixture to a medium bowl and stir in mushrooms. Let stand, stirring occasionally, until mushrooms soften, 3 to 5 minutes. Add chicken, cabbage, radishes, carrot, celery, and mint; toss to combine. Top salad with scallion and serve immediately.

per serving: 267 calories; 10.8 g fat (1.7 g saturated fat); 30.3 g protein; 10.9 g carbohydrates; 2.5 g fiber

GOOD TO KNOW For a more satisfying meal, try incorporating just a small amount of a flavorful high-fat ingredient such as bacon or nuts into the low-calorie mix. Here pancetta is crisped in the oven for hands-off, splatter-free cooking, a method that works well for bacon, too.

SALAD WITH PANCETTA CRISPS, ROASTED BRUSSELS SPROUTS, AND PEAR

SERVES 4 ■ PREP TIME: 15 MINUTES ■ TOTAL TIME: 45 MINUTES

½ pound brussels sprouts, trimmed and quartered lengthwise

¼ cup olive oil

Coarse salt and ground pepper

3 ounces thinly sliced pancetta

¼ cup white-wine vinegar

1 head Boston lettuce (about 1 pound), torn into bite-size pieces

1 firm, ripe red Bartlett pear, halved, cored, and thinly sliced

2 ounces ricotta salata cheese, thinly sliced

1 Preheat oven to 425°F, with racks in upper and lower thirds. On a rimmed baking sheet, toss brussels sprouts with 2 tablespoons oil; season with salt and pepper. Bake on upper rack until tender, 18 to 20 minutes, tossing once. On another rimmed baking sheet, arrange pancetta in a single layer. Bake on lower rack until golden brown, 10 to 12 minutes. Transfer to a paper-towel-lined plate to drain.

2 In a large bowl, whisk together vinegar and remaining 2 tablespoons oil; season with salt and pepper. Add lettuce, pear, and brussels sprouts; toss to combine. Divide among four plates and top with ricotta salata and pancetta. Serve immediately.

per serving: 301 calories; 23 g fat (6.2 g saturated fat); 11.5 g protein; 15 g carbohydrates; 4.5 g fiber

ABOUT PANCETTA
Think of pancetta as the more aromatic, Italian version of bacon. But unlike bacon, pancetta is usually rolled instead of flat, and crusted with spices like fennel seed and black pepper instead of being smoked. Thinly sliced pancetta turns crisp when baked or sautéed. It can also be chopped to give flavor to sauces and stews. Pancetta is available at many supermarkets, either at the deli counter or in packaged slices in the refrigerator case. Refrigerate, wrapped in plastic, up to 1 week, or freeze up to 2 months.

301
CALORIES PER SERVING

203
CALORIES PER SERVING

SMART SUBSTITUTION Unlike white rice, brown rice retains the nutritious bran and germ covering the grain; it has three times the amount of fiber and a host of essential nutrients. Adding brown rice and other whole grains to salads makes them more filling without significantly increasing fat and calories.

BROWN-RICE SALAD WITH SPINACH AND TOMATOES

SERVES 4 ■ PREP TIME: 10 MINUTES ■ **TOTAL TIME: 1 HOUR**

1½ cups water

¾ cup brown rice

Coarse salt and ground pepper

2 tablespoons olive oil

2 teaspoons red-wine vinegar

2 tablespoons chopped fresh dill

1 garlic clove, minced

¼ teaspoon sugar

1 medium cucumber, peeled, halved lengthwise, seeded, and sliced crosswise ¼-inch thick

2 cups baby spinach

1 pint cherry tomatoes, halved

1 Bring the water to a boil in a medium saucepan. Stir in brown rice and 1 teaspoon coarse salt. Cover and simmer over low heat until rice is tender and has absorbed all liquid, about 40 minutes. Remove from heat; let stand 10 minutes, then fluff with a fork.

2 In a large bowl, whisk together oil, vinegar, dill, garlic, and sugar. Season generously with salt and pepper. Add rice, cucumber, spinach, and tomatoes, and toss to combine. Serve immediately.

per serving: 203 calories; 8.1 g fat (1.2 g saturated fat); 4 g protein; 29.9 g carbohydrates; 3.6 g fiber

BUYING AND STORING RICE
Look for brown rice in packages or in the bulk section of the supermarket, alongside white rice. It is more perishable than white rice but will keep for up to 6 months if stored in an airtight container. For longer storage, freeze in a resealable plastic bag for up to 1 year.

This lighter interpretation of a traditional Waldorf salad replaces the sweet mayonnaise dressing with one made from reduced-fat sour cream, white-wine vinegar, and just a hint of sugar.

CELERY AND APPLE SALAD WITH PECANS

SERVES 4 ■ PREP TIME: 15 MINUTES ■ **TOTAL TIME: 15 MINUTES**

¼ cup pecans

2 tablespoons reduced-fat sour cream

1 to 2 tablespoons white-wine vinegar

1 teaspoon sugar

1 pound celery (8 to 10 large stalks), peeled if desired, thinly sliced on the diagonal (about 5 cups)

1 apple, halved, cored, thinly sliced, then slices halved crosswise

Coarse salt and ground pepper

1 Preheat oven to 350°F. Spread pecans on a rimmed baking sheet; bake until lightly browned, tossing halfway through, 5 to 7 minutes. Transfer to a plate to cool.

2 In a medium bowl, whisk together sour cream, vinegar to taste, and sugar until smooth. Add celery and apple; season with salt and pepper. Toss gently to combine. Crumble toasted pecans on top, and serve immediately.

per serving: 98 calories; 6 g fat; 1.8 g protein; 11 g carbohydrates; 3.2 g fiber

98
CALORIES PER SERVING

310
CALORIES PER SERVING

When reducing the amount of fat added to a quick-cooking dish, a few last-minute additions—such as the fresh lemon juice and parsley in this soup—can have a big impact on the overall taste. A topping of shaved Parmesan also improves the end result.

QUICKEST MUSHROOM-BARLEY SOUP

SERVES 4 ■ PREP TIME: 20 MINUTES ■ TOTAL TIME: 30 MINUTES

1 tablespoon olive oil

1¼ pounds white mushrooms, trimmed and sliced

1 medium red onion, finely chopped

2 garlic cloves, minced

½ teaspoon dried thyme

Coarse salt and ground pepper

4½ cups low-sodium store-bought chicken or vegetable broth

2 cups water

1 cup quick-cooking barley

¼ cup fresh flat-leaf parsley leaves, finely chopped

1 tablespoon fresh lemon juice

1 ounce Parmesan cheese, shaved with a vegetable peeler, for garnish

1 In a large saucepan, heat oil over medium-high. Add mushrooms, onion, garlic, and thyme; season with salt and pepper. Cook, stirring occasionally, until vegetables have softened, 6 to 8 minutes.

2 Add broth and the water to pan; bring to a boil over high heat. Reduce to a simmer; add barley and cook until tender, about 10 minutes. Remove soup from heat; stir in parsley and lemon juice. Serve immediately, garnished with Parmesan.

per serving: 310 calories; 6.8 g fat (2.4 g saturated fat); 15.1 g protein; 48.7 g carbohydrates; 8.6 g fiber

ABOUT BARLEY
Pearl barley and quick-cooking barley absorb water faster than regular hulled barley because their bran layers have been removed. The quick-cooking variety, however, has also been presteamed and takes only 10 minutes to cook—more than twice as fast as pearl barley.

WHY IT'S LIGHT French onion soup is usually capped with a molten crown of cheese, but each cup of this trimmer version is topped with a piece of cheese toast instead—a cup of cheese is enough for all eight servings. Well-caramelized onions are the true key to this soup's appeal; be sure to cook them until they turn a deep golden brown.

ONION SOUP WITH CHEESE TOASTS

SERVES 8 ■ PREP TIME: 1 HOUR ■ **TOTAL TIME: 1 HOUR 20 MINUTES**

2 tablespoons unsalted butter

2 tablespoons olive oil

4 pounds onions (about 8 medium), halved and thinly sliced

4 garlic cloves, thinly sliced

   Coarse salt and ground pepper

½ cup port or Marsala wine

2 cans (14.5 ounces each) low-sodium beef broth

2 cans (14.5 ounces each) low-sodium chicken broth

2 cups water, plus more if needed

   Cheese Toasts (recipe follows)

1 In a 5-quart Dutch oven or other heavy pot, heat butter and oil over medium. Add onions and garlic; season with salt and pepper. Cover and cook, stirring occasionally, until onions have softened, 12 to 15 minutes.

2 Uncover and continue to cook, stirring occasionally, until onions are dark golden brown, 25 to 30 minutes more. (If bottom of pot gets too dry, add about ¼ cup water and scrape up browned bits with a wooden spoon.)

3 Add port and cook until syrupy, 2 to 3 minutes. Stir in both broths and 2 cups water, season with salt and pepper, and bring to a simmer. Cook 20 minutes. To serve, divide among eight bowls and top each with a cheese toast.

per serving: 261 calories; 11.6 g fat (5.2 g saturated fat); 10.9 g protein; 26.1 g carbohydrates; 3.7 g fiber

CHEESE TOASTS

8 slices (½-inch-thick) baguette

1 cup coarsely grated Gruyère cheese (4 ounces)

Heat broiler, with rack 4 inches from heat. Place baguette slices on a baking sheet. Divide cheese evenly among the slices, and broil until cheese is golden, 2 to 4 minutes. **MAKES 8**

FREEZING SOUP
Let soup cool completely, then pour into airtight containers, leaving 1 inch of space at top. Freeze up to 3 months. Thaw in microwave or overnight in refrigerator and reheat over low.

261
CALORIES PER SERVING

339
CALORIES PER SERVING

GOOD TO KNOW Hominy, dried corn kernels from which the hull and germ have been removed, adds heft to all kinds of soups and stews, including this dish of Mexico and the American Southwest. Look for canned hominy at Latin food markets or many supermarkets.

CHICKEN POSOLE

SERVES 8 ■ PREP TIME: 20 MINUTES ■ **TOTAL TIME: 1 HOUR 50 MINUTES**

1 whole roaster chicken breast (about 3 pounds)

2 tablespoons olive oil

Coarse salt and ground pepper

2 medium onions, finely chopped

8 garlic cloves, minced

⅓ cup tomato paste

3 tablespoons chili powder

1 teaspoon dried oregano

4 cups water

4 cans (14.5 ounces each) low-sodium chicken broth

4 cans (15 ounces each) white hominy, rinsed and drained

Assorted toppings, such as diced avocado, thinly sliced radishes, and crumbled tortilla chips (optional)

1 Preheat oven to 400°F. Place chicken in a small roasting pan or a large cast-iron skillet. Rub with 1 tablespoon oil and season with salt and pepper. Roast chicken until skin is browned, juices run clear, and an instant-read thermometer inserted in thickest part (avoiding bone) registers 165°F, 50 to 60 minutes. Transfer chicken to a platter. When cool enough to handle, remove skin and shred meat into bite-sized pieces. Discard skin and bones. You should have about 6¾ cups chicken (reserve the rest for another use).

2 Heat remaining 1 tablespoon oil in a 5-quart saucepan over medium heat. Add onions; cook until translucent, 3 to 5 minutes. Add garlic, tomato paste, chili powder, and oregano; cook, stirring constantly, until evenly distributed.

3 Add the water, broth, and hominy. Bring to a boil; reduce heat to a simmer, and cook until fragrant, about 30 minutes.

4 Stir in chicken; season with salt and pepper. Cook until heated through. To serve, divide among eight bowls and serve with toppings, as desired.

per serving (without toppings): 339 calories; 7.4 g fat (2 g saturated fat); 40.9 g protein; 24.9 g carbohydrates; 5 g fiber

FREEZING STEW
Let posole cool completely, then pour into airtight containers, leaving 1 inch of space at top. Freeze up to 3 months. Thaw overnight in refrigerator, and reheat over low (do not microwave, the hominy may burst).

SMART SUBSTITUTION Half-and-half and chicken broth replace the standard heavy cream, lowering the calorie count of this vegetable bisque without diminishing its appeal. For a different flavor, use ground nutmeg or cloves in place of cinnamon, or add a little chili powder for a Southwestern version.

BUTTERNUT BISQUE

SERVES 12 ■ PREP TIME: 15 MINUTES ■ TOTAL TIME: 45 MINUTES

- 3 tablespoons unsalted butter
- 1 medium onion, chopped
- 2 garlic cloves, sliced
- ½ teaspoon dried thyme
- ¼ teaspoon ground cinnamon
- ⅛ to ¼ teaspoon cayenne pepper, plus more for garnish (optional)
  Coarse salt
- 1 large butternut squash (about 4 pounds), peeled, seeded, and cut into 1-inch cubes
- 1 can (14.5 ounces) low-sodium chicken broth
- 1 cup half-and-half
- 3 cups water
- 1 tablespoon fresh lemon juice
- ¾ cup sour cream, for serving

1 In a large saucepan, heat butter over medium. Add onion, garlic, thyme, cinnamon, and cayenne to taste. Season with salt, and cook, stirring occasionally, until onion is softened, 5 to 7 minutes.

2 Add squash, broth, half-and-half, and the water. Bring to a boil; reduce to a simmer, and cook until squash is tender, about 20 minutes.

3 Working in batches, purée in a blender until smooth (do not fill jar more than halfway each time). Stir in lemon juice; season with salt. To serve, divide bisque among bowls and top each with 1 tablespoon sour cream; garnish with additional cayenne, if desired.

per serving: 117 calories; 5.4 g fat (3.3 g saturated fat); 2.6 g protein; 17.1 g carbohydrates; 2.8 g fiber

FREEZING SOUP
Let soup cool completely, then pour into airtight containers, leaving 1 inch of space at top. Freeze up to 3 months. Thaw in microwave or overnight in refrigerator. Heat with a bit of water, stirring occasionally. Add sour cream just before serving.

117
CALORIES PER SERVING

272
CALORIES PER SERVING

WHY IT'S LIGHT A brothy base, lean, mild white fish, and only one tablespoon olive oil keep this dish healthier than heavier seafood stews and chowders. Drizzle just a little extra olive oil over each serving to make the most of the oil's fruity flavor.

SEAFOOD STEW

SERVES 4 ■ PREP TIME: 25 MINUTES ■ **TOTAL TIME: 25 MINUTES**

1 tablespoon olive oil, plus more for serving (optional)

1 garlic clove, finely chopped

1 fennel bulb, trimmed, halved, and thinly sliced, fronds reserved for garnish

1 large tomato, cut into large dice

Coarse salt and ground pepper

4 cups low-sodium store-bought chicken broth

12 ounces skinless striped bass or red snapper fillets, cut into 1-inch pieces

½ pound medium shrimp, peeled and deveined

½ pound sea scallops, large muscle removed

1 In a medium Dutch oven or other heavy pot, combine oil and garlic; cook over medium-high heat, stirring, until garlic is fragrant, about 1 minute. Add fennel and cook, stirring frequently, until slightly softened, about 3 minutes. Add tomato, season with salt and pepper, and cook, stirring frequently, until tomato begins to break down, about 3 minutes.

2 Stir in broth and bring stew to a gentle boil, then reduce to a simmer. Gently fold in seafood. Return to a bare simmer and cook until seafood is opaque throughout, about 3 minutes. To serve, divide stew among bowls and drizzle each with additional oil; garnish with fennel fronds.

per serving: 272 calories; 7.6 g fat (1.5 g saturated fat); 40.4 g protein; 9.7 g carbohydrates; 2.3 g fiber

WHY IT'S LIGHT Naturally lean beans and extra vegetables make this a smarter choice than meat-heavy chili. For a creamy garnish, try a dollop of plain low-fat Greek yogurt rather than sour cream.

VEGETARIAN CHILI

SERVES 6 ■ PREP TIME: 15 MINUTES ■ **TOTAL TIME: 35 MINUTES**

2 tablespoons extra-virgin olive oil

1 medium yellow onion, cut into ½-inch dice

4 garlic cloves, coarsely chopped

1½ teaspoons ground cumin

1 teaspoon chipotle chile powder

Coarse salt and ground pepper

1 medium zucchini, cut into ½-inch dice

¾ cup (6 ounces) tomato paste

1 can (15.5 ounces) black beans, rinsed and drained

1 can (15.5 ounces) pinto beans, rinsed and drained

2 cans (14.5 ounces each) diced tomatoes in juice

1 can (4.5 ounces) chopped green chiles

2 cups water

1 In a large Dutch oven or other heavy pot, heat oil over medium-high. Add onion and garlic; cook, stirring frequently, until onion is translucent and garlic is soft, about 4 minutes. Add cumin and chile powder, season with salt and pepper; cook, stirring, until spices are fragrant, 1 minute. Add zucchini and tomato paste; cook, stirring frequently, until tomato paste is darkened, about 3 minutes.

2 Stir in both beans, the diced tomatoes (with their juice), and green chiles. Add the water and bring mixture to a boil. Reduce to a simmer and cook until zucchini is tender and liquid reduces slightly, about 20 minutes. Season with salt and pepper and serve immediately.

per serving: 232 calories; 6.1 g fat (1 g saturated fat); 10.3 g protein; 35 g carbohydrates; 9.1 g fiber

232
CALORIES PER SERVING

140
CALORIES PER SERVING

FLAVOR BOOSTER The first step in this recipe is about building flavors, so don't try to rush it. Similarly, don't skimp on the handful of chopped parsley added at the end—more than just a garnish, the herb helps brighten and define the other ingredients.

BROCCOLI RABE AND WHITE-BEAN SOUP

SERVES 6 ■ PREP TIME: 30 MINUTES ■ **TOTAL TIME: 50 MINUTES**

2 tablespoons olive oil

2 medium onions, finely chopped

4 garlic cloves, minced

Coarse salt and ground pepper

8 ounces cremini mushrooms, trimmed and thinly sliced

1 bunch broccoli rabe (about 1 pound), trimmed and coarsely chopped

2 cans (14.5 ounces each) low-sodium chicken or vegetable broth

2 cups water

2 cans (15.5 ounces each) cannellini beans, rinsed and drained

¼ cup chopped fresh flat-leaf parsley

1 In a large Dutch oven or other heavy pot, heat oil over medium. Add onions and garlic; season with salt and pepper. Cook, stirring frequently, until onions have softened, 8 to 10 minutes. Add mushrooms; cook, stirring occasionally, until mushrooms begin to release their liquid, 2 to 4 minutes. Add broccoli rabe; cook, stirring, until wilted, 2 to 3 minutes.

2 Add broth and the water; season with salt and pepper. Bring to a boil, then reduce heat to medium-low. Cook, stirring occasionally, until broccoli rabe is tender, 10 to 15 minutes. Add beans and parsley; simmer until warmed through, about 5 minutes. Serve immediately.

per serving: 140 calories; 5.1 g fat (1 g saturated fat); 8.1 g protein; 14.5 g carbohydrates; 4.3 g fiber

WHY IT'S LIGHT The whole eggs in these individual frittatas are supplemented with egg whites for fewer calories and less cholesterol. They still taste rich, though, thanks to a small amount of nutty Gruyère cheese. Customize the recipe by adding fresh herbs, chopped cooked vegetables, or even a bit of cubed ham to the egg mixture before baking.

SPINACH FRITTATA WITH GREEN SALAD

SERVES 4 ■ PREP TIME: 20 MINUTES ■ **TOTAL TIME: 35 MINUTES**

4 large eggs plus 8 large egg whites

½ cup grated Gruyère cheese

3 tablespoons milk

Coarse salt and ground pepper

1 tablespoon plus 1 teaspoon olive oil

2 small shallots, minced

5 ounces baby spinach (about 6 cups)

Nonstick cooking spray

8 ounces mesclun (about 8 cups)

1 teaspoon sherry vinegar

1 Place four 8-ounce baking dishes on a rimmed baking sheet and transfer to oven; preheat oven to 450°F. While oven is heating, in a large bowl, whisk together whole eggs and egg whites, ¼ cup cheese, the milk, 1 teaspoon salt, and ¼ teaspoon pepper.

2 In a large skillet, heat 1 teaspoon oil over medium. Add shallots and cook, stirring occasionally, until softened, 2 to 3 minutes. Add spinach; cook, tossing, until wilted, 3 to 5 minutes. Season with salt and pepper, and stir spinach mixture into egg mixture.

3 Remove baking sheet from oven and coat each dish with cooking spray. Immediately pour egg mixture into dishes, dividing evenly, and top each with 1 tablespoon cheese. Bake until frittatas are puffed up and golden brown, about 15 minutes.

4 Toss mesclun with vinegar and remaining tablespoon oil; season with salt and pepper. Serve frittatas on plates, with salad alongside.

per serving: 226 calories; 12.4 g fat (3.7 g saturated fat); 18.3 g protein; 12.1 g carbohydrates; 4.1 g fiber

226
CALORIES PER SERVING

222

CALORIES PER SERVING

GOOD TO KNOW Cooking in parchment packets is a low-fat, no-mess technique for preparing eggs. Here, mushrooms and spinach—and a mere drizzle of olive oil—are baked along with the eggs for a delicious meal any time of day.

EGGS WITH MUSHROOMS AND SPINACH

SERVES 4 ■ PREP TIME: 15 MINUTES ■ **TOTAL TIME: 20 MINUTES**

1 tablespoon plus 1 teaspoon olive oil, plus more for brushing

1 package (10 ounces) frozen chopped spinach, thawed and squeezed of excess liquid

8 ounces cremini mushrooms, trimmed and coarsely chopped

8 large eggs

Coarse salt and ground pepper

1 Preheat oven to 400°F, with racks in upper and lower thirds. Cut four 24-inch-long pieces of parchment; fold each piece in half, then cut into a half-heart shape. Unfold and place two pieces on each of two rimmed baking sheets.

2 Brush half of each parchment heart with oil. Place spinach and mushrooms on oiled halves of parchment. Crack 2 eggs over each and drizzle each with 1 teaspoon oil. Season with salt and pepper. Fold each packet into a "classic" shape (see page 19).

3 Bake until packets are fully puffed (egg whites will be set), rotating sheets from top to bottom and front to back halfway through, 6 to 9 minutes. Serve immediately.

per serving: 222 calories; 15.2 g fat (3.8 g saturated fat); 16.8 g protein; 6.1 g carbohydrates; 2.5 g fiber

NOTE
This recipe works best with white parchment; the brown type absorbs more heat, leading to overcooked eggs.

WHY IT'S LIGHT This Italian restaurant standby turns virtuous with baked (instead of fried) eggplant and a healthier béchamel made from skim milk, which is then combined with some marinara sauce. Using less cheese also helps; here, the two cheeses are sprinkled only on top, rather than in each layer.

LIGHTER EGGPLANT PARMESAN

SERVES 4 ■ PREP TIME: 20 MINUTES ■ **TOTAL TIME: 45 MINUTES**

1 large Italian eggplant (2 pounds), sliced ½ inch thick crosswise

1 tablespoon olive oil

Coarse salt and ground pepper

1 cup skim milk

3 tablespoons all-purpose flour

2 garlic cloves, minced

1 cup homemade or store-bought marinara sauce

½ cup grated part-skim mozzarella cheese

⅓ cup grated Parmesan cheese

1 Preheat oven to 450°F, with racks in upper and lower thirds. Arrange eggplant in a single layer on two rimmed baking sheets. Brush eggplant on both sides with oil, and season with salt and pepper. Bake until golden brown and very tender, 20 to 25 minutes, turning slices and rotating sheets from top to bottom and front to back halfway through.

2 Meanwhile, in a medium saucepan, whisk together ¼ cup milk, the flour, and garlic. Gradually whisk in remaining ¾ cup milk and ½ cup marinara sauce. Bring to a boil; reduce to a simmer, and cook until sauce has thickened, 2 to 3 minutes.

3 Spread ¼ cup marinara sauce in the bottom of a shallow 2-quart baking dish. Alternate layers of baked eggplant with milk sauce. Dollop with remaining ¼ cup marinara sauce. Top evenly with mozzarella and Parmesan. Bake on upper rack until cheese is browned and sauce is bubbling, 10 to 15 minutes. Serve immediately.

per serving: 229 calories; 9.3 g fat (3.3 g saturated fat); 11.9 g protein; 26.7 g carbohydrates; 8.9 g fiber

229
CALORIES PER SERVING

351

CALORIES PER SERVING

WHY IT'S LIGHT With less oil, fewer nuts, and more basil, this better-for-you pesto cuts calories without sacrificing any of the fabulous flavor. Serve the sauce over whole-wheat pasta for more fiber. Extra pesto freezes nicely, so consider doubling the batch.

WHOLE-WHEAT SPAGHETTI WITH LIGHTER PESTO

SERVES 4 ■ PREP TIME: 10 MINUTES ■ **TOTAL TIME: 15 MINUTES**

Coarse salt and ground pepper

8 ounces whole-wheat spaghetti

Lighter Pesto (recipe follows)

Fresh basil leaves, cut into chiffonade, for garnish (optional)

1 In a large pot of boiling salted water, cook spaghetti until al dente according to package instructions. Reserve ½ cup pasta water; drain pasta and return to pot.

2 Toss pasta with pesto, adding reserved pasta water a little at a time to create a thin sauce that coats spaghetti (you may not need all the water). Season with salt and pepper. Serve immediately, garnished with basil, if desired.

per serving: 351 calories; 16 g fat (2.6 g saturated fat); 11 g protein; 44.9 g carbohydrates; 8.2 g fiber

LIGHTER PESTO

3 cups firmly packed fresh basil leaves (2 ounces)

3 tablespoons walnut pieces

3 tablespoons grated Parmesan cheese

2 garlic cloves (peeled)

1 tablespoon fresh lemon juice

3 tablespoons water

Coarse salt and ground pepper

3 tablespoons extra-virgin olive oil

In a food processor, combine basil, walnuts, Parmesan, garlic, lemon juice, and the water; season with salt and pepper. Purée until a paste forms. With motor running, add oil in a thin stream. Process until very smooth, about 1 minute. Pesto can be refrigerated in an airtight container, with plastic wrap pressed onto the surface to prevent discoloration, up to 3 days. (Or freeze in an airtight container up to 6 months; thaw in the refrigerator.) **MAKES ¾ CUP**

GOOD TO KNOW Hearty and satisfying, bean soups often simmer for hours; this vegetarian stew tastes as if it did, but uses canned beans and broth as shortcuts. To thicken the soup, mash some of the beans with the back of a spoon during cooking.

CUBAN BLACK-BEAN STEW WITH RICE

SERVES 4 ■ PREP TIME: 20 MINUTES ■ **TOTAL TIME: 30 MINUTES**

1½ cups long-grain white rice

1 tablespoon olive oil

1 medium red onion, finely chopped

1 garlic clove, minced

1 red bell pepper, ribs and seeds removed, finely chopped

2 cans (19 ounces each) black beans, rinsed and drained

1 can (14.5 ounces) low-sodium vegetable broth

1 tablespoon cider vinegar

½ teaspoon dried oregano

Coarse salt and ground pepper

Assorted toppings, such as lime wedges, fresh cilantro leaves, and sliced radishes (optional)

1 Cook rice according to package instructions. Meanwhile, heat oil in a large saucepan over medium. Add onion, garlic, and bell pepper. Cook, stirring occasionally, until onion has softened, 8 to 10 minutes.

2 Add beans, broth, vinegar, and oregano. Cook, mashing some beans against side of pan with the back of a spoon, until slightly thickened, 6 to 8 minutes. Season with salt and pepper. Fluff rice with a fork. Serve beans with rice, and with toppings, as desired.

per serving (without toppings): 439 calories; 5.1 g fat (0.6 g saturated fat); 13.8 g protein; 81.4 g carbohydrates; 10.3 g fiber

439
CALORIES PER SERVING

381
CALORIES PER SERVING

WHY IT'S LIGHT Risotto's little secret: It's usually enriched with ample butter at the end. But one bite of this version, which contains just one tablespoon butter, shows how delectable the dish can be without all the extra fat and calories. And rather than adding the squash at the end of cooking, per the usual method, you cook it along with the rice, so it contributes creaminess and sweetness to the final outcome.

BUTTERNUT SQUASH RISOTTO

SERVES 4 ■ PREP TIME: 1 HOUR ■ TOTAL TIME: 1 HOUR

2 cans (14.5 ounces each) low-sodium chicken broth

½ cup water

1 tablespoon unsalted butter

1½ pounds butternut squash, seeded and peeled (see below) and cut into ½-inch chunks

Coarse salt and ground pepper

1 cup Arborio rice

½ cup dry white wine

⅓ cup grated Parmesan cheese, plus more for garnish

1 tablespoon chopped fresh sage, plus more for garnish

1 In a medium saucepan, bring broth and the water to a simmer over medium heat; cover pan.

2 Meanwhile, in a medium Dutch oven or heavy pot, melt butter over medium heat. Add squash; season with salt and pepper. Cook, stirring often, until edges soften, 6 to 8 minutes. Add rice and cook, stirring, until translucent around the edges, about 1 minute.

3 Add wine; cook, stirring, until evaporated, about 1 minute. Reduce heat to medium-low. Add ½ cup hot broth mixture. Cook, stirring, until almost all liquid is absorbed. Repeat process, gradually adding broth, until rice is al dente and liquid is creamy (you may not need to use all the broth), about 25 minutes total.

4 Stir in Parmesan and sage, and season with salt. Serve immediately, garnished with additional Parmesan and sage, if desired.

per serving: 381 calories; 5 g fat (3.4 g saturated fat); 11.2 g protein; 66.4 g carbohydrates; 6.8 g fiber

PREPARING BUTTERNUT SQUASH
With a sharp chef's knife, cut off top and bottom of squash. Halve squash crosswise, then length-wise. Scoop out seeds and fibrous flesh with a spoon and discard. Peel with a vegetable peeler (or sharp knife) and cut as directed in recipe.

GOOD TO KNOW Quinoa—a nutritional powerhouse that's also an excellent source of protein—stars in this vegetarian main; chopped walnuts complement quinoa's nutty taste. Choose short, squat bell peppers that will stand upright easily.

STUFFED RED PEPPERS WITH QUINOA AND PROVOLONE

SERVES 4 ■ PREP TIME: 35 MINUTES ■ TOTAL TIME: 1 HOUR 50 MINUTES

4 red bell peppers
1 tablespoon olive oil
1 medium onion, finely chopped
2 garlic cloves, minced
1 teaspoon ground coriander
  Coarse salt and ground pepper
1 cup quinoa, rinsed
1 cup water
½ cup fresh flat-leaf parsley leaves, coarsely chopped
⅓ cup walnuts, coarsely chopped
1 cup coarsely grated aged provolone cheese (4 ounces)

1 Preheat oven to 450°F, with rack in upper third. Slice a very thin layer from the base of a bell pepper so it sits upright. Slice off top, just below stem, and remove ribs and seeds from top and bottom parts. Repeat with remaining peppers. Discard stems, chop tops, and reserve bottoms for stuffing.

2 In a medium saucepan, heat oil over medium. Add onion, garlic, coriander, and chopped pepper tops; season with salt and pepper. Cook, stirring occasionally, until onion has softened, about 5 minutes.

3 Add quinoa, and cook, stirring, until fragrant, 1 minute. Add the water and bring to a boil. Reduce to a simmer, cover, and cook until water has been absorbed and quinoa is tender, 11 to 13 minutes. Remove from heat. Stir in parsley, walnuts, and ¾ cup provolone; season with salt and pepper.

4 Divide quinoa mixture evenly among peppers; place in a 2-quart baking dish. Cover with parchment, then foil, and bake until peppers are tender, about 1 hour. Uncover and top evenly with remaining ¼ cup provolone; bake until cheese melts, 10 to 15 minutes more. Serve warm.

per serving: 390 calories; 19.3 g fat (6.2 g saturated fat); 15.8 g protein; 41.8 g carbohydrates; 6.4 g fiber

390
CALORIES PER SERVING

330

CALORIES PER SERVING

SMART SUBSTITUTION This savory pie's flaky crust is made with olive oil instead of butter, reducing the amount of saturated fat. The galette is easy to assemble and versatile: If you can't find Broccolini, substitute broccoli florets, or try crumbled goat cheese in place of feta.

BROCCOLINI AND FETA GALETTE

SERVES 6 ■ PREP TIME: 10 MINUTES ■ **TOTAL TIME: 1 HOUR 15 MINUTES**

2 cups all-purpose flour, plus more for dusting

¼ cup olive oil

Coarse salt and ground pepper

⅓ cup cold water

2 bunches Broccolini (1 pound total)

¼ cup grated Parmesan cheese (1 ounce)

⅔ cup crumbled feta cheese (3 ounces)

¼ teaspoon red-pepper flakes

1 large egg, lightly beaten

1 In a medium bowl, combine flour, oil, 1 teaspoon salt, and the water. With a fork, stir to combine. Knead dough 1 minute. Cover with plastic wrap and let rest 30 minutes.

2 Preheat oven to 400°F, with rack in lower third. In a large pot of boiling salted water, cook Broccolini until bright green, about 1 minute. With tongs, transfer to a paper-towel-lined plate.

3 On a lightly floured surface, roll out dough to a 14-inch round; transfer to a parchment-lined baking sheet. Sprinkle dough with Parmesan and top with Broccolini, leaving a 2½-inch border. Top with feta and red-pepper flakes; season with salt and pepper. Fold dough border over filling and brush with beaten egg.

4 Bake until crust is golden brown and topping is heated through, 35 to 40 minutes. Serve warm or at room temperature.

per serving: 305 calories; 13.4 g fat (3.6 g saturated fat); 11.5 g protein; 35.4 g carbohydrates; 1.6 g fiber

WHY IT'S LIGHT Sometimes roast chicken recipes call for softened butter to be spread over—or even under—the skin before putting the bird in the oven. Here, a mixture of parsley and thyme (and not butter) is spread under and on top of the skin of chicken thighs for added flavor, while honey and a small amount of olive oil brushed on top help keep the chicken moist.

ROASTED CHICKEN AND PEARS

SERVES 4 ■ PREP TIME: 25 MINUTES ■ TOTAL TIME: 1 HOUR 25 MINUTES

1 large parsnip (about 8 ounces), peeled, halved lengthwise, and cut into 2-inch lengths

1 large white turnip (about 1 pound), peeled and cut into 1-inch chunks

2 small red onions, cut into 1-inch-wide wedges

2 tablespoons red-wine vinegar

2 tablespoons olive oil

1 teaspoon dried thyme

Coarse salt and ground pepper

2 tablespoons chopped fresh flat-leaf parsley

4 each bone-in, skin-on chicken drumsticks and thighs (about 2 pounds total)

1 tablespoon honey

3 firm, ripe Bosc pears (about 1½ pounds total), halved, cored, and cut into ½-inch-thick wedges

1 Preheat oven to 375°F. On a large rimmed baking sheet (or two small ones), toss parsnip, turnip, and onions with vinegar, 1 tablespoon oil, and ½ teaspoon thyme; season with salt and pepper.

2 In a small bowl, combine parsley and remaining ½ teaspoon thyme; season with salt and pepper. Carefully slide fingers under chicken skin to loosen; spread parsley mixture under and on top of skin. Push vegetables to edges of baking sheet; place chicken pieces in center, and roast 30 minutes.

3 In a small bowl, combine honey and remaining 1 tablespoon oil. Remove baking sheet from oven; add pears and toss with vegetables to combine. Brush top of chicken pieces with honey mixture; roast 30 minutes more, or until thigh juices run clear when meat is pierced. Serve immediately.

per serving: 421 calories; 15.8 g fat (3.3 g saturated fat); 30 g protein; 41.9 g carbohydrates; 8.7 g fiber

421
CALORIES PER SERVING

369
CALORIES PER SERVING

WHY IT'S LIGHT Each serving of this stir-fry has only one teaspoon oil and a tablespoon of roasted peanuts. Lime juice and fresh basil added at the end perk up the dish, so it tastes just as good as (or even better than) more traditional versions.

SPICY CHICKEN STIR-FRY WITH PEANUTS

SERVES 4 ■ PREP TIME: 20 MINUTES ■ **TOTAL TIME: 30 MINUTES**

1 tablespoon plus 1 teaspoon peanut oil

3 boneless, skinless chicken breast halves (6 to 8 ounces each), thinly sliced crosswise

4 garlic cloves, thinly sliced

1 serrano or jalapeño chile, thinly sliced crosswise (ribs and seeds removed for less heat, if desired)

8 ounces snow peas (about 4 cups), stem ends trimmed

Coarse salt and ground pepper

¼ cup fresh lime juice

¼ cup chopped roasted peanuts

¾ cup loosely packed fresh basil leaves, torn

1 In a wok or large nonstick skillet, heat oil over high. Add chicken; cook until browned on one side, 2 to 3 minutes.

2 Turn chicken and add garlic, chile, and snow peas. Cook until chicken is cooked through, 2 to 3 minutes more. Season with salt and pepper; stir in lime juice, peanuts, and basil. Serve immediately.

per serving: 369 calories; 12 g fat (2.1 g saturated fat); 51.5 g protein; 13.2 g carbohydrates; 4.1 g fiber

WHY IT'S LIGHT This rendition of a Tex-Mex favorite uses lean chicken breasts, corn tortillas, and just enough Monterey Jack cheese to create a luscious topping. The gentle, moist heat of pan steaming keeps the chicken breasts juicy and tender without any oil.

LIGHTER CHICKEN ENCHILADAS

SERVES 4 ■ PREP TIME: 20 MINUTES ■ **TOTAL TIME: 45 MINUTES**

3 boneless, skinless chicken breast halves (6 to 8 ounces each)

Coarse salt and ground pepper

2 tablespoons vegetable oil, such as safflower

2 garlic cloves, minced

¼ cup all-purpose flour

1 teaspoon ground cumin

1 to 2 tablespoons minced canned chipotles in adobo

1 can (14.5 ounces) low-sodium chicken broth

½ cup water

8 corn tortillas (6-inch), warmed (see note)

½ cup grated Monterey Jack cheese (2 ounces)

1 In a large skillet, bring 1 inch water to a boil. Add chicken, and season with salt; cover, and reduce heat to medium-low. Simmer 5 minutes; remove skillet from heat. Let chicken steam, covered, until cooked through, 12 to 14 minutes. Transfer chicken to a medium bowl; when cool enough to handle, shred with two forks.

2 While chicken is cooking, in a medium saucepan, heat oil over medium. Add garlic; cook, stirring, until fragrant, about 1 minute. Add flour, cumin, and chipotles to taste; cook, whisking, 1 minute. Whisk in broth and the water; bring to a boil. Reduce to a simmer, and cook, whisking occasionally, until sauce has thickened slightly, 5 to 8 minutes; season with salt and pepper. Transfer 1 cup sauce to bowl with chicken; toss to combine.

3 Preheat oven to 400°F. Spread ¼ cup of remaining sauce evenly in an 8-inch square baking dish. Fill each tortilla with chicken mixture, dividing evenly; roll up tightly, and arrange, seam side down, in baking dish. Cover with remaining sauce, and top with cheese. Bake until cheese is melted and sauce is bubbling, 15 to 20 minutes. Let cool 5 minutes before serving.

per serving: 437 calories; 15 g fat (4.4 g saturated fat); 43.6 g protein; 30.8 g carbohydrates; 3.7 g fiber

NOTE
To warm the corn tortillas, wrap them (stacked) in damp paper towels and microwave 30 to 60 seconds, just until softened. Or you can use tongs to toast them on a gas-stove burner for about 30 seconds per side.

437
CALORIES PER SERVING

463
CALORIES PER SERVING

GOOD TO KNOW One easy way to ensure boneless, skinless chicken breast halves cook up moist and flavorful is to stuff them. Here, a combination of bread, ham, sage, and olive oil does the job in delicious fashion. Sauté broccoli in the same skillet as the chicken for a fast side.

HAM-AND-SAGE-STUFFED CHICKEN WITH BROCCOLI

SERVES 4 ■ PREP TIME: 30 MINUTES ■ TOTAL TIME: 30 MINUTES

- 4 slices white sandwich bread, cut into cubes (about 2½ cups)
- 2 ounces sliced deli ham, coarsely chopped
- ½ teaspoon dried sage
- ¼ cup olive oil

  Coarse salt and ground pepper
- 4 boneless, skinless chicken breast halves (6 to 8 ounces each)
- 2 packages (10 ounces each) frozen broccoli florets, thawed
- 2 garlic cloves, minced
- 1 tablespoon white-wine vinegar

1 In a medium bowl, combine bread, ham, sage, and 2 tablespoons oil; season with salt and pepper.

2 Lay chicken flat on a work surface. Using a paring knife, cut a 2-inch-long slit in the thick side of each breast half. Insert knife and pivot, carefully forming a deep pocket without enlarging opening (or piercing through opposite side). Stuff each pocket with bread mixture, packing tightly; season chicken with salt and pepper.

3 In a large skillet, heat 1 tablespoon oil over medium-high. Add chicken; cook until browned on one side, 6 to 8 minutes. Turn chicken, cover skillet, and reduce heat to medium. Cook until chicken is cooked through, 6 to 8 minutes more. Transfer to a plate; tent with foil to keep warm.

4 In the same skillet, heat remaining tablespoon oil over medium-high; add broccoli and garlic. Cook, tossing, until broccoli is warmed through, 4 to 6 minutes. Remove from heat; stir in vinegar. Serve with broccoli.

per serving: 463 calories; 17.6 g fat (3.2 g saturated fat); 53.5 g protein; 19.2 g carbohydrates; 3.9 g fiber

317

GOOD TO KNOW Even the dark meat of turkey and chicken, such as thighs and legs, can be part of a low-calorie meal; cooking the meat with skin and bones intact yields great flavor, and the skin can be discarded before serving to reduce fat and calories. Serve with steamed green beans tossed with a little melted butter.

APPLE-BRAISED TURKEY THIGHS

SERVES 4 ■ PREP TIME: 30 MINUTES ■ **TOTAL TIME: 2 HOURS 30 MINUTES**

1 tablespoon olive oil

2 turkey thighs (about 2 pounds total)
Coarse salt and ground pepper

2 large shallots, thinly sliced

4 Cortland or Granny Smith apples, peeled, quartered, and cored

2 cups unsweetened apple cider

1 can (14.5 ounces) low-sodium chicken broth

2 teaspoons cider vinegar

1 Preheat oven to 350°F. In a medium Dutch oven or other ovenproof heavy pot, heat oil over medium-high. Pat turkey dry with paper towels and season with salt and pepper. Add to pot, skin side down. Cook until skin is golden and crisp, about 8 minutes. Transfer turkey to a plate.

2 Add shallots to pot and cook, stirring occasionally, until softened, about 5 minutes. Add apples and cook until slightly softened, about 5 minutes.

3 Return turkey, skin side up, to pot; add cider and broth. Bring to a boil, cover, then transfer to oven. Cook 1½ hours. Uncover; cook 30 minutes more.

4 Remove pot from oven and transfer turkey to a cutting board. Skim fat from cooking liquid and stir in vinegar. Slice meat off bones (discard bones); remove skin, if desired. Serve turkey with apples and pan sauce.

per serving: 399 calories; 10.6 g fat (2.8 g saturated fat); 37.3 g protein; 38.6 g carbohydrates; 3.5 g fiber

399
CALORIES PER SERVING

278

CALORIES PER SERVING

FLAVOR BOOSTER A mixture of rosemary, paprika, and lime juice is rubbed over lean turkey before roasting; sweet potatoes cooked alongside soak up the flavorful pan juices, which are also drizzled over each serving. Serve with a side of sautéed leafy greens.

SPICE-RUBBED TURKEY BREAST WITH SWEET POTATOES

SERVES 4 ■ PREP TIME: 10 MINUTES ■ TOTAL TIME: 1 HOUR 20 MINUTES

1½ teaspoons dried crushed rosemary

1 teaspoon sweet paprika

Coarse salt and ground pepper

2 tablespoons fresh lime juice

2 tablespoons olive oil

1 boneless turkey breast half (about 1 pound), skin removed

2 sweet potatoes (about 1 pound total), halved lengthwise

1 Preheat oven to 400°F. In a small bowl, mix together rosemary, paprika, 1½ teaspoons coarse salt, ½ teaspoon pepper, the lime juice, and 1 tablespoon plus 1 teaspoon oil; rub mixture all over turkey. Place in center of a rimmed baking sheet.

2 Brush cut sides of sweet potatoes with remaining 2 teaspoons oil; arrange, cut side down, on sheet around turkey. Roast until an instant-read thermometer inserted in center of breast registers 160°F, about 50 minutes (sweet potatoes should be tender). Remove from oven, and let stand 10 minutes, tented with foil to keep warm (temperature will rise by 5 degrees).

3 Cut turkey into thick slices. Cut sweet potato halves into wedges. Transfer turkey and sweet potatoes to a serving platter, and drizzle turkey with juices from baking sheet.

per serving (without escarole): 278 calories; 3.2 g fat (0.6 g saturated fat); 37.4 g protein; 23.2 g carbohydrates; 3.5 g fiber

SAUTÉED ESCAROLE

2 tablespoons olive oil

3 garlic cloves, smashed and peeled

2 small heads escarole (about 1 pound total), trimmed, leaves torn

Coarse salt

In a large skillet, heat oil over medium. Add garlic and cook until fragrant and light golden, about 3 minutes. Stir in escarole; season with salt. Cook, stirring frequently, until tender, about 10 minutes.
SERVES 4

per serving: 82 calories; 7 g fat (1 g saturated fat); 1.6 g protein; 4.5 g carbohydrates; 3.6 g fiber

SECRET INGREDIENT Beer flavors this robust chicken and vegetable stew. Any light- or medium-colored lager will do, but pilsner—with its pronounced taste of hops—works best.

CHICKEN WITH CORNMEAL DUMPLINGS

SERVES 6 ■ PREP TIME: 35 MINUTES ■ TOTAL TIME: 1 HOUR 15 MINUTES

3 tablespoons unsalted butter

1½ pounds boneless, skinless chicken thighs (about 5), cut into 1-inch pieces

Coarse salt and ground pepper

½ bunch scallions, trimmed and cut into ½-inch pieces

1 green bell pepper, ribs and seeds removed, cut into ½-inch dice

2 celery stalks, cut into ½-inch dice

2 medium carrots, cut into ½-inch dice

1 teaspoon dried thyme

¼ cup all-purpose flour

2 bottles (12 ounces each) pilsner or another light- or medium-bodied lager

1 can (28 ounces) whole peeled tomatoes (with their juice)

1 to 2 tablespoons red-wine vinegar

Cornmeal Dumpling Dough (recipe follows)

1 In a large Dutch oven or other heavy pot, melt 1 tablespoon butter over medium-high. Pat dry chicken and season with salt and pepper. Add to pot, and cook, stirring occasionally, until browned on all sides, about 5 minutes. With a slotted spoon, transfer chicken to a medium bowl.

2 Add remaining 2 tablespoons butter, the scallions, bell pepper, celery, and carrots to pot. Cook, stirring occasionally, until scallions and celery are soft, about 4 minutes. Stir in thyme and flour and season with salt and pepper; cook 1 minute. Whisk in beer and return chicken to pot. With your hands, roughly tear tomatoes and add to pot along with their juices. Bring to a rapid simmer and cook, uncovered, 30 minutes. Season to taste with vinegar.

3 Reduce to a medium simmer and drop dough by rounded tablespoonfuls on top of stew. Cover and simmer until dumplings are cooked through, 7 to 10 minutes. Serve immediately.

per serving: 438 calories; 17 g fat (7 g saturated fat); 26 g protein; 35 g carbohydrates; 3 g fiber

CORNMEAL DUMPLING DOUGH

⅔ cup all-purpose flour

⅓ cup fine yellow cornmeal

1½ teaspoons baking powder

1 teaspoon sugar

¼ teaspoon coarse salt

1 tablespoon unsalted butter

½ cup low-fat buttermilk

In a medium bowl, whisk together flour, cornmeal, baking powder, sugar, and salt. Using your fingers, work in butter until small crumbs form. Stir in buttermilk to form a slightly lumpy batter; do not overmix.

438

CALORIES PER SERVING

212
CALORIES PER SERVING

WHY IT'S LIGHT Rather than cooking this hearty Italian stew on the stove, in the traditional manner, it is prepared in the microwave, using far less oil (because you don't have to brown the chicken thighs first) and in much less time.

CHICKEN CACCIATORE

SERVES 4 ■ PREP TIME: 15 MINUTES ■ **TOTAL TIME: 30 MINUTES**

8 ounces shiitake mushrooms, stems removed, caps cleaned and thinly sliced

5 garlic cloves, thinly sliced

1 tablespoon olive oil

¼ cup water

Coarse salt and ground pepper

1⅓ cups canned crushed tomatoes in juice

3 strips orange zest (each 3 inches long and ½ inch wide)

¼ teaspoon dried rosemary

⅛ teaspoon cayenne

1 pound boneless, skinless chicken thighs, cut into 1-inch pieces

1 In a 2½-quart microwave-safe dish, combine mushrooms, garlic, oil, and the water; season with salt and pepper. Cover and microwave on high, 2 minutes.

2 Stir in tomatoes (with their juice), orange zest, rosemary, cayenne, and chicken until combined. Cover; microwave on high until chicken is just cooked through, 12 to 14 minutes. Remove orange zest, and serve.

per serving: 212 calories; 8.2 g fat (1.7 g saturated fat); 25.3 g protein; 10.1 g carbohydrates; 2.5 g fiber

WHY IT'S LIGHT Serving small, lean steaks—only five to six ounces each—along with a lightly dressed salad of cauliflower and arugula keeps this meal low in calories. The only added oil is used in the dressing. The steak is seared in a dry skillet; the cauliflower is browned in the juices left behind.

FLAT IRON STEAK WITH CAULIFLOWER AND ARUGULA

SERVES 4 ■ PREP TIME: 25 MINUTES ■ **TOTAL TIME: 25 MINUTES**

4 small flat iron steaks (5 to 6 ounces each)

Coarse salt and ground pepper

1 head cauliflower (about 2½ pounds), cored and cut into small florets

2 garlic cloves, smashed and peeled

½ cup water, plus more if needed

2 tablespoons fresh lemon juice, plus lemon wedges for serving

1 tablespoon olive oil

2 bunches arugula (about 10 ounces total), thick stems removed, washed well and dried

1 ounce Parmesan cheese, shaved with a vegetable peeler

1 Heat a large skillet over medium-high. Pat dry steaks and season with salt and pepper. Cook 5 to 6 minutes per side for medium-rare (reduce heat if browning too quickly). Transfer to a cutting board and tent with foil to keep warm.

2 Add cauliflower, garlic, and the water to skillet; season with salt and pepper. Cook, tossing occasionally, until cauliflower is browned and crisp-tender, 8 to 10 minutes. (If bottom of skillet becomes too dry, add ¼ cup more water.)

3 Meanwhile, in a large bowl, whisk together lemon juice and oil; season with salt and pepper. Add arugula, cauliflower, and Parmesan to dressing in bowl; toss (arugula will wilt). Serve steaks and salad with lemon wedges.

per serving: 329 calories; 18.3 g fat (6.3 g saturated fat); 32.8 g protein; 8.8 g carbohydrates; 3.5 g fiber

329

CALORIES PER SERVING

414
CALORIES PER SERVING

GOOD TO KNOW Fiber-rich beans and leafy greens offset the richness of sausages in this Italian-inspired dinner. Broiling makes quick work of cooking the sausages. For an even lighter preparation, substitute chicken or turkey sausages for the pork.

SAUSAGES WITH KALE AND WHITE BEANS

SERVES 4 ■ PREP TIME: 25 MINUTES ■ TOTAL TIME: 25 MINUTES

1½ pounds sweet Italian sausages (about 8 links)

2 tablespoons olive oil

1 large bunch kale (1¼ to 1½ pounds), thick stems removed, leaves coarsely chopped

4 garlic cloves, thinly sliced

½ cup water

Coarse salt and ground pepper

1 can (15.5 ounces) cannellini beans, rinsed and drained

2 tablespoons white-wine vinegar

1 Heat broiler, with rack 4 inches from heat. With a fork, pierce sausages all over; place on a rimmed baking sheet. Broil, turning occasionally, until browned and cooked through, 8 to 10 minutes.

2 Meanwhile, heat oil in a large skillet over medium-high. Add kale, garlic, and the water; season with salt and pepper. Cover and cook, tossing occasionally, until kale is wilted and tender, 10 to 12 minutes. Add beans and vinegar; cook, tossing gently, until beans are heated through, about 2 minutes.

3 Slice sausages and serve over kale and beans.

per serving: 414 calories; 22 g fat (6.6 g saturated fat); 33.1 g protein; 23 g carbohydrates; 4.3 g fiber

FLAVOR BOOSTER After the pork has been roasted, incorporate the flavorful juices and browned bits left in the pan into a savory gravy for serving alongside. Be sure to allow the pork to rest at least ten minutes before slicing (you can make the gravy during this time), for the juiciest meat.

ROASTED PORK LOIN

SERVES 8 ■ PREP TIME: 25 MINUTES ■ **TOTAL TIME: 1 HOUR 15 MINUTES**

2 teaspoons mustard seeds

2 teaspoons dill seeds

1 teaspoon fennel seeds

1 boneless center-cut pork loin (about 3 pounds), tied at regular intervals

1 teaspoon olive oil

Coarse salt and ground pepper

Balsamic Gravy (recipe follows)

1 Preheat oven to 475°F. Crush the mustard, dill, and fennel seeds with a mortar and pestle, or wrap seeds in a kitchen cloth and press with a heavy pan. Place pork in a 9-by-13-inch roasting pan. Rub pork with oil; evenly coat with crushed seeds. Season with salt and pepper.

2 Roast pork until browned, 25 to 30 minutes. Reduce oven temperature to 350°F; continue to roast (tent with foil if browning too quickly) until an instant-read thermometer inserted into thickest part registers 140°F and pork juices run clear, 10 to 20 minutes.

3 Transfer pork to a cutting board (reserve pan for making the gravy; see below). Tent loosely with foil to keep warm. Let rest 10 to 20 minutes. To serve, cut pork against the grain into ¼ inch slices, and serve with gravy.

per serving: 259 calories; 9.6 g fat (2.2 g saturated fat); 38.8 g protein; 1.8 g carbohydrates; 0.4 g fiber

BALSAMIC GRAVY

Juices and browned bits from roasting pan (above)

1 can (14.5 ounces) low-sodium chicken broth

1 tablespoon all-purpose flour

3 tablespoons water

½ teaspoon balsamic vinegar

1 Pour off excess fat from roasting pan (leaving behind dark liquid and browned bits). Add broth to pan; cook over medium-high heat, scraping up browned bits with a wooden spoon, until liquid is reduced by half, 5 to 7 minutes.

2 In a small bowl, whisk together flour and the water. Reduce heat to medium; whisk flour mixture and vinegar into pan until gravy is completely smooth and has thickened, 1 to 3 minutes. **MAKES 1½ CUPS**

259
CALORIES PER SERVING

356
CALORIES PER SERVING

GOOD TO KNOW Tenderloin is the leanest and most tender cut of pork. To keep it from drying out, cook it only until its internal temperature reaches 140°F; the meat will continue cooking as it rests.

BROILED PORK TENDERLOIN WITH BLACK-EYED PEA SALAD

SERVES 4 ■ PREP TIME: 30 MINUTES ■ **TOTAL TIME: 40 MINUTES**

2 cans (15.5 ounces each) black-eyed peas, rinsed and drained

1 avocado, halved lengthwise, pitted, peeled, and cut into ½-inch dice

2 scallions, trimmed and thinly sliced

3 tablespoons finely chopped fresh flat-leaf parsley

1 to 2 tablespoons fresh lime juice
Coarse salt and ground pepper

1 pork tenderloin (about 1 pound)

1 teaspoon olive oil

1 Heat broiler, with rack in top position. In a medium bowl, combine black-eyed peas, avocado, scallions, parsley, and lime juice to taste. Season with salt and pepper and mix well.

2 Line a rimmed baking sheet with foil, then parchment. Rub pork with oil and season with salt and pepper. Place on baking sheet and cook 10 to 12 minutes for medium, turning frequently (an instant-read thermometer inserted in center should register 140°F). Remove from oven; tent with foil and let rest 10 minutes.

3 Slice pork about ¼ inch thick against the grain. Serve with the salad, and drizzle any juices from the baking sheet over pork.

per serving: 356 calories; 12 g fat (2.4 g saturated fat); 28.4 g protein; 35.3 g carbohydrates; 10.5 g fiber

GOOD TO KNOW A stir-fry is an ideal way to cook vegetables: With just a little oil and a short cooking time, the technique helps ensure that vegetables such as broccoli retain their nutrients. Broccoli stalks are as delicious as the florets—use a vegetable peeler to remove the tough skin.

BROCCOLI AND PORK STIR-FRY

SERVES 4 ▪ PREP TIME: 25 MINUTES ▪ **TOTAL TIME: 25 MINUTES**

- 1 teaspoon grated orange zest, plus ¼ cup fresh orange juice
- ¼ cup soy sauce
- ¼ cup rice vinegar (unseasoned)
- 1 tablespoon cornstarch
- 2 teaspoons vegetable oil, such as safflower
- 1 pork tenderloin (about 1 pound), quartered lengthwise and thinly sliced
- 2 garlic cloves, minced
- 3 scallions, trimmed, white and green parts separated and thinly sliced
- 1 head broccoli (about 1 pound), cut into bite-size florets, stalks peeled and thinly sliced
- ½ cup water

1 In a medium bowl, combine orange zest and juice, soy sauce, vinegar, and cornstarch. In a large nonstick skillet, heat 1 teaspoon oil over medium. Working in two batches, cook pork until browned on one side, about 2 minutes (pork will cook more in step 3). Transfer to a plate.

2 Add remaining teaspoon oil, the garlic, and scallion whites to skillet. Cook, stirring occasionally, until scallions wilt, about 2 minutes. Add broccoli and the water; cover, and cook until broccoli is crisp-tender and water has evaporated, 2 to 4 minutes.

3 Add pork (with any juices) and reserved sauce to skillet. Cook, stirring, until pork is cooked through and sauce has thickened, about 2 minutes. Top with scallion greens and serve.

per serving: 218 calories; 6.5 g fat (1.6 g saturated fat); 27.6 g protein; 13 g carbohydrates; 2.2 g fiber

218
CALORIES PER SERVING

254
CALORIES PER SERVING

GOOD TO KNOW Briefly sautéing the rice before adding the broth gives it a nutty flavor. Near-constant stirring as the rice cooks releases its starches, helping the dish become creamy. Here, just two slices of bacon add ample richness, so no butter or oil is needed.

LEEK, BACON, AND PEA RISOTTO

SERVES 4 ■ PREP TIME: 40 MINUTES ■ **TOTAL TIME: 40 MINUTES**

1 leek, white and light-green parts only

6 cups low-sodium store-bought chicken broth

2 slices bacon (2 ounces), cut crosswise into strips

1¼ cups Arborio rice

½ cup dry white wine

⅓ cup frozen peas

¼ cup finely grated Parmesan cheese, plus more for serving

Coarse salt and ground pepper

1 to 2 tablespoons fresh lemon juice

1 Halve leeks lengthwise; wash thoroughly. Pat dry and slice thinly. In a medium saucepan, bring broth to a simmer over medium heat; cover pan.

2 Meanwhile, in a medium Dutch oven or other heavy pot, cook bacon over medium heat, stirring, until lightly browned but not crisp, about 5 minutes. Add leek; cook, stirring, until softened, about 2 minutes. Add rice and cook, stirring, until translucent around edges, about 1 minute.

3 Add wine; cook, stirring, until evaporated, about 1 minute. Reduce heat to medium-low. Add 1 cup hot broth. Cook, stirring, until almost all broth is absorbed. Repeat process, gradually adding broth, until rice is al dente and liquid is creamy (you may not need all the broth), about 25 minutes. Stir in peas after the final addition of broth.

4 Remove skillet from heat and stir in Parmesan. Season risotto with salt, pepper, and lemon juice to taste. Serve immediately with additional Parmesan.

per serving: 254 calories; 7.4 g fat (3.3 g saturated fat); 12.2 g protein; 32.7 g carbohydrates; 1.3 g fiber

FLAVOR BOOSTER Roasting deepens salmon's naturally mild flavor. Brussels sprouts also take especially well to roasting, becoming tender, slightly sweet, and undeniably delicious when seasoned with little more than salt and pepper.

ROASTED SALMON WITH BRUSSELS SPROUTS

SERVES 4 ■ PREP TIME: 10 MINUTES ■ **TOTAL TIME: 35 MINUTES**

1 pound brussels sprouts, trimmed and halved lengthwise

2 tablespoons olive oil

Coarse salt and ground pepper

4 skinless salmon fillets (6 to 8 ounces each)

1 Preheat oven to 450°F. On a rimmed baking sheet, toss brussels sprouts with oil, and season with salt and pepper. Spread in a single layer. Roast, tossing occasionally, until sprouts are browned, 10 to 15 minutes.

2 Season salmon with salt and pepper. Place in center of baking sheet (push sprouts to sides). Roast until salmon is opaque throughout and sprouts are tender, about 10 minutes. Serve warm.

per serving: 351 calories; 17.9 g fat (2.7 g saturated fat); 37.6 g protein; 10.3 g carbohydrates; 4.4 g fiber

351
CALORIES PER SERVING

455
CALORIES PER SERVING

FLAVOR BOOSTER Everyone knows steamed fish is healthy—the trick lies in making it flavorful, too. Here, flounder fillets are spread with Dijon, rolled up, and cooked atop a bed of couscous and vegetables. A drizzle of vinaigrette provides the finishing touch.

STEAMED FLOUNDER WITH VEGETABLE COUSCOUS

SERVES 4 ■ PREP TIME: 15 MINUTES ■ **TOTAL TIME: 20 MINUTES**

1 cup couscous

1 red bell pepper, ribs and seeds removed, finely diced

1 medium zucchini, finely diced

½ teaspoon dried oregano

3 tablespoons olive oil

½ cup water

Coarse salt and ground pepper

1 tablespoon plus 1 teaspoon Dijon mustard

4 flounder fillets (6 to 8 ounces each)

1 tablespoon white-wine vinegar

1 In a 2-quart shallow microwave-safe dish, combine couscous, bell pepper, zucchini, oregano, 1 tablespoon oil, and the water. Season with salt and pepper. Cover and microwave on high until vegetables are crisp-tender, about 3 minutes. Stir mixture.

2 Dividing evenly, spread 1 tablespoon mustard over one side of fish; season with salt and pepper. Roll up each fillet, and place on top of couscous. Cover and microwave on high until fish is almost opaque throughout, about 4 minutes. Let stand, covered, 5 minutes, to finish cooking.

3 Meanwhile, in a small bowl, whisk remaining 1 teaspoon mustard with the vinegar and remaining 2 tablespoons oil. Season with salt and pepper. Drizzle fish and couscous with vinaigrette, and season with pepper. Serve immediately.

per serving: 455 calories; 13 g fat (2.1 g saturated fat); 43.8 g protein; 38.3 g carbohydrates; 3.4 g fiber

GOOD TO KNOW Prepare flavorful sides to complement simply prepared fish (or other lean proteins) without introducing too many extra calories to the meal. Here, roasted tomatoes, potatoes, and a green herb sauce do the trick. If you prefer, remove the skin from the fillets before serving.

SEARED FISH WITH ROASTED POTATOES AND TOMATOES

SERVES 4 ■ PREP TIME: 20 MINUTES ■ TOTAL TIME: 1 HOUR 45 MINUTES

FOR THE SAUCE

- 1 bunch fresh mint, leaves chopped
- 1 bunch fresh flat-leaf parsley, leaves chopped
- ½ bunch fresh basil, leaves chopped
- 1 garlic clove, minced
- 1 tablespoon chopped capers (rinsed and drained)
- 1 tablespoon fresh lemon juice
- 2 tablespoons olive oil
  Coarse salt and ground pepper

FOR THE VEGETABLES AND FISH

- 6 plum tomatoes, halved lengthwise
- ¼ teaspoon sugar
- 1 pound small red potatoes, scrubbed
  Coarse salt and ground pepper
- 3 tablespoons olive oil, plus more for baking sheet
- 4 skin-on striped bass or salmon fillets (6 to 8 ounces each)

1 Make the sauce: In a small bowl, combine mint, parsley, basil, garlic, and capers. Stir in lemon juice and oil; season with salt and pepper. (Sauce can be refrigerated up to 1 week in an airtight container.)

2 Make the vegetables: Preheat oven to 350°F. Arrange tomatoes, cut side up, on two large rimmed baking sheets, and sprinkle with sugar. Bake until softened, about 1 hour. Raise oven to 475°F.

3 While tomatoes are roasting, in a large saucepan, cover potatoes with water. Bring to a boil, and season with salt. Reduce to a simmer, and cook just until tender, about 15 minutes. Drain and let cool slightly.

4 Lightly oil a small rimmed baking sheet. Smash each potato with your palm and place on sheet. Drizzle with 2 tablespoons oil; season with salt and pepper. Roast until crisp, about 20 minutes.

5 Meanwhile, prepare the fish: With a paring knife, score fish skin crosswise in a few places and season fillets with salt and pepper. In a large non-stick skillet, heat remaining tablespoon oil over medium-high. Add fish, skin side down, and cook until browned and crisp, 6 to 8 minutes. Reduce heat to medium; flip fish and cook until opaque throughout, 2 to 4 minutes.

6 Serve fish with potatoes, tomatoes, and green sauce.

per serving: 392 calories; 15.1 g fat (2.4 g saturated fat); 35.6 g protein; 26.3 g carbohydrates; 3.9 g fiber

392
CALORIES PER SERVING

234
CALORIES PER SERVING

SMART SUBSTITUTION Spaghetti squash makes a great, gluten-free stand-in for pasta; after roasting the halved squash until tender, scrape the flesh with a fork into long spaghetti-like strands. Roasted shrimp are brightened with the addition of lemon juice and fresh parsley.

ROASTED SHRIMP WITH SPAGHETTI SQUASH

SERVES 4 ■ PREP TIME: 10 MINUTES ■ TOTAL TIME: 55 MINUTES

1 medium spaghetti squash (about 3 pounds), halved lengthwise

Coarse salt and ground pepper

¾ cup water

1 pound large shrimp, peeled and deveined

1 tablespoon plus 1 teaspoon olive oil

1 tablespoon fresh lemon juice, plus lemon wedges for serving

2 tablespoons fresh flat-leaf parsley leaves, coarsely chopped

1 Preheat oven to 375°F. Season cut sides of squash with salt and pepper. Place, cut side down, in a 9-by-13-inch baking dish. Add the water and bake until tender when pierced with a sharp paring knife, about 45 minutes. Let cool.

2 Meanwhile, on a rimmed baking sheet, toss shrimp with 1 teaspoon oil; season with salt and pepper. Roast until opaque throughout, 8 to 10 minutes.

3 Scoop out seeds from squash and discard. With a fork, scrape flesh into a large bowl. Add shrimp and any cooking juices, lemon juice, and remaining tablespoon oil; toss to combine. Season with salt and pepper, top with parsley, and serve with lemon wedges.

per serving: 234 calories; 6.7 g fat (1.2 g saturated fat); 25.7 g protein; 19.1 g carbohydrates; 4.1 g fiber

GOOD TO KNOW Succulent yet lean, scallops can be seared on the stove without adding much—if any—butter or oil. Be sure to heat the skillet until very hot before adding the scallops, and wait until a crust forms before turning them, to prevent tearing. Browned butter (*beurre noisette* in French) and hazelnuts add richness, without tipping the scales.

SCALLOPS WITH HAZELNUT BROWNED BUTTER

SERVES 4 ■ PREP TIME: 25 MINUTES ■ **TOTAL TIME: 25 MINUTES**

6 tablespoons unsalted butter

¼ cup hazelnuts, toasted to remove skins (see below), coarsely chopped

2 teaspoons white-wine vinegar

Coarse salt and ground pepper

1 pound large sea scallops (about 12), tough muscles removed, halved horizontally

1 to 2 bunches arugula, preferably baby (about ½ pound total), washed well and dried

1 In a large skillet, cook butter over medium heat, stirring frequently, until golden brown and most of the foam has subsided, about 4 minutes. Immediately transfer to a small bowl. Stir in hazelnuts and vinegar; season with salt and pepper. Cover hazelnut butter to keep warm.

2 Wipe skillet with a paper towel. Pat dry scallops and season generously with salt and pepper. Heat skillet over medium-high. In two batches, cook scallops until browned and opaque in center, turning once with a thin metal spatula, about 2 minutes.

3 Divide arugula among plates; top with scallops. Spoon hazelnut butter over scallops and serve immediately.

per serving: 311 calories; 22.6 g fat (11.3 g saturated fat); 21.7 g protein; 6.1 g carbohydrates; 1.6 g fiber

REMOVING HAZELNUT SKINS
Preheat oven to 275°F. Place raw (shelled) hazelnuts in a single layer on a rimmed baking sheet; bake until skins crack, 25 to 30 minutes. Transfer to a clean kitchen towel and roll up. Let steam 5 minutes. Rub the nuts vigorously in the towel until most skins have come off.

311
CALORIES PER SERVING

423

CALORIES PER SERVING

FLAVOR BOOSTER Cooking rice in chicken broth instead of water makes a richer tasting dish, without adding much to the calorie count. Andouille sausage, a Cajun specialty, has a pronounced smokiness; a little goes a long way.

SAUTÉED CAJUN SHRIMP

SERVES 4 ■ PREP TIME: 20 MINUTES ■ **TOTAL TIME: 30 MINUTES**

1 tablespoon olive oil

1 small onion, finely chopped

1 can (14.5 ounces) low-sodium chicken broth

1 cup long-grain white rice

Coarse salt and ground pepper

2 red bell peppers, ribs and seeds removed, sliced lengthwise into thin strips

8 ounces precooked andouille or kielbasa sausage, halved lengthwise and thinly sliced crosswise

1 pound large shrimp, peeled and deveined

1 In a medium saucepan, heat 1½ teaspoons oil over medium. Add onion; cook until softened, stirring occasionally, 3 to 5 minutes. Add broth and bring to a boil. Stir in rice; season with salt and pepper. Cover, reduce heat to low, and simmer until rice is tender, about 20 minutes.

2 Meanwhile, in a large nonstick skillet, heat remaining 1½ teaspoons oil over medium. Add bell peppers and cook until crisp-tender, stirring occasionally, 4 to 6 minutes. Add sausage and shrimp; cook until sausage is heated through and shrimp are opaque throughout, 3 to 5 minutes. Season with salt and pepper.

3 To serve, divide rice among four shallow bowls; top with shrimp mixture, and drizzle with any pan juices.

per serving: 423 calories; 7.6 g fat (1.7 g saturated fat); 35.9 g protein; 49.8 g carbohydrates; 2 g fiber

GOOD TO KNOW The salmon is steamed on a bed of escarole seasoned with onion, garlic, and lemon; lemon slices are also arranged on each fillet. Keep in mind that the escarole—which looks bulky when raw—shrinks substantially when cooked.

SALMON WITH ESCAROLE AND LEMON

SERVES 4 ■ PREP TIME: 20 MINUTES ■ **TOTAL TIME: 35 MINUTES**

2 lemons

1 tablespoon olive oil

1 medium red onion, halved and thinly sliced

2 garlic cloves, thinly sliced

2 heads escarole (2 pounds total), cored, trimmed, and coarsely chopped

½ cup water

4 boneless, skinless salmon fillets (6 to 8 ounces each)

Coarse salt and ground pepper

1 Thinly slice off both ends of one lemon. Cut into 8 thin slices. From remaining lemon, squeeze 1 to 2 tablespoons juice into a bowl.

2 In a 5-quart Dutch oven or other heavy pot, heat oil over medium-high. Cook onion and garlic, stirring occasionally, until golden brown, 6 to 8 minutes.

3 Stir in escarole and the water. Arrange salmon on top; season with salt and pepper. Place two lemon slices on each fillet. Cover and cook over medium-high heat until salmon is opaque throughout, 12 to 14 minutes.

4 Transfer salmon to a plate. Stir lemon juice to taste into escarole mixture. Serve salmon with escarole.

per serving: 323 calories; 14.7 g fat (2.3 g saturated fat); 36.9 g protein; 12.5 g carbohydrates; 7.8 g fiber

OLIVE-OIL MASHED POTATOES

1½ pounds waxy potatoes (about 4 medium), peeled and cut into 1-inch chunks

Coarse salt and ground pepper

2 tablespoons olive oil, plus more for serving (optional)

½ cup skim milk

1 In a large saucepan, cover potatoes with cold water by 2 inches. Bring to a boil; add 1 tablespoon salt. Cook until potatoes are very tender when pierced with a fork, 20 to 25 minutes. Drain; transfer to a large bowl.

2 Using a potato masher or fork, mash potatoes until smooth; add oil and milk, mashing until combined. Season with salt and pepper. Drizzle with more oil before serving, if desired. **SERVES 4**

per serving: **181 calories;** 7 g fat; 3.9 g protein; 25.8 g carbohydrates; 2.6 g fiber

CHILI-ROASTED SWEET POTATO WEDGES

1½ pounds sweet potatoes (2 to 3 medium)

2 tablespoons olive oil

1 tablespoon sugar

1 teaspoon chili powder

Coarse salt and ground pepper

1 Preheat oven to 425°F. Cut each sweet potato lengthwise into 8 wedges; halve long wedges crosswise.

2 On a large parchment-lined rimmed baking sheet, toss sweet potatoes with oil, sugar, chili powder, 1 teaspoon coarse salt, and ¼ teaspoon ground pepper, until coated. Arrange wedges in a single layer, cut sides down.

3 Roast sweet potatoes until browned and tender, 15 to 20 minutes. Season with additional salt, if desired, before serving. **SERVES 4**

per serving: **191 calories;** 3.6 g fat; 2.8 g protein; 37.8 g carbohydrates; 5.4 g fiber

BALSAMIC-BAKED POTATOES

1½ pounds small potatoes, scrubbed and halved or quartered

¾ cup low-sodium store-bought chicken broth

¼ cup balsamic vinegar

8 garlic cloves, smashed and peeled

5 sprigs thyme

Coarse salt and ground pepper

Preheat oven to 425°F. In an 8-inch square baking dish, combine potatoes, broth, vinegar, garlic, and thyme; season with salt and pepper. Bake until potatoes are tender and liquid is reduced to a glaze, about 1¼ hours, tossing twice. **SERVES 4**

per serving: **155 calories;** 0.3 g fat (0.1 g saturated fat); 4.7 g protein; 34.3 g carbohydrates; 3.9 g fiber

ROASTED MUSHROOMS AND POTATOES

10 ounces oyster or cremini mushrooms, trimmed (halved if using cremini)

2 tablespoons extra-virgin olive oil

Coarse salt and ground pepper

1 pound small red potatoes, scrubbed and quartered

¼ cup packed fresh flat-leaf parsley leaves

2 to 3 teaspoons sherry or red-wine vinegar

2 tablespoons capers, rinsed (optional)

1 Preheat oven to 450°F, with racks in upper and lower thirds. On a rimmed baking sheet, toss mushrooms with 1 tablespoon oil; season with salt and pepper. On another rimmed baking sheet, toss potatoes with remaining tablespoon oil; season with salt and pepper.

2 Roast until mushrooms are browned and potatoes are cooked through, about 20 minutes, tossing once and rotating sheets from top to bottom and front to back halfway through. Transfer to a bowl and toss with parsley, vinegar to taste, and capers, if desired. Serve warm. **SERVES 4**

per serving: **160 calories;** 7.4 g fat (1 g saturated fat); 4.9 g protein; 19.1 g carbohydrates; 3.6 g fiber

SECRET INGREDIENT Made by draining yogurt to remove excess moisture, yogurt cheese is a tangy, low-fat alternative to sour cream. Once you've discovered how easy it is to prepare, you'll find many ways to use it—on top of baked potatoes, spread on crackers or bread, or served as a dip for chips or blanched vegetables. Try it plain or flavored with the variation that follows.

BAKED POTATOES WITH YOGURT CHEESE

SERVES 4 ■ PREP TIME: 5 MINUTES ■ TOTAL TIME: 1 HOUR (PLUS DRAINING TIME)

2 cups plain low-fat yogurt
½ teaspoon coarse salt
¼ teaspoon ground pepper
4 medium russet potatoes, scrubbed

1 Line a fine sieve with a coffee filter or paper towel and set over a large glass measuring cup or deep bowl. Fill sieve with yogurt. Cover with plastic wrap, and refrigerate at least 8 hours (or up to 24 hours).

2 Discard liquid that has collected in the measuring cup; transfer yogurt cheese to a bowl. Stir in ½ teaspoon salt and ¼ teaspoon pepper.

3 Preheat oven to 400°F. Prick potatoes in several places with a fork; place on a baking sheet (or directly on oven rack). Bake until tender when pierced with a paring knife, 45 to 60 minutes (depending on size).

4 Split potatoes open with a fork; serve with yogurt cheese.

per serving: 199 calories; 2 g fat (1.3 g saturated fat); 7.2 g protein; 40.7 g carbohydrates; 4 g fiber

VARIATION
YOGURT CHEESE WITH GARLIC AND CHIVES
Cook 1 garlic clove in boiling water 1 minute; remove, and chop finely. Stir garlic and 3 tablespoons finely chopped fresh chives into yogurt cheese.

STORING YOGURT CHEESE
Yogurt cheese can be refrigerated up to 1 week in an airtight container. Before serving, pour off any liquid that may have accumulated.

199
CALORIES PER SERVING

APPLE-PARSNIP MASH

1 pound parsnips, peeled and cut into ½-inch pieces

1 pound apples (such as Honeycrisp or Fuji), peeled, cored, and cut into ½-inch pieces

1 cup water

1 tablespoon unsalted butter

Coarse salt and ground pepper

In a medium saucepan, combine parsnips, apples, and the water. Cover and bring to a boil over medium-high heat. Reduce heat to medium, and cook until parsnips are completely tender, 25 to 30 minutes. Transfer mixture to a food processor, add butter, and process until smooth. Season with salt and pepper. Reheat in pan over medium if necessary before serving. **SERVES 4**

per serving: **156 calories;** 3.3 g fat (1.9 g saturated fat); 1.5 g protein; 33 g carbohydrates; 7.4 g fiber

ACORN SQUASH WITH ONIONS AND YOGURT

1 acorn squash (about 1 pound), halved, seeded, and cut into 8 wedges

1 medium red onion, cut into 8 wedges

2 tablespoons extra-virgin olive oil

Coarse salt and ground pepper

½ cup full-fat plain Greek-style yogurt

2 teaspoons fresh lemon juice

¼ cup loosely packed fresh mint leaves

1 Preheat oven to 375°F. On a rimmed baking sheet, toss squash and onion with oil; season with salt and pepper. Roast until squash is tender, 30 to 35 minutes.

2 In a small bowl, combine yogurt and lemon juice; season with salt and pepper. Transfer squash and onion to a serving plate. Top with yogurt and mint; sprinkle with pepper. **SERVES 4**

per serving: **138 calories;** 8.5 g fat (2 g saturated fat); 2.1 g protein; 15.2 g carbohydrates; 2.3 g fiber

GREEN BEANS WITH HAZELNUTS

⅓ cup hazelnuts, toasted to remove skins (see page 346), coarsely chopped

1¼ pounds green beans, stem ends trimmed

Coarse salt and ground pepper

1 tablespoon unsalted butter

1 In a small skillet, toast hazelnuts over medium heat until golden brown, tossing occasionally, about 5 minutes. Transfer to a bowl to cool.

2 Cook beans in a pot of boiling salted water until crisp-tender, 4 to 6 minutes; drain. Return to pan; toss with butter and half the hazelnuts. Season with salt and pepper. Transfer to a serving dish, and sprinkle with remaining hazelnuts. **SERVES 4**

per serving: **129 calories;** 8.8 g fat (2.3 g saturated fat); 4 g protein; 11.7 g carbohydrates; 5.7 g fiber

PINTO BEAN AND SPINACH SALAD

3 tablespoons olive oil

1 tablespoon grated lemon zest, plus 2 tablespoons fresh lemon juice

½ teaspoon Dijon mustard

Coarse salt and ground pepper

3 cups canned pinto beans (drained and rinsed)

8 ounces spinach, tough stems trimmed, washed well and dried

½ cup fresh flat-leaf parsley leaves, finely chopped

1 tablespoon capers, rinsed and drained

2 scallions, trimmed and thinly sliced

1 In a large bowl, whisk together oil, lemon juice, and mustard; season with salt and pepper. Stir in pinto beans.

2 In a medium pot, bring 1 inch water to a boil; add salt and spinach. Cover and cook until wilted, 2 to 4 minutes. Drain spinach, and transfer to bowl with beans. Add parsley, capers, scallions, and lemon zest; toss to combine and serve. **SERVES 4**

per serving: **355 calories;** 11.6 g fat (1.7 g saturated fat); 17.4 g protein; 48.8 g carbohydrates; 17.3 g fiber

GOOD TO KNOW Sweet-tasting butternut squash is easier to prepare than some other hard-skinned winter squashes, and is even sweeter when roasted until it caramelizes. It's also extremely versatile: Toss it into a salad, slice it into "fries" and dust with spices, or drizzle roasted halves with maple butter.

BUTTERNUT SQUASH, FETA, AND ARUGULA SALAD

- 1 medium butternut squash, halved lengthwise, seeded, peeled, and cut into ¾-inch cubes
- 2 teaspoons olive oil

  Coarse salt and ground pepper
- ¼ cup crumbled feta cheese (1 ounce)
- 1 bunch arugula (5 ounces), washed well and dried, tough ends trimmed, torn into bite-size pieces

Preheat oven to 425°F. In a roasting pan, combine squash and oil; season with salt and pepper. Toss to coat, and spread in a single layer. Roast until tender when pierced with a knife, 35 to 45 minutes. Transfer squash to a bowl; gently toss with feta and arugula and serve. **SERVES 4**

per serving: **128 calories;** 4 g fat (1.2 g saturated fat); 3.3 g protein; 23.1 g carbohydrates; 6.7 g fiber

BUTTERNUT SQUASH FRIES

- 1 medium butternut squash, halved lengthwise, seeded, peeled, and cut into ½-inch-wide sticks
- 2 teaspoons olive oil
- ½ teaspoon ground cumin

  Coarse salt and ground pepper
- 1 tablespoon fresh lime juice
- 1 tablespoon coarsely chopped fresh cilantro

Preheat oven to 425°F. On a rimmed baking sheet, combine squash with oil and cumin; season with salt and pepper. Toss to coat and spread in a single layer. Roast until tender when pierced with a knife, 45 minutes to 1 hour. Sprinkle with lime juice and cilantro and serve immediately. **SERVES 4**

per serving: **108 calories;** 2.5 g fat (0.4 g saturated fat); 2 g protein; 22.7 g carbohydrates; 6.6 g fiber

BUTTERNUT SQUASH WITH MAPLE BUTTER

- 1 medium butternut squash, scrubbed
- 2 tablespoons unsalted butter
- 1 tablespoon plus 1 teaspoon pure maple syrup

  Coarse salt and ground pepper

Preheat oven to 425°F. Halve squash lengthwise; scoop out seeds. Place in a roasting pan, cut side up (if necessary, slice a thin strip from each skin side to help it sit level). Dividing evenly, fill each cavity with butter and maple syrup; season with salt and pepper. Roast until tender when pierced with a knife, 45 minutes to 1 hour. Halve squash again lengthwise; spoon butter mixture from pan over tops (skins are edible). **SERVES 4**

per serving: **153 calories;** 5.9 g fat (3.7 g saturated fat); 2 g protein; 26.8 g carbohydrates; 6.5 g fiber

107
CALORIES PER SERVING

GOOD TO KNOW There are few good no-fat options for dessert, but sorbet is among them, and it's definitely one of the most refreshing. It is also simple to prepare at home, and with less sugar than store-bought varieties. You can experiment with other types of fruit juices, alone or in combination, following the formula below.

CRANBERRY AND APPLE-CIDER SORBET

MAKES 1 QUART ■ PREP TIME: 15 MINUTES ■ **TOTAL TIME: 4 HOURS 30 MINUTES (WITH FREEZING)**

2 cups 100% cranberry juice
1½ cups unsweetened apple cider
½ cup sugar
1 tablespoon fresh lemon juice

1 In a large saucepan, bring juice, cider, and sugar to a boil over medium-high heat. Cook, stirring, until sugar is dissolved, about 3 minutes. Remove from heat; stir in lemon juice.

2 Transfer to a 9-by-13-inch nonreactive baking dish. Freeze for 2 hours, then mash with a fork. Cover with plastic wrap and return to freezer until set, at least 2 hours or up to 1 day.

3 Purée sorbet in a food processor until smooth. Transfer to an airtight container and freeze until set, at least 2 hours (or up to 1 week), before serving.

per ½ cup: 107 calories; 0.1 g fat; 0 g protein; 27.4 g carbohydrates; 0.1 g fiber

FLAVOR BOOSTER Naturally sweet, pears become even more so when baked until very tender. They are delicious on their own or topped with a dollop of rich mascarpone cheese and crumbled almond-flavored cookies for a slightly more lavish treat.

ROASTED PEARS WITH AMARETTI COOKIES

SERVES 8 ■ PREP TIME: 10 MINUTES ■ **TOTAL TIME: 45 MINUTES**

4 firm, ripe Bartlett pears (red or green), halved lengthwise and cored (unpeeled)

2 tablespoons fresh lemon juice

2 tablespoons sugar

Pinch of coarse salt

¼ cup water

½ cup mascarpone cheese

8 amaretti cookies (Italian almond macaroons)

1 Preheat oven to 375°F. In a 9-by-13-inch baking dish, toss pears with lemon juice, sugar, and salt; arrange halves in a single layer, cut side down. Add the water, cover dish tightly with foil, and bake until pears are easily pierced with the tip of a paring knife, 25 to 30 minutes.

2 Place each pear half, cut side up, on a plate, and top with 1 tablespoon mascarpone and 1 crumbled cookie. Drizzle with juices from baking dish, and serve.

per serving: 196 calories; 13.7 g fat (7 g saturated fat); 2.7 g protein; 18.2 g carbohydrates; 2.2 g fiber

HALVING PEARS
For a fresh-picked look, try to leave stems intact as you halve each pear lengthwise. Then use a melon baller or a small spoon to scoop out the core.

196
CALORIES PER SERVING

58
CALORIES PER SERVING

WHY IT'S LIGHT Since they contain no butter or oil, these crunchy, nut-studded treats are significantly lower in fat than other cookies. Whole-wheat flour gives the wholesome biscotti extra fiber.

WHOLE-WHEAT WALNUT-RAISIN BISCOTTI

MAKES 24 ■ PREP TIME: 10 MINUTES ■ **TOTAL TIME: 1 HOUR 10 MINUTES (PLUS COOLING)**

Vegetable oil, for baking sheet
- ¾ cup whole-wheat flour
- ½ cup all-purpose flour, plus more for dusting
- ⅓ cup sugar
- 1 teaspoon baking powder
- ¼ teaspoon salt
- ½ cup walnut halves
- ¼ cup golden raisins
- 2 large eggs
- 1 teaspoon pure vanilla extract

1 Preheat oven to 350°F. Brush a baking sheet with oil. In a medium bowl, whisk together both flours, sugar, baking powder, and salt; stir in walnuts and raisins. In a small bowl, whisk together eggs and vanilla. Add to flour mixture; stir just until combined.

2 On a lightly floured surface, with floured hands, pat dough into a loaf about 1 inch thick, 2½ inches wide, and 7 inches long; transfer to prepared baking sheet. Bake until risen and firm, 20 to 25 minutes; remove from oven and let cool completely on sheet. Reduce oven to 300°F.

3 Transfer loaf to a cutting board, and using a serrated knife, cut diagonally into ¼-inch-thick slices; place slices in a single layer on sheet. Bake, turning once, until dried and slightly golden, 25 to 30 minutes, rotating sheet halfway through. Transfer sheet to a wire rack and let cool completely. Biscotti can be stored in an airtight container at room temperature 1 week.

per cookie: 58 calories; 1.9 g fat (0.3 g saturated fat); 1.7 g protein; 9.2 g carbohydrates; 0.7 g fiber

SECRET INGREDIENTS Replacing butter with applesauce and reduced-fat sour cream lightens these brownies, while a double helping of chocolate means you won't feel the least bit deprived. For the deepest flavor, use high-quality cocoa powder.

LIGHT CHOCOLATE-CHUNK BROWNIES

MAKES 16 ■ PREP TIME: 20 MINUTES ■ **TOTAL TIME: 55 MINUTES (PLUS COOLING)**

2 tablespoons vegetable oil, such as safflower, plus more for pan

4 ounces bittersweet chocolate, coarsely chopped

¾ cup all-purpose flour

½ cup unsweetened cocoa powder

½ teaspoon salt

¼ teaspoon baking soda

1 cup packed dark-brown sugar

½ cup unsweetened applesauce

½ cup reduced-fat sour cream

2 large eggs

1 Preheat oven to 350°F. Brush a 9-inch square baking pan with oil; line with parchment, leaving an overhang on two sides. Brush parchment with oil. Heat half the chocolate in a small bowl in the microwave, stirring every 30 seconds, until melted.

2 In a medium bowl, whisk together flour, cocoa powder, salt, and baking soda. In another bowl, whisk together brown sugar, applesauce, sour cream, melted chocolate, eggs, and oil until combined; add flour mixture, and mix just until moistened.

3 Spread batter in prepared pan; sprinkle evenly with remaining chopped chocolate. Bake until a toothpick inserted in center of cake comes out with a few moist crumbs attached, 30 to 35 minutes.

4 Let cool completely in pan. Use paper overhang to lift from pan; peel off paper, and cut into 16 squares. Brownies can be stored in an airtight container at room temperature up to 3 days.

per brownie: 154 calories; 6.8 g fat (2.7 g saturated fat); 2.8 g protein; 24.3 g carbohydrates; 1.7 g fiber

154
CALORIES PER SERVING

111
CALORIES PER SERVING

WHY IT'S LIGHT Vegetable oil, with no saturated fat, replaces butter in these drop cookies. The dough—which can be whipped up in just ten minutes—also features equal parts whole-wheat and all-purpose flours. (In fact, you can substitute whole-wheat flour for up to half of the all-purpose flour in many recipes for baked goods without compromising flavor or texture.)

HEALTHY OATMEAL COOKIES

MAKES 18 TO 20 ■ PREP TIME: 10 MINUTES ■ **TOTAL TIME: 35 MINUTES**

½ cup whole-wheat flour

½ cup all-purpose flour

1 teaspoon baking powder

⅓ cup vegetable oil, such as safflower

⅔ cup packed dark-brown sugar

1 large egg

1 teaspoon pure vanilla extract

½ cup old-fashioned rolled oats (not quick-cooking)

½ cup dried currants or raisins

1 Preheat oven to 350°F, with racks in upper and lower thirds. In a medium bowl, whisk together both flours and baking powder. In a large bowl, whisk together oil, sugar, egg, and vanilla. Add flour mixture and stir to combine; mix in oats and currants.

2 Using 2 tablespoons dough per cookie, roll into balls; place 1½ inches apart on two parchment-lined baking sheets. Bake until lightly browned, 15 to 17 minutes, rotating sheets from top to bottom and front to back halfway through.

3 Let cool 5 minutes on sheets, then transfer cookies to a wire rack to cool completely. Cookies can be stored in an airtight container at room temperature up to 5 days.

per cookie: 111 calories; 4.4 g fat (0.5 g saturated fat); 1.6 g protein; 17.3 g carbohydrates; 0.8 g fiber

WHY IT'S LIGHT Fruit makes a naturally healthy dessert; here, lightly sweetened fresh pears and berries are embellished with only a thin layer of crunchy oatmeal topping. The topping can be made ahead and chilled until ready to use; refrigerate it in an airtight container up to five days.

PEAR AND BERRY CRISP

SERVES 8 ■ PREP TIME: 30 MINUTES ■ **TOTAL TIME: 1 HOUR 40 MINUTES**

1 bag (12 ounces) frozen mixed berries (do not thaw)

3 pounds ripe pears (5 to 7), peeled and cut into ¾-inch pieces

1 tablespoon fresh lemon juice

3 tablespoons sugar

2 tablespoons all-purpose flour

Oatmeal Topping (recipe follows)

Vanilla frozen yogurt, for serving (optional)

1 Preheat oven to 450°F. Spread frozen berries in a single layer on a paper-towel-lined baking sheet; thaw 30 minutes at room temperature.

2 In a large bowl, combine thawed berries, pears, lemon juice, sugar, and flour; toss well. Transfer to a shallow 2-quart baking dish. Sprinkle evenly with chilled topping.

3 Bake until fruit is tender and topping is golden, about 45 minutes. Let cool at least 20 minutes. Serve warm with frozen yogurt, if desired.

per serving: 242 calories; 6.7 g fat (3.6 g saturated fat); 2.1 g protein; 46.8 g carbohydrates; 5.1 g fiber

OATMEAL TOPPING

¼ cup all-purpose flour

¼ cup packed light-brown sugar

2 tablespoons granulated sugar

¼ teaspoon ground allspice

Pinch of salt

½ cup old-fashioned rolled oats (not quick-cooking)

4 tablespoons cold unsalted butter, cut into small pieces

In a large bowl, mix together flour, both sugars, allspice, and salt. Stir in oats. Using a pastry blender, two knives, or your fingers, work butter into flour mixture until large, moist clumps form. Refrigerate, covered, until ready to use.
MAKES ¾ CUP

242
CALORIES PER SERVING

ACKNOWLEDGMENTS

We are most grateful to all the editors and art directors who have helped create the award-winning *Everyday Food* magazine since it was first launched. Editor in chief Anna Last and her team of food editors—Khalil Hymore, Heather Meldrom, Samantha Seneviratne, and Lesley Stockton—carry on the tradition of developing delicious recipes with an eye toward ease of preparation and with good health always in mind. Thank you to the design team of Chi Lam and Kirsten Hilgendorf, in conjunction with the wonderful photographers listed on page 373, for continuing to present the food in such an appealing and approachable light.

A heartfelt thanks to the Special Projects Group at MSLO for creating this wonderful book. Editorial director Ellen Morrissey and executive editor Evelyn Battaglia, with the able support of assistant editor Stephanie Fletcher, sifted through a wealth of magazine content to select the rich (but light!) collection of recipes contained on these pages. Design director William van Roden and associate art director Jeffrey Kurtz created the signature clean, modern look with invaluable guidance from creative director Eric A. Pike.

Thanks as well to chief creative officer Gael Towey and others at MSLO who provided ideas and support, including: Denise Clappi, Alison Vanek Devine, Erin Fagerland, Catherine Gilbert, Heloise Goodman, Kellee Miller, Michele Outland, Ayesha Patel, Lucinda Scala Quinn, Megan Rice, and Maggie Ruggiero.

As always, we thank our longtime publishing partners at Clarkson Potter for their support of and dedication to our brand, including Amy Boorstein, Angelin Borsics, Doris Cooper, Terry Deal, Derek Gullino, Maya Mavjee, Mark McCauslin, Marysarah Quinn, Lauren Shakely, Patricia Shaw, Jane Treuhaft, and Kate Tyler, for working together to build our library of inspiring, how-to books.

PHOTO CREDITS

ROLAND BELLO 69, 86, 136, 203, 219, 246, 247, 255 top left, 352 top right

EARL CARTER 102, 272, 288, 319, 336, 337, 352 bottom right

LISA COHEN 97 bottom right, 151, 187 right, 267 left

CHRIS COURT 66, 67, 70, 71, 72, 167, 188, 192, 193, 268, 320, 364

REED DAVIS 207, 274, 275, 303, 334, 335

DANA GALLAGHER 90, 91, 298, 299, 316, 317

RAYMOND HOM 6, 171, 218, 332, 344

KARL JUENGEL 183

JOHN KERNICK 124, 255 top right, 256 bottom left, 260, 264 bottom left, 286, 287, 315, 328, 331, 340, 343, 356 top right & bottom left, 368

YUNHEE KIM 5, 38, 42, 43, 92, 93, 110, 113, 147, 159, 187 left, 256 top right, 263, 292, 307, 367

DAVID LOFTUS 23, 77, 139, 175, 179 bottom right, 252, 283, 324, 327, 360

JONATHAN LOVEKIN 58, 59, 348

WILLIAM MEPPEM 32, 33, 267 right, 355

JOHNNY MILLER 97 bottom left, 101 top left, 132, 162, 163, 180 top left & bottom left, 256 bottom right, 291, 312

MINH + WASS 46, 47, 156, 304, 305, 359

MARCUS NILSSON 25, 37, 40, 41, 49, 54, 73, 74, 106, 107, 127, 164, 200, 201, 204, 208, 211, 212, 216, 222, 223, 231, 239, 240, 243, 244, 245, 248, 251, 255 bottom left, 256 top left, 264 top right, 300, 351

AMY NEUNSINGER 264 bottom right, 279

KANA OKADA 64, 65, 101 bottom right, 116, 128, 140, 179 top left & top right, 180 bottom right, 232, 280, 281

VICTORIA PEARSON 94, 95, 120, 220

CON POULOS 15, 17, 19, 21, 50, 62, 81, 82, 85, 98, 101 top right, 105, 109, 119, 122, 123, 135, 152, 153, 155, 168, 179 bottom left, 184, 191, 228, 236, 276, 277, 295, 296, 308, 310, 311, 347, 356 top left

JOSE MANUEL PICAYO RIVERA 45, 60, 61, 88, 89, 97 top left, 227, 235, 259, 352 bottom left, 363

KIRSTEN STRECKER 131

CLIVE STREETER 53, 78, 180 top right, 224, 255 bottom right, 264 top left, 352 top left, 371

BRETT STEVENS 176, 214, 215

PETRINA TINSLAY 57

JONNY VALIANT 143, 148, 356 bottom right

MIKKEL VANG 34, 35, 97 top right, 199, 284, 339

ANNA WILLIAMS 101 bottom left, 144, 160, 161, 172, 195, 323

INDEX